Betzy Dinesen was born in 1945 into a family of Danish, French and Polish origins, and was brought up in Surrey, the second of four children. She read French literature at university and then started working in publishing in London. She took her MA at Birkbeck College, London, which caters for evening students. She has worked in publishing for the last eleven years and is at present technical editor in a research organization. *Rediscovery* is her first book, arising out of her two principal interests, literature and the women's movement.

About *Rediscovery*:
'The great female virtues – a strong social sense, unpleasantly sharp observation and occasional bursts of unwanted candour – are here celebrated'   *Guardian*

REDISCOVERY
300 years of stories by and about women

Edited by
BETZY DINESEN

The Women's Press

First published by The Women's Press Limited 1981
A member of the Namara Group
124 Shoreditch High Street, London E1 6JE
Reprinted 1984

Printed in Great Britain by Nene Litho
Bound by Woolnough Bookbinding
Both of Wellingborough, Northants

British Library Cataloguing in Publication Data

Rediscovery: 300 years of stories by and about women
  1. Short stories – Women authors
  I. Dinesen, Betzy
  808.83'1   PN6069.W/

ISBN 0-7043-3879-3

CONTENTS

I would like to thank, among other friends, Lindsay Miller, Margaret Crowther and Kathryn Swift for their sympathetic interest and help while I was preparing this book.

The stories in this collection have been structured around the life cycle of a woman, from birth to old age, and are intended to be read in the order in which they appear.

Introduction

There came to my mind's eye one of those long streets somewhere
south of the river whose infinite rows are innumerably populated ... I
saw a very ancient old lady ... close on eighty; but if one asked her
what her life has meant to her, she would say that she remembered the
streets lit for the battle of Balaclava, or had heard the guns fire in
Hyde Park for the birth of King Edward the Seventh. And if one
asked her, longing to pin down the moment with date and season, but
what were you doing on the fifth day of April 1868, or the second of
November 1875, she would look vague and say that she could
remember nothing. For all the dinners are cooked; the plates and cups
washed; the children sent to school and gone out into the world.
Nothing remains of it. All has vanished. No biography or history has
a word to say about it. And the novels, without meaning to, inevitably
lie. All these infinitely obscure lives remain to be recorded, I said ...
feeling in imagination the pressure of dumbness, the accumulation of
unrecorded life.

Virginia Woolf, *A Room of One's Own*

One of the most enjoyable areas of feminist studies is to uncover the
little-known records of these obscure lives from a tradition of
women's writing. Women have written about the domestic fabric of
their lives, creating a strand of fiction that is both authentic and
relevant, illuminating as it does, not moments of war or social
upheaval but the underside of history and the quality of women's lives
in the private sphere. All this has not vanished or gone unrecorded but
much of it has gone out of print and is there to be reclaimed. Rescuing
this lost literature is not an esoteric task. A certain amount can be
found in public libraries with the guidance of a good bibliography,
such as those in Ellen Moers, *Literary Women*, Elaine Showalter, *A
Literature of their Own* and the *Women and Literature* bibliography.[1]
From the eighteenth century on, there is a great quantity of published
fiction by women, much of it trite and ephemeral, but reassuring in its
demonstration that women were speaking, if not for posterity, then
for their own generation. Most of it is of no great interest today,

except in so far as it shows that women writers were responsive towards a growing literary market and that a female literary tradition was already establishing itself.

The stories in this collection outline briefly this developing tradition, with an emphasis on psychological and domestic realism. They range across a variety of cultures and periods, not so much as a search for the essence of women's lives as an attempt to show representative aspects of female experience. The collection is structured around the life cycle of a woman with the earlier stories describing experiences of childhood and adolescence, followed by stories portraying women reaching maturity with differing experiences of maternity, marriage or celibacy. The final stories represent middle life and old age. The stories have been written over a period of three hundred years, though the chronological order of writing is not reflected in the structure of the book and there is a movement backwards and forwards from the seventeenth to the twentieth century.

Women have, until comparatively recently, been restricted to activities in the private sphere or to low-prestige work outside the home. Women's writing has largely reflected these activities, opening them to the charge of narrowness of vision. Our exclusion from battlefields, except as camp followers, and from political and commercial power has, men argue, limited our vision. But this supposes that the experience of and ability to describe social and political development are the stuff of literature rather than history and introduces unhelpful categories of 'major' and 'minor' which bear little relation to the concerns of most people. Men have written more of 'great' events, but what of it? A more useful criterion may be one of relevance and, using this touchstone, women's literature, with its vision – epic, domestic or other – can often be very satisfying.

The stories reflect this historical reality of restricted experience. They show us women with limited options suffering oppression and uninvigorating defeat. Caroline Norton's Kate Bouverie, for example, is too individualistic and spirited to win approval on the marriage market. But reality, or an author's rendering of it, also gives us proof of long-experienced dissatisfaction of women at social injustices and proof that some women have always resisted stereotyping and social oppression and have used their perceptions creatively. So we have Elizabeth Robins describing a working-class family welcoming with grudging joy an illegitimate child, Mary Wilkins describing a choice of celibacy rather than marriage, Margaret Cavendish creating a character who insists on a single moral standard within marriage for both partners.

The stories in this book have been selected to highlight certain areas of experience, biological destiny and reactions to it, conditioning to social roles, repression and revolt, and the stories are linked by common threads, presenting a female perception of women's lives. They are all written by women, with either a female narrator (except for the shadowy male narrator of 'A Wagner Matinée') or an omniscient narrator, sympathetic to women.

Before women were identifying their own social disadvantages in print, they often transposed their sense of injustice to other issues, such as working-class poverty or slavery. Even their moral sense of justice over women's rights was often more advanced than their ideology. Margaret Oliphant, for example, led a very independent life and deplored the way in which her publisher dominated his more intelligent wife, but she was not formally committed to women's rights and considered female suffrage a 'mad notion'. Yet her 'Story of a Wedding Tour' is full of latent sympathy for women's struggle for independence and this in spite of its somewhat retributive ending. Similarly, in 'Two Cousins', Eliza Linton presents a role reversal of a competent, talented woman educating an effete, swooning man to be a fit partner for her, but in her own life she cut herself off from other women to show herself worthy of the success accorded to her by men. The unconscious feminism of these stories transcends the explicit beliefs of the writers, who were simply of their time. Ironically, the more advanced and politically committed writers have not always created the most successful fiction. Explicitly feminist commitment became evident with the First Wave of the women's movement and two of the writers in this collection, Elizabeth Robins and Evelyn Sharp, were activists in the women's suffrage movement. Their suffrage stories are not included here as they sag under the weight of a didactic burden too heavy for the fictional framework and Evelyn Sharp's 'The Game that Wasn't Cricket', included here, is slightly marred by this fault. A fictional recreation of women's oppression can carry its own political meaning, often beyond the conscious intention of the writer.

This collection emphasizes what is specific about female experience and what constitutes a type of experience which is separate and distinct from male experience. Some of the stories root the experience firmly in an explanation of biological destiny, the inevitable consequences of being born female. Growing up female, experiencing adolescence and menstruation, pregnancy and maternity, provide an initial clear identification of female experience. Clara Schiavolena in 'Clementina' describes the relationship between a foetus and its mother

Menstruation had, before Doris Lessing's *The Golden Notebook*, rarely been referred to directly in fiction (uniquely female as this experience is, it is doomed to forego universal application, that dubious yardstick of great art). The onset of menstruation is described here in the single contribution which is not fiction. The extract by Greta Lainer (from *A Young Girl's Diary*) is a story adapted from an apparently authentic diary of an adolescent girl in Vienna early this century, though it has been suggested that the diary was retouched, and it may in this sense be considered as an imaginative recreation of adolescence. Even if it is authentic, which cannot now be proved, diaries provide a training-ground for writers of fiction, calling for a shaping of events, just as fiction does. Alix Kates Shulman's contribution to this sequence of stories on physical aspects of being female is 'A Story of a Girl and her Dog', which gives an example of childhood sexuality of an unusual and exclusively female kind.

These are female experiences which do not in themselves provide a complete definition of women's lives. Although our biologically determined experiences bring some fulfilment, they may also mean denying other parts of ourselves. Women's experiences are not limited to childbirth and childrearing, and women cannot be defined simply in terms of their biology, a definition which would rob them of other areas of female identity. Kate Chopin's character, Mrs Sommers, in 'A Pair of Silk Stockings', starts by defining herself exclusively in terms of her maternity, her social role a direct extension of her biological role. In the course of the story she discovers a separate identity, and this ability to transcend our purely biological identity is part of a shared female experience which the stories also illustrate. Our biological identity provokes ambiguous responses. Henry Handel Richardson's girl bathing recoils from knowledge of her own future at the sight of two middle-aged women bathing naked, maturity and maternity bringing only, in her eyes, hideous physical deformity.

Maternity is dealt with here in the stories by Aphra Behn, Mary Delarivière Manley, and Elizabeth Robins. The seventeenth and eighteenth-century stories, by the first two authors, present a grim picture of women punished for conceiving without the legal protection of marriage, even when seduced or raped. Only in 'Gustus Frederick', Elizabeth Robins's story written in 1896, is the picture reversed.

A large part of female experience is our reaction to biological roles and conditioning to social roles. We are of course programmed to our roles as women. What female nature might possibly be, if it were not so intensively socialized, remains obscure, and our reactions to our socialization are a significant part of our experience. We are socialized from early childhood, and Evelyn Sharp's competitive, resourceful cricket-player in 'The Game that Wasn't Cricket' is knocked into suitable feminine submissiveness. Other writers, Caroline Norton and Eliza Haywood, for example, illustrate the penalties of a failure to be acceptably socialized and appropriately feeble or, alternatively, and more optimistically, like Mary Wilkins and Sarah Orne Jewett, hold out the hope of a successful revolt.

It is a source of frustration and injustice for women to gain social acceptance only through their relationship with a man, lacking, in his absence, economic security, being punished for bearing children outside marriage, and requiring a husband for any status. Having an identity only in this reflected status and being defined only in terms of a relationship with a man is humiliating, and this collection tries to move away from these degrading definitions. Love can make these definitions seem desirable, of course, but the subject of love between men and women has been amply treated elsewhere in fiction and is not, except in the Eliza Linton story, approached in this collection.

Marriage needs no idealizing (a conventional upbringing and pulp fiction have done so sufficiently for most women), nor, indeed, the realistic exposure of these stories, since marriage has been seriously treated in fiction. Old age can do with both. Sarah Orne Jewett and June Arnold emphasize the positive aspects of old age, refusing to conjure up its traditional concomitants of either serenity or senile decay, and they draw an enticing picture of vigour, initiative and, unexpectedly, enhanced sexuality. Sarah Orne Jewett gets near to a cosy interpretation; June Arnold writes more experimentally, and is able to break the double taboo of writing about sex, and sex between women, in old age.

Marriage, if not love, however, is treated here, and in the stories selected, it is shown, unromantically, to be at best a chafing bridle and at worst a weapon of oppression. Women are forced into marriage as the only economic and socially acceptable option and are shown reacting variously to it, rebelling against the option ('A Story of a Wedding Tour'), refusing it altogether ('A New England Nun'), being rejected for failing to conform to the stereotype of society wife ('Kate Bouverie'), escaping from it when it crushes personal growth ('Marie') and accepting it only on terms of fairness and equality ('The Matrimonial Agreement').

Other stories look at experiences of unmarried working women, competing in a market where women are cheap labour, and low wages mean dreary living conditions and genteel poverty, illustrated in the stories of Mary Webb and Dorothy Richardson.

The older stories in this book are both of their time and ahead of it. They are progressive in presenting characters and conflicts which are still recognizable today. Conversely, they are of their time not only because their authors sometimes shared the prejudices of the period, as in the case of Margaret Oliphant and Eliza Linton, but also in their style and choice of themes. The style of the earlier writers is not always accessible, and partly for this reason, as well as for reasons of space, the stories by Mary Delarivière Manley and Eliza Haywood have been abridged, and only very short pieces by Margaret Cavendish and Aphra Behn included. The themes used also show the preoccupations of the age: the eighteenth-century concern with the innocent girl's ruin, the sombre Victorian belief in retribution, the twentieth-century interest in childhood perceptions. The need to conform to contemporary tastes and views has meant that some stories, which begin promisingly, appear to compromise in their endings. Some survive better than others, but the intention of this collection is not to uncover great art which transcends the ages. The stories are of interest because they enable us to rediscover the perceptions of women writers of the past and present, illustrating how these women have responded to the restrictions and exploited the opportunities, both literary and social, of their age.

Note
1   Ellen Moers, *Literary Women*, New York, Doubleday & Co Inc, 1977, London, W.H. Allen, 1977, The Women's Press 1978 (paperback); Elaine Showalter, *A Literature of Their Own: British Women Novelists from Brontë to Lessing*, Princeton and London, Princeton University Press, 1977, London, Virago, 1978 (paperback); The Women & Literature Collective, *Women and Literature: An Annotated Bibliography of Women Writers*, 3rd ed, 1976, Box 441, Cambridge, Mass 02138.

CLARA SCHIAVOLENA

Clementina

Translated by Miranda Miller

Clara Schiavolena was born in Sicily into a middle-class family, with one sister and one brother, whom she was close to, who died young. Her great-grandmother was a Victorian English eccentric who settled in Italy. Clara Schiavolena went to university in Palermo. She was married briefly to a painter, and has one daughter. During the Second World War, she went to Rome, where she has lived ever since. She has written two volumes of poetry and a novel, L'Età successiva and has contributed to the literary magazine Il Caffé. She is interested in foretelling the future and has compiled a dictionary of dreams. 'Clementina' is her first work to be published in the English language.

I'm sure to be beautiful, when I'm born, because both my parents are good looking, I thought. My mother was tall and slim with a regal way of carrying herself. She had chestnut hair and eyes that were dark, with a suggestion of violet. I fell in love with her straight away – at first sight – as soon as I was conceived.

My father was medium height, skinny and dried up. There wasn't an ounce of fat on his stomach. He had black hair that contrasted with his green eyes. As soon as she was certain that she was pregnant, my mother told her husband. He looked annoyed. He doesn't want me, I thought, and I felt a bit disappointed.

My aunt, my mother's twin sister, was delighted at the news. I thought she seemed sincere. The two sisters were incredibly alike, except for that haze in their dark eyes. My aunt's eyes had a stone-coloured haze.

My father's parents brought my mother a bottle of vintage wine to celebrate. They toasted her health, and mine.

After two months I got to know my relatives' habits. My aunt was an usher in an elementary school, and went to work at eight every morning. My mother finished all her chores and started to sew. She worked at home, as a dressmaker. My father was a bricklayer who left at dawn and got home at about seven.

I grew peacefully in this harmonious atmosphere. During the day I slept deliciously, waking up in the evening when my father came home. After supper he talked to my mother. Often my aunt, who lived with us, was there as well. He loved to remember his past, and talked about it sadly and imaginatively. He was born in a poor Sicilian village, and his childhood had been very tough. His father's house and land had been buried beneath the lava during a violent eruption of Etna. It had happened when he was tiny, but he could still remember the disaster.

Having lost his land, and in order to survive, his father had to work for practically nothing, picking chicory in fields that belonged to other people or to nobody at all. His mother had had two sons in quick succession, both of whom had died of diarrhoea. Somehow or other my father had survived the heat, malnutrition and misery. Perhaps God wanted him to. He also went to school, which was a real sacrifice for his parents, and when he was older he helped his father pick chicory. One day, he swore, he would find a job and earn a decent living for himself and for his parents, who were getting old. He wanted to pay them back for all they had done for him.

The opportunity came. He had a friend who had found work in Avellino. This friend had written to him, saying that he was enjoying himself and that my father could join him, if he wanted to. There was a job going at the Town Hall, where they needed a door-keeper. The friend could recommend him to the Mayor. At this my father was in seventh heaven and felt as if he had suddenly become immensely rich. He gathered together his few possessions, his old parents and some provisions, and loaded them all into an ancient, decrepit jeep (left behind during the last war by an American soldier who was killed in a minefield) and left Sicily forever. No! he declared, he would never go back to that place, where he remembered only hunger and misery.

When he had crossed the Straits of Messina he felt as if he had crossed the Atlantic, and he thought he was setting foot on a safer land. But he took the wrong road and instead of taking the road to Avellino, he followed a little road that wasn't even marked on the map. Hopelessly lost, he stopped in the middle of the country and pitched camp, to rest a bit and change his plans. The khaki tents were American army surplus like the jeep, they camouflaged him, and his parents, and their belongings. But that night while they were asleep they were all attacked and robbed by some thugs, who all but cut their heads off as they slept. They stole everything, even the money hidden in the mattress. The only thing they left was my father's guitar, because he was using it as a pillow.

My father reported the robbery to the police in the nearest town, and demanded compensation. 'They're not thugs,' the police told him. 'We know them. They're just kids who want to show off to their girlfriends, trying to be rebels.' They got two months in prison.

They weren't able to give back what they had stolen. They had given away the luggage to some peasants they had met in the countryside, and lost the money playing bowls and shooting at a rifle-range. They apologised to my father and promised to help him find a job as soon as they came out of prison. They were well-connected, and the father of one of them was a surveyor who had his own firm.

Because of all these apologies and promises, my father stayed in the town. He settled down in a prefabricated house which a stranger let him rent very cheaply. He found a job sooner than he expected, because the surveyor was ashamed of what his son had done and wanted to make it up to my father. He employed him as a hodman. Then, finding that he was intelligent and full of ideas, even though he was a bit lazy, he promoted him to bricklayer.

A few months later my father met my mother. By pure chance, as so often happens. The pipes in her house weren't working and water was leaking from her kitchen down to the floor below where the surveyor, my father's employer, lived. It was a difficult job because the house was old and badly built.

He worked there for several days, and made friends with my mother. She told him about her life: she was a dressmaker, she had no brothers, and a twin sister who was exactly like her. The house belonged to both sisters, who had inherited it when their mother died. My mother couldn't remember her father. Under fascism he had resigned from his job as a clerk working for the state railways. He was a communist, and had gone to live abroad. He hadn't written for years.

My father got used to my mother's voice. It was a bit raucous, but pleasing. One day after he had finished the plumbing job he went to see her. Her sister was there too. He was amazed at the resemblance, but he noticed the different coloured haze in their eyes. He said he would never swap one for the other.

My father always ended the story with the same words. 'You're more beautiful,' he would say to my mother, when my aunt wasn't there. 'I don't know what it is, but you're different!' My mother preened herself, and hugged him. She loved it when he talked about their meeting, and what had happened afterwards. She joined in, lovingly remembering all the details with a languor which communicated itself to me.

Every night their love-making went on for hours. My father went to sleep satisfied, sleeping heavily and snoring loudly. My mother found it difficult to sleep. The love-making which he enjoyed exhausted her, wore her out. I watched her with love and concern, in all her enthusiasm and disappointments, in her exhaustion and her doubts.

Things had now been going badly for some time. My father didn't have much work and my mother said to him, 'I'll be careful not to spend too much.'

In the evenings, after supper, they did their accounts. My father grumbled. My mother was having a difficult pregnancy and felt dizzy and sick. Maybe my father was disgusted. He tried to be kind, because he still loved her, but he started going out. One night he had a drink with a friend in the osteria. He went there again, and played cards with the friend's friends. He lost his meagre wages and came home blind drunk, in a filthy temper. It was that night that the quarrels began.

For the first time my mother reproached him. Why play cards? Why drink? Why didn't he concentrate on getting work? Write to his friend in Avellino? My father, smelling of alcohol, replied, 'You trapped me, with your sexy voice. You've tied me, hand and foot. But I'm leaving this place, I've had enough of it, ever since those kids fleeced me. I just want to be free, that's all I want!'

His anger worried me. I'd never heard him talk like that before. My mother was alarmed, too, as well as surprised, and she shut up. Perhaps she had already said too much. That's bad luck, I thought, having parents who quarrel.

The rows continued, and my mother and I put up with them together. I had started kicking inside her belly and she complained, 'Why can't you keep still? You should be ashamed of yourself!' I wanted to tell her how much I loved her. But I didn't have a voice. I rolled myself up into a tiny ball, with my chin on my knees, so as not to bother her. I was nearly born a hunchback. I knew, by now, that she was feverish every day, so I forgave her for nagging me. She stuffed herself with barley and honey sweets to soothe the cough that racked her. She liked those sweets. I liked them too.

My mother had her first attack of shaking. She took her temperature and was frightened when she saw what it was. She knew of a doctor who came to our town every Saturday and Thursday. The shaking increased. She looked at the calendar: it was Saturday, surgery day. There was no time to lose. She put on a woollen shawl, touched her belly to make sure I was still there and took me with her.

At first the doctor wasn't sure. But when my mother said 'ninety-nine', he knew. My mother was consumptive. TB was already gnawing her lungs, and she didn't have long to live.

My mother didn't tell her husband what her doctor had said. She knelt down instead and prayed to Jesus, asking him to look after me. She cried for a long time. And I cried with her.

She often used to wake up with nightmares, disturbing my father. Not knowing that she was ill, he would ask, yawning, 'What's the matter?' In between periods of sleep he would fondle her, and to calm her down he would say, 'Don't worry. If something goes wrong when you're in labour, they'll give you some penicillin. They'll bring it to you fresh, all the way from America.'

When my mother woke him up like that he still wanted to make love to her, but he knew it was dangerous during the last months of her pregnancy. He didn't feel like turning to other women, not because he loved my mother but because he couldn't be bothered. He was basically lazy.

My aunt made the most of this situation. She was engaged to a worker who had found a job in Germany, but they hadn't written to each other for a long time. There was something going on, and I couldn't work it out. My aunt often looked at my mother enviously and said, 'Lucky you, you're married!'

She tried to seduce my father, who took no notice of her at first. She persisted and he, hungry for sex as he was, gave in. He used to take her down to the poultry pen, in the garden shared by all the tenants in the block. One of them saw what was going on and was thoroughly scandalized. My aunt was betraying her fiancé, who was slaving away for her in Germany. She had no feeling for her sister. My father was a bastard to be unfaithful to his wife when she was in that state – and apart from anything else, they hadn't been married long.

When she knew for certain that it was true, my mother didn't react violently. Instead she collapsed. One day she asked herself, what's the point of living? She swallowed lots of brown pills and was rushed to hospital, where they pumped out her stomach and restored her to health and sanity. But I had a bad liver.

For a while I stopped loving my mother because of her crazy gesture. Apart from her own life, she had risked mine. My mother went to the priest to make her confession. He absolved her after some hesitation. Why didn't she ask me to absolve her too? Why couldn't she even have said to me, 'Forgive me'?

My mother looked at herself naked in the mirror. She saw how swollen and ugly she was, and forgave her husband for his infidelity. He was quite right to prefer his sister-in-law. Without leaving the house, he had found the ideal mistress, exactly like his wife. Hearing her talk like this, I wondered, can love do that to you? Can jealousy turn you into an idiot?

Every day my father grew more distant from my mother. He took to going out more often after supper. His sister-in-law's vivacious presence excited him, and he didn't want to give in to his weakness for her too often. He wasn't altogether insensitive and made excuses to my mother before going out. There was a possibility of an important job, he said, and he had to discuss it. Then he went to the osteria where he drank and played cards with friends. If he lost, he came home with his tail between his legs. If he won, he bought drinks for all his friends. Either way, he never had any money.

Like a penitent, he went down on his knees to my mother. He asked her to forgive him and kissed the hem of her dress, saying, 'I'm weak. Feckless. I drink and spend money like a maniac. But you'll see, I will change! I'll get things together, I'll start tomorrow and find a proper job and save some money. For you and the child. And with my first week's wages I'll buy you a lovely shirt. Hand embroidered.' Meanwhile he fondled her breasts, unaware of the TB that was nibbling at her, ignoring the cough that made her shake.

I wondered, why isn't my father interested in her health? Why doesn't he ask about her cough? Why does he tell so many lies and make so many impossible promises? I never answered my own questions. I came to believe that my father was despicable, false as Judas, and from then on I smothered every affectionate feeling towards him.

My mother grew worse and gave up her work as a dressmaker. When she bent down she felt an agonizing pain in her breasts. One day she spat blood. She wiped her mouth on a handkerchief which she burnt straight away so as to obliterate every trace, out of a fear that her husband would be more repelled by her. After that, she spat blood into the lavatory.

I was consumed by grief for her; and I was exhausted because I was trying desperately to find a way to make her suffer less. By chance, I succeeded. For days I had been sleeping a lot, and I felt better for it. My memory was sharpened by all that healthy rest, so much so that I could remember my dreams.

The first one indicated a change in my mother's destiny. I found myself in a cemetery full of deserted benches which were white. The melancholy, dying paths were bordered with poplars and weeping willows. If I'd known how to draw, I would have put in brightly coloured flowers to brighten the landscape and to prove my love for dead things. Meanwhile my father and mother were alive. They were sitting on a bench kissing, holding each other tightly. They were whispering incoherently, exchanging promises of love. My father was bolder, my mother more cunning. They were playing together sensually on their white marble seat, more like lovers than a married couple. I enjoyed the scene immensely although I found the landscape unnaturally neat, ghastly in its cleanness. It was like a Surrealist painting.

I woke up with a start at the sullen bang of a door slammed shut by the wind.

My mother got up sleepily. She was all dishevelled and had gone to bed fully dressed after yet another row with her husband. She paused in the middle of the room, as an afterthought. She went to look at herself in the mirror on the chest of drawers and gazed at herself for some time. She smoothed her untidy hair and bent her head, smiling slightly. She scrutinized herself again, as if she wanted to confide a guilty secret to herself.

The banging door awoke my father, too. He saw his wife admiring herself in the mirror, with that smile on her lips.

'What's the matter?' he asked rudely.

'I'm happy,' she replied. 'I had a wonderful dream last night.'

My father stared at her, amazed. He had done nothing but nag! He wondered why on earth she was in such a good mood, with her cheeks flushed a fiery red, as if she had just made love. But as far as he remembered, they hadn't.

The next dream, with its destructive, ambiguous language, made my flesh creep.

I stood at the foot of a high mountain, looking up at its peak. A cloud of huge, malevolent birds towered above me, dominating the world below. They were predatory, with gleaming black feathers. I shivered at the sight of them. I certainly wouldn't have been afraid of them if I had seen them in real life instead of masked in a dream. I was terrified they would pounce on me. I couldn't breathe and clung to my mother's womb. Meanwhile I was thinking, it's extraordinary how dreams vary. The last one left me feeling calm and satisfied, whereas I'll be surprised if I get out of this one alive! I wailed at the birds, so that they would know I was there and show some compassion for me. My breath ruffled their feathers and they saw in this a sign of the fate from which they were fleeing. In pelting rain, they disappeared.

I woke up drenched with sweat. My mother woke too, as the tide overflowed onto her.

'I feel sick,' she said to her husband.

'You're always feeling sick,' he replied sleepily.

'It's not like before,' she insisted.

My father lifted her up by her armpits and put two pillows behind her back. Then he went straight to sleep. My mother got up and sat in an armchair where she stayed, awake and in pain, for the rest of the night.

I was upset by her reactions and was convinced that my dreams influenced my mother's health. Our dreams were as closely connected as we were to one another. The violent ones made her feel sick, living as she was in a highly nervous state, and the happy ones brought a warmth and flush to her cheeks, a marvellous vitality that had been lacking in her for months, either because of her illness or because of my father's behaviour.

So I did something about it.

With incredible will-power, so that my brain nearly burst from the strain, I filtered my dreams before I communicated them to her, giving her a gilded version of the world. I gave her back her past, idyllic moments of her adolescence. How lovely she was at sixteen! And at thirteen, still a child, running gaily through the fields with school friends. The wind blew their skirts up and they tried to push them down, shyly. She relived the honesty and openness of that period.

She still had a vague memory, distant like a sweet rustling in her ears, of the happiness that first dream had given her, when she held my father tight on that lovers' bench. And I discovered that I had that dream in my keeping, with all the peace and serenity it brought with it, when the right moment came to give it to her again.

My mother didn't think it was worth quarrelling with her husband. She thought it was useless to fight with her sister, who felt guilty about her and who often confided in her. Recently she had told her how she had made love to her fiancé, when he had returned from Germany to help his parents with the olive harvest. She was pregnant, she said, from that encounter.

My mother listened, distractedly. She didn't reply. Absorbed in her own thoughts, sunk in the rickety armchair (which my father had promised to mend), my mother gazed at the olive tree. The peach tree was just about to blossom. She probably wouldn't pick its fruit. She would probably die before her child was born.

This event came to seem timeless to her, as if she had nothing to do with it. She stopped counting her missed periods and didn't answer precisely when people asked about her pregnancy. She stroked her belly and waited. The serenity that my filtered dreams had communicated to her gave her faith.

My father grumbled, 'It's just my luck to marry a woman like that! Lounging around in a chair all day! Thinking about God knows what!'

One day he found her unconscious. My aunt had gone to see her future parents-in-law, as she often did since she had discovered she was pregnant. My father was alarmed. He shook his wife, and hit her to help her to recover.

My mother, once she regained consciousness, didn't believe that he was genuinely concerned. She was shrewder than before, more mature. She didn't lose the serenity she had acquired.

I was born under Aries, the sign of the ram. The same sign that had given me an unfaithful father made my birth my mother's death. We were alone in the house. She felt the labour pains begin and lay down on the bed. Then she became frightened that there wouldn't be anybody to help her. She shouted with all her strength, and some fellow who was on the stairs promised to run to fetch the midwife. A friend who lived on the floor above heard her too and came down and told the man to get the doctor as well. 'This is serious,' she whispered to him, 'she can hardly breathe, she looks as if she's dying!'

I drew my own conclusions from all this chaos, and thought, if I want to live, I'd better act fast. My mother might die while I'm being born. I chose the best position, head down, legs in the air, and I was like that when the midwife arrived.

'Now where have we got to?' she asked my mother. She came to the bed where my mother lay moaning and lifted the sheet. Furious, I hurled a stinking yellowy liquid in her face. She pulled me by my head.

The doctor arrived, out of breath. 'Everyone out of the room,' he said to my father and all the relations and friends who had meanwhile invaded our house.

'It's just the right moment to cut the cord,' the midwife said to him.

The doctor took off his jacket. Carefully, he rolled his shirt-sleeves up his hairy arms. He took off his tie and put on his white coat. He didn't seem to be in any hurry.

I thought, what a lazy sod! What a waste of time! And I bet he'll charge an enormous fee! I came into the world shivering with cold and rage, while my mother was already half dead.

The midwife and the friend from upstairs washed me in a bowl. They nearly flayed me, the water was so hot. They bundled me up in scratchy, heavy clothes – it was still cold in our mountain town, although it was early spring. I needed to be cared for and warmed with hot water bottles. The doctor asked my father to come in. He stood with him in a corner and told him the truth. There was no hope for my mother, whose lungs were damaged. My father looked at me with hatred. 'Little wretch!'

I hadn't come into a world where I was loved. The friends and relations gathered around my mother's bed ignored me, too, hating me already. Only my aunt showed a little interest. She took me in her arms and said to them all, 'It's not her fault that her mother is dying.'

The latest medical discoveries did no good whatsoever. After two hours of agony, my mother died.

The priest came with his altar boy. He administered extreme unction, said 'Amen' and went away.

Immediately after, two men turned up. They looked like a couple of policemen, and were armed with hammers and nails. They carried a rough wooden box into which they put my mother. Then they took her away. Right under my eyes, took her away. They didn't even ask my permission, or what I thought: they didn't bother about me, choking with grief beneath the stuffy swaddling clothes and the cold hot water bottles. They snatched her away from me forever, before she could kiss me good night, before I saw the colour of her eyes, before she saw the colour of mine, before we could exchange views on life, on the world's miseries, on ingratitude and men's follies. 'Damnation! Damnation!' That's the best word I can find without blaspheming. I can't do that, my mother was religious. She wore the Madonna on a chain around her neck. Those policemen didn't take it off, because they didn't see it. And she couldn't even leave it to me to remember her by. All I had left were my eyes to cry with.

HENRY HANDEL RICHARDSON

The Bathe

Henry Handel Richardson (1870-1946) was born in Melbourne, Australia, of an Irish father and English mother. She was christened Ethel Florence Lindesay, and took her pseudonym from her family tree. She had an unsettled childhood as her father struggled to make a living as a doctor, and at the age of eight went to live outside Melbourne on the coast where her father encouraged her and her sister in an active outdoor life. After her father's death in a lunatic asylum, her mother supported the family by working up country in a post office, and she received, for the period, a good academic education in a boarding school in Melbourne, an experience she used in The Getting of Wisdom *(1910). Her mother succeeded in selling some property and took her daughters to Leipzig where they studied music at the Conservatorium, Henry Handel Richardson giving up her studies when she got engaged to be married. She spent most of her married life in London, and after her husband's death in 1933 settled in Sussex where she lived until her death with a friend, Olga Roncoroni, whose agoraphobia she had helped to cure years earlier. Her novels include the trilogy* The Fortunes of Richard Mahony *(1917-29).*

Stripped of her clothing, the child showed the lovely shape of a six-year-old. Just past the dimpled roundnesses of babyhood, the little body stood slim and straight, legs and knees closely met, the skin white as the sand into which the small feet dug, pink toe faultlessly matched to toe.

She was going to bathe.

The tide was out. The alarming, ferocious surf, which at flood came hurtling over the reef, swallowing up the beach, had withdrawn, baring the flat brown coral rocks: far off against their steep brown edges it sucked and gurgled lazily. In retreating, it had left many lovely pools in the reef, all clear as glass, some deep as rooms, grown round their sides with weeds that swam like drowned hair, and hid strange sea-things.

Not to these pools might the child go; nor did she need to prick her soles on the coral. Her bathing-place was a great sandy-bottomed pool that ran out from the beach, and at its deepest came no higher than her chin.

Naked to sun and air, she skipped and frolicked with the delight of the very young, to whom clothes are still an encumbrance. And one of her runs led her headlong into the sea. No toe-dipping tests were necessary here; this water met the skin like a veil of warm silk. In it she splashed and ducked and floated; her hair, which had been screwed into a tight little knob, loosening and floating with her like a nimbus. Tired of play, she came out, trickling and glistening, and lay down in the sand, which was hot to the touch, first on her stomach, then on her back, till she was coated with sand like a fish bread-crumbed for frying. This, for the sheer pleasure of plunging anew, and letting the silken water wash her clean.

At the sight, the two middle-aged women who sat looking on grew restless. And, the prank being repeated, the sand-caked little body vanishing in the limpid water to bob up shining like ivory, the tips of their tongues shot out and surreptitiously moistened their lips. These were dry, their throats were dry, their skins itched; their seats burned from pressing the hot sand.

And suddenly eyes met and brows were lifted in a silent question. Shall we? Dare we risk it?

'Let's!'

For no living thing but themselves moved on the miles of desolate beach; not a neighbour was within cooee; their own shack lay hid behind a hill.

Straightway they fell to rolling up their work and stabbing it with their needles.

Then they, too, undressed.

Tight, high bodices of countless buttons went first, baring the massy arms and fat-creased necks of a plump maturity. Thereafter bunchy skirts were slid over hips and stepped out of. Several petticoats followed, the undermost of red flannel, with scalloped edges. Tight stiff corsets were next squeezed from beneath their moorings and cast aside: the linen beneath lay hot and damply crushed. Long white drawers unbound and, leg by leg, disengaged, voluminous calico chemises appeared, draped in which the pair sat down to take off their boots – buttoned boots – and stockings, their feet emerging red and tired-looking, the toes misshapen, and horny with callosities. Erect again, they yet coyly hesitated before the casting of the last veil, once more sweeping the distance for a possible spy. Nothing stirring, however, up went their arms, dragging the balloon-like garments with them; and, inch by inch, calves, thighs, trunks and breasts were bared to view.

At the prospect of getting water playmates, the child had clapped her hands, hopping up and down where she stood. But this was the first time she had watched a real grown-up undress; she was always in bed and asleep when they did it. Now, in broad daylight, she looked on unrebuked, wildly curious; and surprise soon damped her joy. So this was what was underneath! Skirts and petticoats down, she saw that laps were really legs; while the soft and cosy place you put your head on, when you were tired ...

And suddenly she turned tail and ran back to the pool. She didn't want to see.

But your face was the one bit of you you couldn't put under water. So she had to.

Two fat, stark-naked figures were coming down the beach.

They had joined hands, as if to sustain each other in their nudity ... or as if, in shedding their clothes, they had also shed a portion of their years. Gingerly, yet in haste to reach cover, they applied their soles to the tickly sand: a haste that caused unwieldy breasts to bob and swing, bellies and buttocks to wobble. Splay-legged they were, from the weight of these protuberances. Above their knees, garters had cut fierce red lines in the skin; their bodies were criss-crossed with red furrows, from the variety of strings and bones that had lashed them in. The calves of one showed purple-knotted with veins; across the other's abdomen ran a deep, longitudinal scar. One was patched with red hair, one with black.

In a kind of horrid fascination the child stood and stared ... as at two wild outlandish beasts. But before they reached her she again turned, and, heedless of the prickles, ran seawards, out on the reef.

This was forbidden. There were shrill cries of, 'Naughty girl! Come back!'

Draggingly the child obeyed.

They were waiting for her, and, blind to her hurt, took her between them and waded into the water. When this was up to their knees, they stooped to damp napes and crowns, and sluice their arms. Then they played. They splashed water at each other's great backsides; they lay down and, propped on their elbows, let their legs float; or, forming a ring, moved heavily round to the tune of: *Ring-a-ring-a-rosy, pop down a posy!* And down the child went, till she all but sat on the sand. Not so they. Even with the support of the water they could bend but a few inches; and wider than ever did their legs splay, to permit of their corpulences being lowered.

But the sun was nearing meridian in a cloudless sky. Its rays burnt and stung. The child was sent running up the beach to the clothes-heaps, and returned, not unlike a depressed Amor, bearing in each hand a wide, flower-trimmed, dolly-varden hat, the ribbons of which trailed the sand.

These they perched on their heads, binding the ribbons under their chins; and thus attired waded out to the deep end of the pool. Here, where the water came a few inches above their waists, they stood to cool off, their breasts seeming to float on the surface like half-inflated toy balloons. And when the sand stirred up by their feet had subsided, their legs could be seen through the translucent water oddly foreshortened, with edges that frayed at each ripple.

But a line of foam had shown its teeth at the edge of the reef. The tide was on the turn; it was time to go.

Waddling up the beach they spread their petticoats, and on these stretched themselves out to dry. And as they lay there on their sides, with the supreme mass of hip and buttock arching in the air, their contours were those of seals – great mother-seals come lolloping out of the water to lie about on the sand.

The child had found a piece of dry cuttlefish, and sat pretending to play with it. But she wasn't really. Something had happened which made her not like any more to play. Something ugly. Oh, never . . . never . . . no, not ever now did she want to grow up. *She* would always stop a little girl.

ALIX KATES SHULMAN

A Story of a Girl and her Dog

Alix Kates Shulman was born in the mid-west of the United States, in Cleveland, Ohio. She studied philosophy at Columbia University, and took her master's degree in the humanities at New York University. She worked as an editor on the Encyclopedia of Philosophy *while her children were small, after an earlier career as an encyclopedia editor. She began writing in 1967, at about the same time that she became an active feminist. She has written short stories, articles on feminist and literary subjects, a biography of Emma Goldman and several children's books. Her first novel,* Memoirs of an Ex-Prom Queen, *was published in 1972; her second,* Burning Questions, *a political novel, in 1978. She has taught writing and feminist theory courses since 1972. She has two children and lives in New York City.*

Lucky Larrabee was an only child, and unpredictable. At eight, she was still trying to sail down from the garage roof with an umbrella. She never ate ice cream without a pickle. She was afraid of nothing in the world except three boys in her class and her uncle Len who patted her funny. She brought home every stray dog in the neighbourhood. She upset the assistant principal by participating in the Jewish Affair.

Naturally her parents worried; but they adored her nevertheless and all the more.

There is little Lucky, wearing red anklets with stripes down the sides and poorly tied brown oxfords while everyone else has on loafers, her hair hanging down in strings, her chin thrust out, absolutely refusing to sing the words, Jesus or Christ. Why? Two Jewish girls in her class will not sing, and though she has never been Jewish before, Lucky has joined them. She says it is a free country and you can be anything you like. I'm a Jew, she says and will not sing Jesus.

Everyone knows she's no more Jewish than their teacher. It is ridiculous! But she insists and what can they do? She is ruining the Christmas Pageant. They'll get her at recess, they'll get her after school, they'll plant bad pictures in her desk, they'll think of something. But it won't work. Incorrigible little fanatic!

Okay. She doesn't have to sing. But will she just mouth the words silently during the programme please? No one will have to know.

No, she won't. If they try to make her, she swears she'll hold her breath until she faints instead. Perhaps she'll do it anyway! Perhaps she'll hold it till she's dead! That'll show them who's a Jew and who isn't.

Is something wrong at home, Mrs Larrabee? Does Lucky eat a good enough breakfast? Get enough sleep? She is very thin. Has she grown thinner? Not meaning to alarm you, but Lucky has been unusually sullen in class lately – doesn't participate in the class discussions as she used to, doesn't volunteer her answers, no longer seems interested in current events, spends too much time daydreaming, picking at scabs, being negative. She doesn't seem to be trying. Her fingernails. Is there any known source of tension at home? The school likes to be kept informed about these matters as we try to keep parents informed about progress at school. Don't you agree, parents and teachers ought to be working closely together in harmony, for the benefit of the child. The only concrete suggestion the school can make at this time is some companionship and diversion for Lucky. Another child perhaps, or a dog. Meanwhile, we'll just keep an eye on her. Thank you so much for coming in. These conferences are always helpful in any case, even if they do no more than clear the air.

As the Larrabees had been half considering buying a dog for Christmas anyway, they decided it would do no harm to seem accommodating and took the step. They waited until a month had elapsed after the Christmas Pageant so Lucky would not suspect a connection, and then, piling into the new family Nash, backing out of the cinder drive, they drove straight out on Main Street beyond the city limits and continued on into the country to buy a dog.

Naturally, Lucky was permitted by the concerned Larrabees to pick out the pup herself, with only one restriction. It had to be a boy dog, they said, because if they took home a girl dog, sooner or later they would have to have her spayed, which would be cruel and unnatural and would make her into a fat, lazy and unhappy bitch, or they'd have to let her have babies. For keeping her locked up during heat (also cruel and unnatural) couldn't be expected to work forever; creatures have a way of eluding their jailors in quest of forbidden knowledge – witness the fate of Sleeping Beauty, Bluebeard's wives, etc., and the unwanted litters of the neighbourhood bitches. And if they let her go ahead and have her babies, well, either they'd have to keep the puppies (a certain portion of which could be expected to be females too), generating an unmanageable amount of work, anxiety, and expense, even supposing they had the facilities, which of course they did not. Or they'd have the wrench the pups away from their mother (equally cruel and unnatural as well as a bad example for a child) and worry about finding a decent home for each of them besides. No, no, it could be any pup she chose as long as it was male.

The seven mongrel puppies from which she was permitted to choose one were to her untutored eyes and arms indistinguishable as to sex unless she deliberately looked. So she was perfectly happy to restrict her choice to the four males, though she did feel sorry for the females who, it seemed, were condemned to suffer a cruel and unnatural life or else bring on, like Eve, more trouble than they were worth – particularly since cuddling them in the hollow between her neck and shoulder felt quite as wonderful as cuddling the males. But such, she accepted, was family life.

She chose neither the runt she was temperamentally drawn to but upon whom her father frowned, nor the jumper of the litter over whom her mother voiced certain reasonable reservations, but instead picked from the two remaining males the long-eared, thoughtful-eyed charmer who endeared himself to her by stepping across three of his siblings as though they were stepping stones in order to reach her eager fingers wiggling in the corner of the box and investigate them with his adorable wet nose. Curiosity: the quality her parents most admired in Lucky herself. He sniffed and then licked her fingers in a sensual gesture she took for friendship, and although she continued to examine all the pups for a considerable time, picking them up and cuddling them individually, deliberating at length before rendering her final decision, she knew very early the one she would take home. It pained her to reject the others, particularly the runt and a certain female who tickled her neck lovingly when she held her up and was pure when she peeked underneath. But by eight Lucky had already learned through experience that one could not have everything one wanted, that every choice entailed the rejection of its alternatives, and that if she didn't hurry up and announce her selection, much as she enjoyed playing with all the puppies, she'd provoke her father's pique and lose the opportunity to decide herself.

She named the dog Skippy because of the funny way he bounced when he walked. An unimaginative name perhaps, but direct (a quality she instinctively valued) and to her inexperienced mind which did not know that the dog would stop bouncing once it got a few months older, appropriate. Her parents thought she might have selected a name with more flair, but naturally they said nothing.

The day of Lucky's brightening (her word, for no one ever taught her another) seemed like an ordinary late-summer Saturday. Unsuspectingly, she was just finishing a treasured bath, where she had spent a long time sending the water back and forth between the sides of the tub to simulate ocean waves. She was studying the movement of the water, its turbulence, its cresting at the edges and doubling back, trying to imagine how the process could possibly illuminate, as her father declared, the mysteries of the ocean's waves and tides; and afterwards when her brain had grown weary of encompassing the continental coasts, which she had never seen, the earth and the moon, she filled her washcloth with puffs of air which she could pop out in little explosions into the water sending big bubbles rippling through the bath like porpoises.

Up through the open bathroom window drifted the familiar sounds of her father setting up the barbecue in the backyard and her mother bringing out the fixings on a tray. Next door Bertie Jones was still mowing the lawn while from the Jones's screened-in porch the ballgame droned on. Summer days; dog days.

Lucky climbed reluctantly from the tub, now cold, and examined herself in the mirror. Whistle gap between her front teeth, a splash of freckles, short protruding ears, alert: Lucky herself. If she had known what delights awaited her in the next room, she would not have lingered to peel a strip of burnt skin from her shoulder or scratch open a mosquito bite. But she was a nervous child who had never, from the day she learned to drop things over the edge of her high chair for her mother to retrieve, been able to let well enough alone. Three full minutes elapsed before she finally wrapped herself in a towel and padded into her bedroom where Skip, banished from the backyard during dinner preparations, awaited her with wagging tail.

'Skippy Dip!' she cried, dropping to her knees, and throwing her arms around him. She hugged his neck and he licked her face in a display of mutual affection.

She tossed the towel at the door, sat down on the maple vanity bench, made a moue at her freckly face in the mirror, and in a most characteristic pursuit, lifted her left foot to the bench to examine an interesting blister on her big toe, soaked clean and plump in her long bath.

Suddenly Skip's wet little nose, as curious as on the day they had met, delved between her legs with several exploratory sniffs.

'Skip!' Lucky giggled in mock dismay. 'Get out of there,' pushing his nose aside and quickly lowering her foot, for she did know a little. Skip retreated playfully but only until Lucky returned (inevitably) to the blister. For like any pup who has not yet completed his training, he could hardly anticipate every consequence or generalize from a single instance. You know how a dog longs to sniff at things. When Lucky's knee popped up again, exposing that interesting smell, Skip's nose returned as though invited.

Suddenly Lucky felt a new intriguing sensation. '*What's this?*'

She had once, several years earlier, felt another strange sensation in the groin, one that had been anything but pleasant. She and Judy Jones, the girl next door, had been playing mother and baby in a game of House. As Lucky lay on the floor of that very room having her 'diaper' changed by a maternal Judy, the missing detail to lend a desired touch of verisimilitude to the game struck Lucky. 'Baby powder!' she cried. 'Sprinkle on some baby powder!'

'Baby powder?' blinked Judy.

'Get the tooth powder from the bathroom shelf. The Dr Lyons.'

In the first contact with Skip's wet nose, Lucky remembered her words as if they still hung in the room. She didn't stop to remember the intervening events: how Judy obediently went to the bathroom but couldn't find the Dr Lyons; how, after finally finding it she could barely manage to get the tin open. Lucky's memory flashed ahead to the horrible instant when the astringent powder fell through the air from a great (but not sufficiently great) height onto the delicate tissue of her inner labia and stung her piercingly, provoking a scream that brought her poor mother running anxiously from a distant room.

But the sensation produced by her pal Skippy was in every respect different. It was cool not hot; insinuating not shocking; cosy, provocative, delicious. It drew her open and out, not closed in retreat. No scream ensued; only the arresting thought, *What's this?* Like the dawning of a new idea or the grip of that engaging question, What makes it tick? If she had had the movable ears of her friend's species, they would have perked right up. *What's this?* The fascination of beginnings, the joy of the new. Something more intriguing than a blister.

She touched Skip's familiar silky head tentatively, but this time did not quite push it away. And he, enjoying the newness too (he was hardly more than a pup), sniffed and then, bless him, sniffed again. And following the natural progression for a normally intelligent dog whose interest has been engaged – as natural and logical as the human investigator's progress from observed phenomenon to initial hypothesis to empirical test – the doggie's pink tongue followed his nose's probe with a quizzical exploratory lick.

What would her poor parents have thought if they had peeked in? They would have known better than to see or speak evil, for clearly these two young creatures, these trusting pups (of approximately the same ages when you adjust for species), were happy innocents. They would probably have blamed themselves for having insisted on a male pup. They might even have taken the poor animal to the gas chambers of the ASPCA and themselves to some wildly expensive expert who would only confuse and torment them with impossibly equivocal advice until they made some terrible compromise. At the very least, there would have been furious efforts at distraction and that night much wringing of hands.

Fortunately our Adam and Eve remain alone to pursue their pragmatic investigations. The whole world is before them.

The charcoal is now ready to take on the weenies. Mrs Larrabee kisses her husband affectionately on the neck as she crosses the yard towards the house. She opens the screen door, leans inside, and yells up the stairs, 'Dinner.'

'Just a minute,' says Lucky, squeezing her eyes closed. One more stroke of that inquisitive tongue – only one more! – and Lucky too will possess as her own one of nature's most treasured recipes.

Waves and oceans, suns and moons, barbecues, bubbles, blisters, tongues and tides – what a rich banquet awaits the uncorrupted.

EVELYN SHARP

The Game that Wasn't Cricket

Evelyn Sharp (1869-1955) was brought up in London and Bucking-hamshire, one of nine children, and she later regretted that the size of her family kept her mother a stranger to her until she was an adult. She had a happy Victorian childhood, with summer holidays in Brighton and the country. She was educated in London, and would have liked to have gone on to university, which was then still uncommon for women. When she left school, she spent half a year in Paris with two of her sisters, sightseeing and attending open lectures at the University of Paris. On her return to England, she persuaded her parents to let her work, which was unusual for middle-class women at the time. She settled in London, supporting herself first by teaching and later by journalism. She quickly became established as a writer, contributed to the Yellow Book *and broke into literary circles. While she was covering a conference of women workers for the* Manchester Guardian *she heard Elizabeth Robins speak on suffrage for women, and was immediately inspired to join the Women's Social and Political Union. She worked with Elizabeth Robins for many years as an active suffragist and had two terms of imprisonment in Holloway. She continued her suffragist activities during the First World War and was a founder member of the United Suffragists. She refused to pay her income tax as a voteless woman, and her possessions were vindictively seized and sold by the Bankruptcy Court. After the war and the limited enfranchisement of women, she travelled widely in Germany, Holland and Ireland, and in 1922 she went to Russia, working as part of a Quaker famine relief programme. She married Henry Nevinson at the age of sixty-four. All her life she continued to be interested in political and social problems, and worked for the Labour Party, the National Council for Civil Liberties and the Council for the Abolition of the Death Penalty. Her writing includes fiction for children and adults, and an autobiography,* Unfinished Adventure *(1933).*

Down the alley where I happen to live, playtime draws a sharp line between the sexes. It is not so noticeable during working hours, when girls and boys, banded together by the common grievance of compulsory education, trot off to school almost as allies, even hand-in-hand in those cases where protection is sought from the little girl by the little boy who raced her into the world and lost – or won – by half a length. But when school is over sex antagonism, largely fostered by the parent, immediately sets in. Knowing the size of the average back yard in my neighbourhood, I have plenty of sympathy for the mother who wishes to keep it clear of children. But I always want to know why, in order to secure this privacy, she gives the boy a piece of bread-and-dripping and a ball, while the girl is given a piece of bread and dripping and a baby. And I have not yet decided which of the two toys is the more destructive of my peace.

Every evening during the summer, cricket is played just below my window in the hour preceding sunset. Cricket, as played in my alley, is less noisy than football, in which anything that comes handy as a substitute for the ball may be used, preferably an old, jagged salmon tin. But cricket lasts longer, the nerves of the parents whose windows overlook the cricket ground being able to stand it better. As the best working hour of my day is destroyed equally by both, I have no feeling either way, except that the cricket, as showing a more masterly evasion of difficulties, appeals to me rather more. It is comparatively easy to achieve some resemblance to a game of football even in a narrow strip of pavement bordered by houses, where you can place one goal in the porch of the model dwellings at the blind end of the alley, and the other goal among the motor traffic at the street end. But first-class cricket is more difficult of attainment when the field is so crowded as to make it hard to decide which player out of three or four has caught you out, while your only chance of not being run out first ball is to take the wicket with you – always a possibility when the wicket is somebody's coat that has a way of getting mixed up with the batsman's feet.

In spite of obstacles, however, the cricket goes on every evening before sunset; and all the while, the little girl who tripped to school on such a gay basis of equality with her brother only a few hours back, sits on the doorstep minding the baby. I do not say that she actively objects to this; I only know with acute certainty that the baby objects to it, and for a long time I felt that it would be at least interesting to see what would happen if the little girl were to stand up at the wicket for a change while her brother dealt with the baby.

And the other evening this did happen. A mother, making one of those sorties from the domestic stronghold, that in my alley always have the effect of bringing a look of guilt into the faces of the innocent, shouted something I did not hear, picked up the wicket, cuffed somebody's head with it and made him put it on, gave the baby to a brother, and sent his sister off to the oil-shop with a jar in one hand and a penny tightly clasped in the other. The interruption over, the scattered field reformed automatically, somebody else's jacket was made into a mound, and cricket was resumed with the loss of one player who, by the way, showed an astonishing talent for minding the baby.

Then the little girl came back from the oil-shop. I know not what spirit of revolt entered suddenly her small, subdued soul; perhaps the sight of a boy minding the baby suggested an upheaval of the universe that demanded her instant co-operation; perhaps she had no distinct idea in her mind beyond a wish to rebel. Whatever her reasons, there she stood, bat in hand, waiting for the ball, while the baby crowed delightedly in the unusual embrace of a boy who, by all the laws of custom, was unsexing himself.

Another instant, and the air was rent with sound and fury. In front of the wicket stood the Spirit of Revolt, with tumbled hair and defiant eyes, breathless with much running, intoxicated with success; around her, an outraged cricket team, strong in the conventions of a lifetime, was protesting fiercely.

What had happened was quite simple. Grasping in an instant of time the only possible way of eluding the crowd of fielders in the narrow space, the little impromptu batswoman had done the obvious thing and struck the ball against the wall high over their heads, whence it bounded into the open street and got lost in the traffic. Then she ran till she could run no more. Why wasn't it fair? she wanted to know.

''Cause it ain't – there!' was one illuminating reply.

''Cause we don't never play that way,' was another upon which she was quick to pounce.

'You never thought of it, that's why!' she retorted shrewdly.

She was desperately outnumbered. It was magnificent, but it wasn't cricket; moreover, her place was the doorstep, as she was speedily reminded when the door reopened and avenging motherhood once more swooped down upon the scene. A shake here, a push there – and the boy was back again at the wicket, while a weeping baby lay unheeded on the lap of a weeping Spirit of Revolt.

And the queer thing is that the innovation made by the small batswoman in her one instant of wild rebellion has now been adopted by the team that plays cricket down my alley, every evening before sunset.

GRETA LAINER

From, A Young Girl's Diary

A Young Girl's Diary, *from which the following extracts are taken, was published in 1919, edited by Dr Hermine von Hug-Hellmuth. The anonymous diarist, who is given the name Greta Lainer, gave her diary to her friend Dr Hug-Hellmuth when she got engaged to be married, knowing of the doctor's interest in child psychology. When the First World War broke out, Greta became a nurse on the Serbian front, but suffered a breakdown and died during the war. Dr Hug-Hellmuth showed the diary to Freud before it was published. He responded warmly, calling it a 'gem', and urged her to publish it, praising the candid way in which 'we are shown how the mystery of the sexual life first presses itself vaguely on the attention, and then takes entire possession of the growing intelligence, so that the child suffers under the load of secret knowledge but gradually becomes enabled to shoulder the burden. Of all these things we have a description at once so charming, so serious, and so artless, that it cannot fail to be of supreme interest to educationalists and psychologists'. Extracts from Freud's letter appeared as a preface to the original edition of the diary, but, after publication, suggestions were made that the diary might have been retouched and in later editions his incautious accolade of the artlessness of the diary was not reprinted.*

Greta Lainer lived in Vienna before the First World War with her parents, her older brother Oswald and her older sister Dora (nicknamed Inspee). Her closest friend in Vienna was Hella; Ada was a friend she saw during summer holidays in the country. Greta's mother died of cancer during the time she was keeping this diary, and her aunt came to live with the family.

First Year: Age Eleven
October 10th. I'm in a great funk, I missed my gymnastic lesson

yesterday. I was upstairs at Hella's and without meaning it I was so late I did not dare to go. And Hella said I had better stay with her, that we would say that our sum was so difficult that we had not got it finished in time. Luckily we really had a sum to do. But I said nothing about it at home, for tomorrow Oswald is going to G. to Herr S's. I thought that I knew all about it but only now had Hella really told me everything. It's a horrible business this . . . I really can't write it. She says that of course Inspee has it already, had it when I wrote that Inspee wouldn't bathe, did not want to bathe; really she had it. Whatever happens one must always be anxious about it. *Streams of blood* says Hella. But then everything gets all bl . . . That's why in the country Inspee always switched off the light before she was quite undressed, so that I couldn't see. Ugh! Catch me looking! It begins at 14 and goes on for 20 years or more. Hella says that Berta Franke in our class knows all about it. In the arithmetic lesson she wrote a note: Do you know what being un . . . is? Hella wrote back, of course I've known it for a long time. Berta waited for her after class when the Catholics were having their religion lesson and they went home together. I remember quite well that I was very angry, for they're not chums. On Tuesday Berta came with us, for Hella had sent her a note in class saying that I knew *everything* and she needn't bother about me. Inspee suspects something, she's always spying about and sneering, perhaps she thinks that she's the only person who ought to know everything.

October 21st. Berta Franke says that when one is dark under the eyes one has *it* and that when one gets a baby then one doesn't have it any more until one gets another. She told us too how one gets it, but I didn't really believe what she said, for I thought she did not know herself exactly. Then she got very cross and said, 'All right, I won't tell you any more. If I don't know myself.' . . . Men have *it* too, but very seldom. We see a lot of Berta Franke now, she is an awfully nice girl, perhaps Mother will let me invite her here next Sunday.

Second Year: Age Twelve
April 1st. Today Dora told me a lot more. She is quite different now from what she used to be. One does not say P[eriod], but M[enstruation]. Only common people say P-. Or one can say one's *like that*. Dora has had M- since August before last, and it is horribly disagreeable, because men always know. That is why at the High School we have only three men professors and all the other teachers are women. Now Dora often does not have M- and then sometimes it's awfully

bad, and that's why she's anemic. That men always know, that's frightfully interesting.

April 4th. We talk a lot about such things now. Dora certainly knows more than I do, that is, not more but better. But she isn't quite straightforward all the same. When I asked her how she got to know about it all, whether Erika told her or Frieda, she said, 'Oh, I don't know; one finds it all out somehow; one need only use one's eyes and one's ears, and then one can reason things out a little.' But seeing and hearing don't take one very far. I've always kept my eyes open and I'm not so stupid as all that. One must be told by someone, one *can't* just happen upon it by oneself.

Third Year: Age Thirteen

August 14th. Just a word, quickly. Today, when Ada was having a bath Mother said to *us two*, 'Girls, I've something to tell you; I don't want you to get a fright in the night. Ada's mother told me that Ada is very nervous, and often walks in her sleep.' 'I say,' said I, 'that's frightfully interesting, she must be *moonstruck*; I suppose it always happens when the moon is full.' Then mother said, 'Tell me, Gretel, how do *you* know about all these things? Has Ada talked to you about them?' 'No,' said I, 'but the Frankes had a maid who walked in her sleep and Berta Franke told Hella and me about it.' It has just struck me that Mother said: how do you know about all *these* things? So it must have something to do with *that*. I wonder whether I dare ask Ada, or whether she would be offended. I'm frightfully curious to see whether she will walk in her sleep while she is staying here.

August 24th. Today I ventured to ask Ada about the sleep-walking, and she said that it was really so, when she walked in her sleep it was always at *that time* and when the moon is full. The first time, it was last year, she did it on purpose in order to frighten her mother, when her mother had first told her she would not be allowed to go on the stage. It does not seem to me a very clever idea, or that she is likely to gain anything by it. The day after tomorrow someone is coming to fetch her home, and for that reason she was crying all the morning.

December 16th. Owing to Mother's illness I've had simply no time to write anything about the school, although there has been a *great deal* to write about, for example that Prof W. is very friendly again although he no longer gives us lessons, and that most of the girls can't bear the Nutling because she makes such favourites of the Jewish girls. It's quite true that she does, for example Franke, who is never any good, will probably get a Praiseworthy in Maths and Physics; and

she lets Weinberger do anything she likes. I always get Excellent both
for school work and prep, so it really does not matter to me, but
Verbenowitsch is frightfully put out because she is no longer the favourite as she was with Frau Doktor St. The other day it was quite unpleasant in the Maths lesson. In the answer to a sum there happened to
be ⅓, and then the Nutling asked what ⅓ would be as a decimal fraction; so we went on talking about recurring [periodic] decimals and
every time she used the word *period*, some of the girls giggled, but
luckily some of them were Jews, and she got perfectly savage and
simply screamed at us. In Frau Doktor St's lesson in the First, some of
the girls giggled at the same thing and she went on just as if she had
not noticed it, but afterwards she always spoke of *periodic places*, and
then one does not think of the real meaning so much. Frau Doktor F.
said she should complain to Frau Doktor M. about our unseemly behaviour. But really all the girls had not giggled, for example, Hella
and I simply exchanged glances and understood one another at once. I
can't endure that idiotic giggling.

January 5th. Most important, Hella since yesterday evening
— — — — ! She did not come to school yesterday, for the day before
she felt frightfully bad, and her mother really began to think she was
going to have another attack of appendicitis. Instead of that!!! She
looks so ill and interesting, I spent the whole afternoon and evening
with her; and at first she did not want to tell me what was the matter.
But when I said I should go away if she did not tell me, she said, 'All
right, but you must not make such idiotic faces, and above all you
must not look at me.' 'Very well,' I said, 'I won't look, but tell me
everything about it.' So then she told me that she had felt frantically
bad, as if she was being cut in two, much worse than after the appendicitis operation, and then she had frantically high fever and shivered
at the same time, all Friday, and yesterday — — — tableau!! And
then her mother told her the chief things, though she knew them
already. Earlier on Friday the doctor had said, 'Don't let us be in a
hurry to think about a relapse, there may be *other*!! causes.' And then
he whispered to her mother, but Hella caught the word *enlighten*.
Then she knew directly what time of day it was. She acted the innocent to her mother, as if she knew nothing at all, and her mother
kissed her and said, now you are not a child any more, now you
belong among the grown-ups. How absurd, so I am still a child! After
all, on July 30th I shall be 14 too, and at least one month before I shall
have it too, so I shan't be a *child* for more than six months more.
Hella and I laughed frightfully, but she is really a little puffed up

about it; she won't admit that she is, but I noticed it quite clearly. The only girl I know who did not put on airs when that happened was Ada. Because of the school Hella is awfully shy, and before her father too. But her mother has promised her not to tell him. If only one can trust her!!!

January 7th. Hella came to school to-day *in spite of everything*. I kept on looking at her, and in the interval she said, 'I have told you already that you must not stare at me in that idiotic way, and this is the second time I've had to speak to you about it. One must not make a joke about such things.' I was not going to stand that. One must not look at her; very well, in the third lesson I sat turning away from her; then suddenly she hooked one of my feet with hers so that I nearly burst out laughing, and she said, 'Do look round, for that way is even stupider.' Of course Dunker promptly called us to order, that is, she told Hella to go on reading, but Hella said promptly that she felt very unwell, and that what she had said to me was, she would have to go home at 12. All the girls looked at one another, for they all know what *unwell* means, and Frau Doktor Dunker said Hella had better leave directly, but she answered in French – that pleases Dunker awfully – that she would rather stay till the end of the lesson. It was simply splendid!

June 15th. Hella thinks that I shall soon be 'developed' too, because I always have such black rings under my eyes.

July 2nd. My goodness, to-day I have . . . no, I can't write it plain out. In the middle of the Physics lesson, during revision, when I was not thinking of anything in particular, Fräulein N. came in with a paper to be signed. As we all stood up I thought to myself: Hello, what's that? And then it suddenly occurred to me: 'Aha!!' In the interval Hella asked me why I had got so fiery red in the Physics lesson, if I'd had some sweets with me. I did not want to tell her the real reason directly, and so I said, 'Oh no, I had nearly fallen asleep from boredom, and when Fräulein N. came in it gave me a start.' On the way home I was very silent, and I walked so slowly (for of course one must not walk fast *when* . . .) that Hella said, 'Look here, what's up today, that you are so frightfully solemn? Have you fallen in love without my knowing it, or is it *at long last* . . . ?' Then I said '*Or is it at long last!*' And she said 'Ah, then now we're equals once more,' and there in the middle of the street she gave me a kiss. Just at that moment two students went by and one of them said, 'Give me one too.' And Hella said: 'Yes, I'll give you one on the cheek which will burn.' So they hurried away. We really had no use for them: to-day!! Hella wanted me to tell her *everything about it*; but really I hadn't anything to tell, and yet she believed that I *wouldn't* tell. It is really very unpleasant, and this evening I shall have to take frightful care because of Dora. But I must tell Aunt because I want a San— T—. It will be frightfully awkward. It was different in Hella's case, first of all because she had such frightful cramps before it began so that her mother knew all about it without being told, and secondly because it was her *mother*. I certainly shan't tell Dora whatever happens, for that would make me feel still more ashamed. As for a San— T—, I shall never be able to buy one for myself even if I live to be 80. And it would be awful for Father to know about it. I wonder whether men really do know; I suppose they must know about their wives, but at any rate they can't know anything about their daughters.

July 3rd. Dora does know after all. For I switched off the light *before* I undressed, and then Dora snapped at me, 'What on earth are you up to, switch it on again directly.' 'No I won't.' Then she came over and wanted to switch it on herself; 'Oh do please wait until I've got into bed.' 'O-o-h, is that it,' said Dora, 'why didn't you say so before? I've always hidden my things from you, and you haven't got any yet.' And then we talked for quite a long time, and she told me that Mother had commissioned her to tell me everything *when* — — — Mother had told her all about it, but she said it was better for one girl to tell it to another, because that was least awkward. Mother knew too that in January Hella had . . . But how? I never let on! It was midnight before we switched off the light.

ELIZA HAYWOOD

Aliena's Story

Eliza Haywood (1693?-1756) appears to have been the daughter of a small shopkeeper in London, and was better educated, she later claimed, than most girls of her time. She married a clergyman much older than herself, and in 1720 ran away from her husband who, the following year, advertised that he would not be responsible for her debts. By then she was already earning a living, and her first novel Love in Excess *(published in three parts in 1719 and 1720) went through six editions by 1725. She is reputed to have had two illegitimate children. Her early attempts at plays were not particularly successful, though her occasional appearances on the stage aroused interest, and she concentrated on fiction, maintaining a very high output of romances of passion in the 1720s. She then turned to novels of contemporary scandal, retailing, in thinly veiled fiction, gossip about celebrities of the period. This earned her notoriety as well as powerful enemies, led by Pope, who managed to damage her reputation, and her once high production dwindled in the 1730s. In the 1740s, she re-established herself and founded the* Female Spectator *which was originally published in monthly parts between 1744 and 1746. It was supposedly produced by an editorial team of four women, but there is no evidence that her co-editors actually existed, and the essays, didactic stories and miscellanies were presumably all her own. She had a brief, apparently unsuccessful, venture as a bookseller and publisher. In the 1750s she wrote her best remembered novels,* The History of Betsy Thoughtless *(1751) and* The History of Jemmy and Jenny Jessamy *(1752), having regained her public, if not her reputation. She justified the content of her books – chiefly love intrigue – on the grounds that, as a woman, she lacked formal education, but had nonetheless an intuitive knowledge of love, and she was not slow to identify and exploit her market. 'Aliena's Story', which purports to be a letter from a reader of the* Female Spectator, *is a watered-down version of the popular eighteenth-century theme of the innocent girl's*

*ruin, but indicates the genuine oppressiveness of a censorious society.
The story has been abridged and the spelling and punctuation have
been modernized.*

Ladies,
You cannot be insensible how little compassion the woes occasioned
by love find from this iron-hearted age; nor how ready everyone is, on
the least breach of decorum, to censure and condemn, without considering either the force of that passion or what particular circumstances may have concurred to ensnare a young creature into a forgetful-
ness of what she owes to herself. I am sure you are too generous not to
make some allowances for heedless youth, when hurried on by an
excess of passion to things which cooler reason disapproves.

In this confidence I take the liberty to give you the narrative of an
adventure, which, though exactly true in every circumstance, has in it
something equally surprising with any that the most celebrated
romance has presented to us.

The heroine of it, whom I shall distinguish by the name of Aliena, is
the daughter of a gentleman descended of a very ancient family; and
as he had several children besides this Aliena, none of them, excepting
the eldest son, could expect any other fortunes than their education,
which he indeed took care should be very liberal.

But though his paternal tenderness seemed equally divided among
them all, and Aliena had no more opportunities of improvement than
her other sisters, yet did she make a much greater progress in everything she was instructed in than any of them; and as nature had
bestowed on her a much greater share of beauty, so was also her
genius more extensive than that which either one which was elder, and
another a year younger than herself, had to boast of.

In fine, dear ladies, she was at fourteen one of the most charming
creatures in the world. As her father lived in London, she went
frequently to public places, and those diversions which were too
expensive for the narrowness of her circumstances were, however, not
denied her: she was never without tickets for the masquerades,
ridottoes, operas, concerts, and plays, presented to her by her friends.

Aliena was the darling of all that knew her; wherever she came a
general and unfeigned pleasure diffused itself in every face through
the whole company. It is scarce possible to say whether she was more
admired by the men, or loved by the women: a thing wonderful you
will own, and what some people take upon them to say is incompat-
ible, yet so in reality it was.

Among the number of Aliena's admirers, there was a commander of one of his majesty's ships, a gentleman of good family, agreeable person, and handsome fortune, exclusive of his commission; whether he had more the art of persuasion than any of his rivals, I will not pretend to say, but it is certain that either his merit or good fortune rendered everything he said to her more acceptable than the most courtly address of any other person.

To be brief, she loved him: his manner, whatever it was, ensnared her young heart, and the society of her dear captain was preferable to her than any other joy the world could give.

I am very well assured his pretensions were on an honourable footing, otherwise they had been rejected at the first; all her acquaintance expected every day to hear of the completion of their wishes by a happy marriage; when contrary to her and it may be to his expectations, he was ordered to sail for the West Indies, and to be stationed there for three years. How terrible a rebuff this was to her dearest hopes anyone may judge, and the more so as he did not press her to complete the marriage before his departure.

I will not pretend to be so well acquainted with his thoughts as to say positively he had never loved her; but I believe you will be of the opinion with me, that this behaviour was far from being the indication of a sincere and ardent passion.

She had too much wit not to perceive this slight, but too much tenderness to resent it as she ought to have done; and when he told her, as he sometimes vouchsafed to do, that he depended on her constancy, and that he should find her at his return with the same inclination as he left her possessed of his favour, she always answered that it was impossible for time, absence, or any other solicitations ever to prevail on her to call back that heart she had given him.

At length the cruel day of taking leave was come. Never parting had more the show of mournful: I say the show, because I cannot think the captain had any real grief at heart, but on the side of Aliena it was truly so. For some days she shut herself up, gave a loose to tears and complainings, and scarce could be prevailed upon to take needful nourishment; her father's commands, however, and remonstrances, how much this conduct would incur the ridicule of the world at last made her assume a more cheerful countenance, and she consented to see company, and appear abroad as usual; but while we all thought her grief was abated, it preyed with greater violence by being restrained, and inspired her with a resolution to sacrifice everything she had once valued herself upon rather than continue in the condition she was.

In short, one day, when she was thought to be gone on a visit to one of her acquaintance, she went to a sale-shop, equipped herself in the habit of a man, or rather boy, for being very short, she seemed in that dress not to exceed twelve or thirteen years of age at most.

Thinking herself not sufficiently disguised even by this, she made her fine flaxen hair be shaved, and covered her head with a little brown wig, which wrought so great a change in her that had her own father happened to have met her, he would not have known her after this transformation.

But it was not her intention to run that hazard, nor had she taken all these pains to live concealed in London; she always knew she loved the captain, but knew not till now with how much violence she did so; or that for the sake of being near him, she could forego all that ever had or ought to have been dear to her.

Not able to support life without the presence of him who had her heart, she seemed with her habit to have thrown off all the fears and modesty of womanhood: the fatal softness of our sex alone remained; and that, guided by the dictates of an ungovernable passion, made her despise all dangers, hardships, infamy, and even death itself.

She went directly to Gravesend, where her lover's ship lay yet at anchor, waiting his arrival, who was gone into the country to take leave of some relations. This she knew, and resolved, if possible, to get herself entered on board before he came, being unwilling he should see her till they were under sail. She was a great admirer of an old play of Beaumont and Fletcher's, called *Philaster; or Love Lies a Bleeding*; the character of Bellario, who, disguised like a page, followed and waited on her beloved prince in all his adventures strangely charmed her; and she thought, as her passion was equal to that of any woman in the world, it would become her to attest it by actions equally extravagant.

As she had often heard the captain talk of his first lieutenant with a great deal of friendship, she thought him the most proper person to address; accordingly she waited till he came on shore, and went to his lodgings, where being easily admitted, she told him she had a great inclination to the sea; she begged to be received in the station of a cabin-boy; she added she had heard such extraordinary praises of the captain's humanity and gentleness to all belonging to him that she had an extreme ambition to attend on him, if such a favour might be granted her.

The lieutenant eyed her attentively all the time she was speaking, and was seized with a something which he had never felt before, and at that time was far from being able to account for; and this secret impulse it was that made him unable to refuse her request, though he knew very well that a sufficient number of boys had been already entered; he told her, however, that he could not give her any assurance of being employed about the captain's person till he had spoke to him concerning it.

She thanked the lieutenant a thousand times over, and was ready to fall at his feet in token of her gratitude; but entreated he would continue his goodness so far as to order her to be put on board, lest he should, in the hurry of his affairs, forget the promise he had made, and they should sail without her. To which he answered that she had no need to be under any apprehensions of that sort, for he should send his servant with her to a house where there were several boys of the same station, and he believed much of the same age, and that the long boat would put them all on board that evening.

He called his man and sent him to conduct her to the house he had mentioned. There she found several youths ready equipped for their voyage, and whose rough athletic countenances and robust behaviour became well enough the vocation they had taken upon them, but rendered them very unfit companions for the gentle delicate Aliena.

The discourse they had with each other, the oaths they swore, and the tricks they played by way of diverting themselves frighted her almost out of her intention; but she was much more so when they began to lay their hands on her, to make her one in their boisterous exercises. The more abashed and terrified she looked, the more rude they grew, and pinching her on the ribs, as boys frequently do to one another, one of them found she had breasts, and cried with a great oath that they had got a girl among them: on this they were all for being satisfied, and had doubtless treated her with the most shocking indecency, had not her cries brought up the woman of the house, who, being informed of the occasion of the uproar, took Aliena from them, and was going to carry her into another room, in order to learn the truth of this adventure, when the lieutenant entered, and found his new sailor all in tears, and the rest in a loud laugh.

The cause of all this was soon explained to him, but the greatest mystery was still behind; Aliena begged that as her design had miscarried, by her sex being so unfortunately discovered, they would permit her go without making any further enquiry concerning her. But this request the lieutenant would by no means comply with; he now no longer wondered at those secret emotions, which had worked about his heart at first sight of her, and avowed the force of nature, which is not to be deceived, though the senses may, and frequently are.

He now indulged the admiration of her beauty, and told her in a gay manner that as he had entered her on her earnest desire, he could not consent to discharge her without knowing something more of her than that she was a woman.

'Nay,' added he, 'even of that I am not quite assured: I have only the testimony of two or three boys, who, in such a case, are not to be depended upon – I think that I ought, at least, to satisfy myself in that point.'

In speaking these words he offered to pluck her towards him, and the vile woman of the house, who had no regard for anything but her own interest in obliging her customers, guessing the lieutenant's designs, and perhaps thinking them worse than they were in reality, went out of the room and left them together.

This, indeed, quite overcame all the resolution of Aliena; she thought she saw something in the eyes of the lieutenant, that, even more than his words, threatened her with all a maid of honour and condition had to dread; and after having struggled with all her might to get loose of the hold he had taken of her, threw herself at his feet, and with a flood of tears, and broken trembling voice, conjured him to have pity on her, and suffer her to depart.

The lieutenant, who, as it luckily proved for her, was really a man of honour, raised her from the posture she had been in, with more respect than, indeed, considering all things, she could in reason have expected; desired she would not be under any apprehensions of his behaviour to her in a manner she could not be brought to approve; but in return for that self-denial, he still insisted she should make him the confidant of the motive which had obliged her to expose herself to the dangers she had done.

To this poor Aliena answered little but with tears; and while he continued pressing, she evading, a sailor came in to acquaint him the captain was arrived; on which he hastily took leave, but before he left the house, charged the landlady, as she valued his friendship, not to let the seeming boy stir out of the room.

This Aliena was ignorant of, till, imagining herself at liberty, she was going downstairs, in order to quit a place where she had nothing but ruin to expect; she was met by the woman of the house, who obliged her to return back, and then locked her into a room, telling her she must stay till the return of the lieutenant.

Now had this unfortunate creature full liberty to reflect on the mischiefs she had brought upon herself: night came on, and every moment came loaden with new horrors. A thousand different ideas rose in her almost distracted brain: she feared the lieutenant, and saw no way to avoid him but by the protection of the captain, and how to acquaint him with anything of what had passed she knew not; at last she bethought herself of attempting to do it even by the lieutenant himself; and accordingly when he came, as he did pretty early in the morning, she said to him, with all the courage she could assume, 'Sir, you insist on knowing who I am, which I am determined to die rather than comply with: there is but one way by which you have a chance of gratifying your curiosity. Be the bearer of a letter from me to your captain; he knows me, and if he thinks fit, will inform you of everything.'

The lieutenant on this began to guess somewhat of the truth, and agreed to do as she desired, and immediately called for pen, ink, and paper for her; which being brought, she was not long writing these lines:

> To Capt. –
> Unable to support your absence, I followed you in disguise, desirous of no other happiness than to enjoy concealed your sight. An unlucky accident has discovered me; your first lieutenant, whose prisoner I now am, can tell you by what means – for heaven's sake deliver me from his power, that I may either return to my father, if he will receive me after this adventure, or die with shame of it in some obscure corner of the world.

She subscribed no name, nor was there any occasion for doing it to one so well acquainted with the character of her handwriting; the lieutenant suffered her to seal it without once asking to see the contents, and gave his word and honour to deliver it the same hour into the captain's hand, and bring whatever answer should be returned.

He hurried away to his lodgings, where he was strangely surprised to find a great crowd of officers, and other people, about the door, and on his going upstairs saw the captain, and three gentlemen, whom he knew not, engaged in a very warm dispute. The cause of it was this.

The family of Aliena had no sooner missed her, than strict search was made for her all over the town; accident at last discovered where she had exchanged her habit, and the disguise she had made choice of made them naturally conjecture on what design she was gone; but not being able to imagine that so young and artless a maid should have undertaken an enterprise of this bold kind, concluded she must have her advisers and exciters to it: and who but the captain could they suspect of being so. They complained of the insult, and obtained an order to search the ship, and force her from this betrayer of her honour; to this end, they brought proper officers with them to Gravesend, and had the assistance of others belonging to that place.

Before they proceeded to extremeties, however, they went to the captain's lodgings. At first, the father, an uncle, and a cousin of Aliena's remonstrated to him, in terms tolerably mild, how ungentleman-like an action it was, to delude a young girl of good family to accompany him in so shameful a manner; but finding he denied all they accused him of, they began to grow extremely rough, and their mutual rage was expressing itself in the highest terms when the lieutenant entered.

'Gentlemen,' cried he to the kindred of Aliena, 'your passion has transported you too far. I am the only person capable of clearing up this mystery; but before I do so, beg leave to give a letter to my captain, put into my hands this morning, for the safe delivery of which I have pawned my honour.'

The captain, taking the letter hastily out of his hands, and having read it with a great deal of real amazement walked several times about the room with a confused emotion; the father and the uncle of Aliena still crying out he must produce the girl made him throw the letter upon the table in an abrupt manner. The father, finding it his daughter's hand, read it with a shock which is not to be expressed, and having given it to his brother, cried, 'Where, who is the lieutenant into whose power my unhappy girl has fallen?'

'I am the person,' said the lieutenant; 'and but to clear my captain from any imputation of a base design, should not have spoke what I now find myself obliged to do.' He then related in what manner Aliena came to him, the earnestness with which she begged to be entered on board; and in fine, neither omitted nor added to anything of the truth.

The lieutenant conducted them where they found the unfortunate Aliena walking about the room in her boy's clothes, distracted in her mind at what reception her letter would find from the captain, but little thinking of the new guests who entered her chamber. At seeing them thus all together, she fell into faintings, from which she was recovered but to relapse again, and the first words she spoke were, 'I am ruined for ever. Oh wretched! wretched am I in every way, by all deservedly abandoned.'

The condition they saw her in disarmed her kindred of great part of the indignation they before had been full of, and hearing the captain testify an abundance of tender concern for the hazards to which she had exposed herself for his sake, they desired the captain to go with them into another room; which request he readily complying with, the father of Aliena told him that as he had courted his daughter, he thought it would become him to silence the reproaches of the world by marrying her before he embarked.

To which the captain replied that he desired no greater happiness in life than being the husband of Aliena provided the duties of his post had not called him so suddenly away, but as he must not only immediately be snatched from her arms, but also be absent thence for so long a time, he thought it inconsistent, either with love or reason, to leave her a wife under such circumstances: 'As constancy more than vehemence of affection is requisite to render the conjugal state a happy one, it is time alone can assure me of felicity with the lady in question, for which reason I must not think of entering into any bonds of the nature you mention till after my return.'

This answer, determinate as it was, did not make them give over; but all they urged was preaching to the wind, and the more they seemed to resent his refusal, the more obstinately he persisted in it; and they were obliged to leave Gravesend, taking with them the disconsolate Aliena, no less dissatisfied in their minds than when they came to it.

How changed is now the fate of this young lady! The idol once of her acquaintance, the pity now of some, and the contempt of others! Her father and brothers look on her as a blemish to their family, and her sisters take every opportunity to reproach her. The captain has never wrote to her since he went, though several letters from him have been received by others. All I can say gives but a faint idea of it; yet such as it is, I flatter myself, will be sufficient to induce you to make her innocence as public as possible, by inserting this faithful account of the whole affair.

I am, ladies,
Your sincere well-wisher
And most humble servant,
Claribella

Red Lion Square
March 29, 1745

CAROLINE NORTON

Kate Bouverie

Caroline Norton (1808-77) was the granddaughter of the playwright Richard Sheridan. She was launched in London Society at the age of eighteen, and the following year married George Norton, who had first wanted to marry her when she was only sixteen. Her father was now dead and she had no dowry, so she had to marry to secure her future. It was an unsuccessful marriage from the start, exacerbated by the dislike of both families for each other, and their political differences, as the Nortons were Tories and the Sheridans an old Whig family. Caroline Norton approached Lord Melbourne, then Home Secretary, for an appointment for her husband, and Melbourne became a frequent visitor at the Nortons' home. Caroline Norton aspired to holding a political and literary salon, and was a published author. After her marriage broke down, George Norton brought an action against Melbourne for seducing his wife, motivated possibly by a wish to provoke political scandal and discredit Melbourne, as well as by personal vindictiveness towards Caroline. Norton lost the case but, despite Caroline's innocence, she had no legal access to her three children. For six years, she saw them only a few times, in harrowing circumstances. Her successful lobbying led to a change in the law on infant custody, giving legally innocent mothers limited access to their children, but by that time Norton had sent the children to Scotland which was outside English jurisdiction. Caroline Norton finally succeeded in gaining access to her children, though in her absence her youngest son, who had been taken from her at the age of two, had died of blood poisoning from a neglected scratch. The couple continued to quarrel over money for many years, and Caroline's further campaigning led to improvement for women in marriage and divorce laws. Later in life, she had care of her two grandchildren who lived with her. After Norton's death, Caroline remarried at the age of sixty-nine. She wrote poetry and novels and contributed to and edited periodicals.

'Well, my dear Harry, I declare you're handsomer than even your father was at your age; if Kate does not lose her heart to you at first sight, I shall be much surprised.' Such were the words addressed by the widow of Colonel Bouverie to her only son; and as she closed the sentence she dropped the eye-glass through which she had attentively considered his features, and gave a sigh of regret, partly to the memory of her husband, and partly to the recollection of her own past loveliness, which a mirror opposite told her, had sadly faded during the three-and-twenty years which had matured the rosy infant into the young man by her side.

'I hear Kate is rather odd, mother.'

'What do you mean, my dear boy? She is a charming girl with a large fortune, and you have been engaged to her these twelve years. What *do* you mean?' and again the eye-glass assisted the perception of the fair widow.

Henry Bouverie did not explain what he meant; but he bit his lip and looked out of the window, and then his eyes wandered to his two sisters, the younger of whom, Pamela, was lying half asleep on the sofa, her long black eyelashes all but closed on the pinkest cheek in the world; while the elder, Annette, sat apparently reading, but occupied less with her book than the subject of conversation; of which, however, she took no further notice than by meeting her brother's glance with a meaning and *espiègle* smile.

'We shall start for Scotland next week,' said Mrs Bouverie, in a displeased tone, fixing her eyes on the *piquant* countenance of her rebellious daughter.

'So soon, mamma!' murmured Pamela; and opening her wide blue eyes in astonishment at the idea of anything being performed in a week, she again resigned herself to a state of drowsy enjoyment, strongly resembling that in which an Angola cat passes its summer day.

Annette made no reply, but the smile which had offended still lurked and quivered round the corners of her mouth.

'I wonder how Gertrude has turned out,' thought the widow, as she withdrew her glance. 'She was handsomer than either of her sisters: no – nothing *can* be handsomer than Pamela,' and the eye-glass was allowed complacently to rest on the exquisitely proportioned form and beautiful face of her youngest daughter, while a vague and rapid calculation of the different sort of match she might expect for each of the girls passed through her mind.

Pamela was already a duchess, when a visitor arriving turned her thoughts into another channel.

When Mrs Bouverie ran away with her penniless husband, and married him at Gretna Green, as much from love of the frolic as from love of the man, she acted upon impulse; but having her own reasons, in later life, for disapproving of such motives of action, she had vowed that she never *would*, and it was her boast that she never *did*, 'do anything without a plan.'

She had successfully formed and executed a number of small plans, but her expected master-stroke was to marry her son to his cousin Kate, who was to inherit the whole of the Bouverie property.

In furtherance of this plan she has sent her daughter Gertrude to stay with General Bouverie and his daughter, during her own residence in Italy, for Pamela's health: in furtherance of this plan, her letters to her absent child had always contained the most miraculous accounts of Harry's sweet temper, talents, and anxiety to return from the continent; and in furtherance of this plan she was now about to visit Scotland, for the treble purpose of reclaiming her daughter, introducing her son, and paying a visit to the old General, who, pleased with the prospect of marrying his child to a Bouverie, and thus keeping the property in the family, looked forward with eager satisfaction to their arrival.

Kate, too, anticipated with tranquil joy the fate which had been chalked out for her in infancy, and which appeared to promise all human happiness. She was already in love with Mrs Bouverie's descriptions of her cousin; and forgetting that he was but a little fair shy boy when she had last seen him, believed the ideal Harry to be the counterpart of the object of her affections.

Lady Catherine Bouverie, the General's wife, ran away from him soon after her marriage, and her husband was for a length of time inconsolable. He gave up all society, shut himself up in a wild and romantic place he had in Northumberland, and devoted his whole time to his little girl.

Kate Bouverie became in consequence, at a very early age, the companion and friend of her father. She would sit with him when he had letters to write, and copy, in a clear neat hand, dry directions respecting farm business, and show cattle, without ever wearying, or appearing to consider it as a task.

Latin, geography, and arithmetic, were the studies pointed out to her by her father; she had no governess (General Bouverie cursed accomplishments as the cause of a woman's ruin), but she was an excellent French scholar, and took sketches from nature without any other assistance than what was afforded by intuitive talent. Such studies, however, occupied but a small portion of her time.

Slightly formed, but well knit and vigorous in limb, her naturally good constitution strengthened by constant exercise, and the enjoyment of heaven's pure air, she would follow her father with a light step and a merry heart, in most of his shooting excursions; and when that father caught her glowing cheek and fearless eye, he felt as much tenderness and pride in her beauty as ever monarch in his newly-crowned child. Kate was also an incomparable horse-woman: no road was too dangerous, no steed too spirited, for her nerves. The risk was to her a source of wild and intense enjoyment.

With this being, strange and eccentric in her habits, romantic and enthusiastic in her disposition, Mrs Bouverie's second daughter, Gertrude, had spent the four last years of her girlhood.

Taken from amongst very worldly people, at an age when the youthful heart is most susceptible of strong impressions, no wonder if Gertrude, whose feelings were naturally warm, became ardently attached to this strangely fascinating being, the first *she* had ever seen who was perfectly natural.

The merits of Kate Bouverie (and she had many) were perfections; her faults were not such in the eye of her youthful companion. Indeed, the latter became gradually as much the objects of imitation, as the more worthy points of her character; for Gertrude, with the same degree of ardent feeling, had few of her cousin's better qualities; headstrong, rebellious, gifted with intense vanity, and with something peculiar of harshness and coarseness in her ill-trained mind, she copied the habits, without being able to seize the virtues of Kate Bouverie; and the consequence was such as might be expected.

The same words and actions which acquired a wild charm from the native sweetness and originality of Kate, became perfectly odious when copied by Gertrude; and the utter want of tact she displayed, joined with her strange manners, made her conversation as galling to the feelings as it was revolting to the delicacy of those who were her occasional associates. Even Kate, who had sighed for a female companion to share her tasks and her sports, could scarcely be said to be fond of her present associate. Before Gertrude had been a fortnight at Heathcote Lodge, Kate heartily wished herself alone again, in spite of flattery, open and expressed, and the more silent and more gratifying flattery of imitation. What did Kate care whether others thought her handsome, when her father's eyes silently told her how much rather he would look on her countenance than on any other in the universe? What did she care that her horsemanship was admired, as long as her little Arab, Selim, carried her over the wild moor with the speed of lightning – the blue arch of heaven over her, and the free air of heaven round her head?

At length the day of meeting arrived. Mrs Bouverie and her family (after being twice overturned) drove up the long avenue, and never, perhaps, did so uncongenial a party assemble round the dinner table as met that night.

The affected worldly mother; the conceited, talkative, half-French, half-English Annette; the foolish, languishing beauty, Pamela; and, opposite to these, the wild, but graceful and kind-hearted Kate, the shy, handsome Captain Bouverie, and Gertrude, half-contemptuous, and half-jealous, as she looked at the manner and attire of her sisters.

Every day increased the mutually repellent nature of the qualities each was endowed with, by making them more known to each other; and it was with difficulty that Mrs Bouverie concealed her dislike in order to forward a marriage so much to the advantage of her son.

His sisters were not so cautious: Annette, with a keen perception of the ridiculous, and considerable talent, occupied herself daily, almost hourly, in ridiculing – not Kate – she had tact enough to see that it would be a dangerous attempt – but the clumsy imitation of Gertrude she visited with unsparing satire; and the consequent coldness between the sisters drew the two cousins more together, and opened Kate's heart more towards the faulty Gertrude than four years of constant companionship.

The unheard-of insolence of her niece, who christened the younger Miss Bouverie 'the squirrel and the dormouse', made their affectionate mother ill for two days; and the ejaculation of the old General, who said, on seeing Annette and Pamela enter the apartment in their baptiste dresses, 'I wish to God, Mrs Bouverie, you would put something decent on those girls.' at length determined the crafty widow on making her own escape at least, and leaving her son to pay his court to his eccentric bride at his leisure.

To Captain Bouverie she spoke of the errors of her niece in a kind, indulgent, *motherly* way, assuring him she was convinced that time and instruction, and her own valuable society, would make his wife all he could wish. Captain Bouverie's only reply was a deep sigh; and they parted.

It was agreed, after much entreaty, that Gertrude should still remain at Heathcote Lodge, and return under her brother's escort, Mrs Bouverie comforting herself by the reflection that, when once Gertrude was at home again, she should be able to re-model her manners.

After the departure of the trio, the party at Heathcote Lodge were more happy, more companionable; but Harry Bouverie was disappointed, and he could neither conceal it from himself nor from his sister, nor even in a degree from Kate herself.

Shy, vain, and with an insupportable dread of ridicule, the impression made by the beauty, warm-heartedness, and evident affection of his cousin, was always painfully contrasted in his mind with what *others* would think and say of her. He figured her introduced to the world – his world – as his wife. He imagined to himself the astonished stare of his well-bred friends, the affected disgust of his *fine* female acquaintances, and at such moments he loathed the sight of Selim, hid his face from the sunshine and the breeze, and groaned when Kate passed her fingers through the short curls of her distinguished-looking head – though that hand was small and white, and her hair bright and glossy. Annette's letters were by no means calculated to improve his feelings in this respect. 'I see her,' said this amiable sister, 'entering the rooms at D——e House; all eyes bent upon her; all tongues murmuring her praise. I see her in the park, Selim not quietly entering the ride by the posts intended for that purpose, but *franchissant les bornes* (as her mistress does) at one free leap, from long habit which, as you know, is second nature. I am practising the song, "*Mein Schatz ist ein reiter*," as I doubt not it will become a great favourite of yours, and only beg of you to be careful not to go *more* than forty miles a day, as it will be sadly injurious to your health and looks, frère Adonis; and you know that any alteration in the *latter* would bring the (grey?) hairs of my mother with sorrow to the grave.'

The slave to the opinions of others retired to rest, full of recollections inspired by that letter. 'From the force of habit, which is second nature,' muttered he, as he turned for the twentieth time on his restless pillow. He fell asleep, and dreamed that he was married, and that his brother officers rose from the mess-table to drink Kate's health. Just as he was lifting the glass to his lips, he saw Kate enter; she was dressed in a long green riding-habit: she passed her taper fingers rapidly through her hair: he remonstrated; he entreated her to leave the mess-room; but she only laughed: he rose from his place, and, walking to the spot where she stood, endeavoured to persuade her to go. Suddenly, he thought she turned and kicked him, and the little well-turned, firmly-knit ankle was unaccountably transformed into Selim's hoof. He started in violent pain, and woke.

Full of mingled irritation and sadness, Harry Bouverie sat alone that day in his uncle's library, leaning his aching head on his hand,

and gazing listlessly from the window on a long avenue of lime trees, which opened on the moor.

He was interrupted by the entrance of Gertrude, who, tapping him lightly on the shoulder with her whip, exclaimed, 'Why, Harry, what are you musing about? Come, come, and take a ride with us.'

Harry shook his head. 'Oh, come, there's a good fellow; cheer up, drive away black thoughts, and let Romeo be saddled quickly, for my horse and Selim will take cold standing so long.'

'For God's sake,' said Captain Bouverie, impatiently, 'do strive to be less like that anomalous being they intend for my wife.' Then suddenly turning, he added, 'Oh, Gertrude, if I marry that girl, we shall both be miserable!'

There was a breathless silence; for, as Harry turned, he beheld, standing within two paces of him, his cousin Kate. The eloquent blood rushed as rapidly to that glowing cheek as if the sun had never touched and mellowed its original tint of pure rose, and the big tears stood for a moment in those clear, kind, blue eyes; then a deadly paleness overspread her face, and Captain Bouverie thought she would have fainted. He sprang forward, but the moment his hand touched hers, she started from him; and before they could follow her to the door, the fleet foot of Selim had borne his mistress far over the wild moor, which was her favourite ride.

For long weary miles she galloped on at full speed, till even the little Arab relaxed its exertions, and, unchecked by the bridle, slackened its pace. The alteration recalled Kate Bouverie to herself. She stopped and dismounted, and, gazing far round on the barren heath, as if to assure herself that no human eye could witness her weakness, she flung herself on the ground, and wept bitterly.

'My God!' exclaimed the unhappy girl, as she clasped her hands and raised her eyes to heaven, 'what have I done to make him hate me?' and as the speech she had heard again rung in her ears, she contrasted the affection she had borne him ever since she could remember – the pleasure with which she looked forward to sharing his home – the many resolutions never to suffer her past liberty to tempt her to dispute his will, and to keep a careful watch over that rebellious heart which was his alone – with the sentiments of dislike, almost of disgust, which he had openly expressed towards her. Again she repeated to herself, 'What *have* I done?' and again she wept, till, weary and exhausted, she sunk into a profound slumber.

When she woke, the calm glow of sunset was on the moor, and Selim was feeding quietly at a little distance. She mounted her favourite, for the first time without a caress, and for the first time she turned towards home with a slow step and a heavy heart.

At dinner, Kate Bouverie was in wild spirits, and though her cheek was pale, and her eyes dim, her manner repelled all attempt at explanation or consolation, even from Gertrude. She retired early to rest, pleading a bad headache to her anxious father.

The next morning the following note was brought to her by her maid:

> My dear Kate,
> For God's sake, see and hear me patiently for a few minutes, and be to me what, except in my hours of madness and folly, I have always hoped to see you.
>
> HARRY BOUVERIE

She was just struggling against the temptation of once more conversing with her beloved cousin, when a tap at the door announced Gertrude. 'Come in,' said she, in a low voice. Gertrude obeyed the summons.

'Heavens! Kate, how ill you look,' exclaimed she; 'and you have not been to bed last night. Oh, Kate! how can you be so foolish for a little quarrel.'

'A *little* quarrel, Gertrude,' said her companion; and a slow bitter smile crept round her mouth – 'but sit down, and say what you came to say, for I must go to my father.'

Gertrude came as her brother's ambassador, and earnestly did she endeavour to promote peace, for she loved Harry, and almost worshipped his betrothed wife; but she had none of the tact necessary for the performance of such a task. While she wounded the feelings of the sensitive girl she addressed, by the constant allusion to her brother's distaste for her manners and habits; she also bluntly reasoned upon the impossibility of his feeling otherwise, when he looked forward to presenting her to the world, because he knew that the world would judge harshly of her; and with natural coarseness of mind, she seemed to suppose that nothing more than a mutual concession of certain points, an apology on the part of Harry, and a sort of 'kiss-and-be-friends' ceremony, was necessary to establish them exactly in the situation they were before.

But she spoke a language Kate Bouverie did not understand. What could it signify to Harry what the world, that strange world, thought of her, as long as he himself was satisfied of her affection, and pleased with her society? What had the opinions of others to do with the comfort of his home? the opinions of others, too, none of whom he appeared to respect, and many of whom he openly avowed to be worthless? No, *that* could not be the reason of his dislike; and she resented the supposed attempt to impose on her understanding.

Had Gertrude had to deal with one of her own disposition, the task would have been comparatively easy. Had her cousin been angry, she could have soothed her; but vanity had no place in Kate Bouverie's heart – it is the vice of society, and she had lived alone almost from childhood. It was her heart that was crushed, and it would have required a tenderer and far more skilful hand to have healed the blow.

By his sister's hands, Harry received an answer to his appeal; it was as follows:

After what passed yesterday, dear Harry, it can serve no good purpose to comply with your request, but will only give great pain to both of us. I shall tell father I cannot marry you, as it would grieve him were he to know how differently others can think of his only child. I am at a loss to know how I have forfeited your good opinion; but of this I am very sure, that I have never *voluntarily* given you a moment's displeasure. We are not likely to meet often again, but I shall always be glad to hear good news of you, and always feel an interest in all that concerns you. I would not wish to end with a reproach, but I would fain you had *told* me what chance discovered to me. Did you intend to marry me under the conviction that our union would tend to the misery of both? If it is because you are attached to another that you have dealt thus strangely by me, I will hope your present freedom may conduce to your future happiness. If it is really and truly for the reasons Gertrude gave me, may that world, dear Harry, of which you are a worshipper, be able to repay you for your submission to its opinion!

It was with tolerable composure that Kate Bouverie wrote and despatched this note; but with her father the fountain of her tears again burst forth. The General was electrified; he had never seen her weep before; for in that happy home she had had no cause for sorrow, and her tears made an impression on him that erased from his memory the long-cherished plan of continuing the property in the family by this much-desired union. He himself informed Captain Bouverie of his daughter's decision, and that information was accompanied with expressions of regret.

Years rolled on. Kate Bouverie continued unmarried, in spite of the offers of more than one suitor for her hand. Gertrude remained at home, under the auspices of her careful parent. But though self-love and vanity did what her mother's advice would most assuredly not have done, and she soon began to conform in some degree to the tastes of the people she was amongst; still her real and acquired faults were not indicated, and '*as odd as Ger. Bouverie*' became a by-word by no means pleasing to the rest of the family.

Taunted and reproached at home, alternately caressed and sneered at abroad, Gertrude always entered a ballroom with a vague spirit of defiance against uncommitted injuries. At once affecting to scorn, and making faint endeavours to conciliate the world; beautiful in person; harsh in manner; fearless by nature; she said everything, and did everything that came into her head, and the consequence was as might be expected. She was flattered by those she amused; courted by those to whom her notice gave a sort of notoriety; admired by many; and abused by the whole of her acquaintance.

Pamela's drowsy existence was by no means interrupted or disturbed by her sister's strange ways; but Annette, while by dint of mocking, she unconsciously caught something of the gesticulating manner and audible tone of voice which accompanied Gertrude's speeches, resented as an injury the notoriety she thus obtained, and visited it with the whole force of her wit; while forgetting how far different the copy was from the original, Harry Bouverie never ceased to congratulate himself on his escape from the matrimonial snare prepared for him.

While things were in this state, Mrs Bouverie received a letter one morning, which forced an ejaculation even from her little, cold, compressed lip, and sent a momentary flush of emotion to her faded cheek. 'Your cousin Kate is dead,' said she, turning to her daughters; and then, as if seeking to excuse her own emotion as she felt the rush of tears to her eyes, she added, 'but – she is dead in such a shocking way!' The letter was read, and it was with bitter feelings that Harry Bouverie listened to its contents.

Since the departure of her cousin, poor Kate's whole character seemed to have changed. Wild with a sort of delirious gaiety at one time – dejected and incapable of occupying herself at another, she seemed always the slave of some unintelligible caprice. Her eye grew dimmer, her figure thinner and less graceful; her very voice – that low, laughing voice which had given a charm to all she said – acquired a sharpness and shrillness which was foreign to it.

Gloom sat on her brow like shadows in a sunny place, and while her father merely remarked that Kate's temper was not so good as it had been – the old nurse declared that her child was dying of a broken heart.

But it was not by slow degrees – by the sapping and mining of grief – by the wasting away of the body's strength under the soul's weakness, that one so full of life and energy was to die. Suddenly, in the flower of her youth, she was to be cut off, as if it were vain to wait till decay should creep into so slight a heart, and within so bright a form.

Amongst other changes, Kate had become very absent; frequently she forgot she was in the presence of others, and with a low, moaning exclamation, would hide her head and weep. Frequently she would remain out on the sunny moors for hours, and wander home, unconscious that the day was drawing to a close, and that her father was waiting her return. At such times she would fling her arms around his neck, and give way to an hysterical burst of mingled tears and laughter at her own thoughtlessness, and then put on the wild gaiety of a child.

There came a day when her father waited in vain – when the look that pleaded for pardon – the voice that soothed – the laugh that cheered him – were lost to him for ever; and that hurrying step which was the signal for the old man to rise and advance to fold his daughter in his arms, was silent in the desolate corridors of his house.

All that was ever known of Kate's death was told by a peasant girl who, while waiting for her young sister to cross the moor, saw a horse with a lady on it flying at full speed down the narrow road which skirted it. She ran as fast as she was able to the foot of a little bridge, which made a sudden and short angle from the road. She stood still and listened, but the dashing and murmuring of the waters prevented her hearing the approach of the horse's hoofs. She called, but nothing except a faint echo, muffled, as it were, by the branches which shadowed the wild and rocky stream, answered her cry. She waited, knowing that the road had no other turn, but all remained sleeping in the quiet sunshine as before. Suddenly a sick and horrible fear crossed the girl's heart; she turned and looked far down into the bed of the stream, and there, among the broken granite and white stones, she distinctly saw some dark object; and while her heart beat so loud as almost to stifle the sound, she fancied that a faint wailing cry swept past on the wind.

Slowly, and with cautious steps, she crept down round by the bridge, over the bank, swinging by a branch, or letting herself slip down the steep and broken ground. At length she descended into the torrent, which ran meagre, and half dried up by the summer sun –

struggling over and under and round the stones in its course, murmuring and complaining as it went. There lay the little Arab Selim, with the last life-pulse faintly quivering through its limbs; and there, with her face hidden, and the stream rippling through the curls of her golden hair, lay poor forsaken Kate.

The girl stopped; a natural and unconquerable horror made her pause before she would venture to turn round and lift what she doubted not was the face of a corpse, bruised and horrible. At length she approached, and, with shuddering hands, raised the head of the unhappy girl from the waters. No bruise was there; pure and calm, with closed eyes and parted lips, and the glistening drops hanging on the still fresh pink of her cheek, she lay – but death was in her face.

Years rolled on: Annette's more successful plan for her brother's advancement was put into execution, and Harry became the easy husband of the all-accomplished and beautiful Lady Sarah Davenel, the chosen companion and confidante of the sprightly Miss Bouverie.

Lady Sarah was a duke's daughter; she therefore thought herself entitled to treat her husband as her inferior. She was a beauty and a spoilt child, and she therefore conceived herself at liberty to accept the homage of those around her, and to show off sundry little airs of wilfulness and vanity, just as if she had not married the handsomest man in England, as she was in the habit of calling Henry. She was headstrong and violent, and the same adherence to her own fancies, which led her to oppose her doting father on the subject of her marriage, led her now to oppose her husband. She was frivolous and heartless, but she was a strict observer of the rules of etiquette. Maradan Carçon made her dresses, Cavalier dressed her hair, and *the world* declared she was a charming woman.

Five years after his marriage, accident brought Harry Bourverie to the spot where his young cousin, with whom from his infancy he had expected to pass his life, had died unseen, alone, without one to hear her last word. He was with a party of pleasure, and their loud laughing voices rang in his heart as he bent over the little bridge, and with straining eyes looked downwards, as if he could still see the light form which for years had mouldered in the grave. 'Is that a good trout stream, Bouverie?' asked one of the gentlemen.

Harry turned hastily away, and catching Lady Sarah by the arm, he muttered – 'Come away; it was here that Kate died – they will drive me wild!'

'You are always sentimentalising about that girl,' said his wife pettishly; 'I am sure it is no great compliment to me, the way you regret her.' She moved on, and joining the party, walked forwards.

'Oh! Kate, Kate!' exclaimed Harry Bouverie, as rushing tears dimmed his view of that death scene, 'was it for such a heart I scorned you?'

APHRA BEHN

The Adventure of the Black Lady

Aphra Behn (c1640-89) was born in Kent. She appears to have received a conventional female education of the period, but later resented that she had been denied a classical education, a male prerogative. As a young woman, she went out to Surinam in South America, then a small and hazardous English colony. She later used her experiences in Surinam in her novel Oroonoko *(1688), which showed her progressive attitude towards slavery. On her return to London, she married a City merchant of Dutch ancestry, named Behn, about whom little is known and who died shortly afterwards, possibly a victim of the plague of 1665. She was recruited into Charles II's intelligence service and went to Antwerp to investigate Dutch intentions towards the English. Kept short of funds, and her intelligence reports ignored or undervalued, she borrowed money for her journey home and returned to London, where, unable to repay the loan, she was imprisoned for debt for a time. She turned to writing plays, and her first play* The Forced Marriage *was produced in 1670. She was the first English woman to earn her living by writing. This, together with the bawdy content of some of her plays, characteristic of the Restoration, gained her a notoriety which lasted up to the twentieth century. She was, however, popular at the time. She was arrested again when an epilogue she had written for an anonymous play offended the king by its political content. Her love for the cultured and rakish lawyer John Hoyle was only partially returned: he was bisexual, and demanded fidelity from her without giving it himself. Her poem 'To the Fair Clarinda, Who Made Love to me, Imagined More than Woman' suggests that she may also have had a relationship with a woman. Towards the end of her life, she began to write fiction, and 'The Adventure of the Black Lady' contains some of her disenchanted views on marriage. The spelling and punctuation have been modernized.*

About the beginning of last June (as near as I can remember)
Bellamora came to town from Hampshire, and was obliged to lodge
the first night at the same inn where the stage coach set up. The next
day she took coach for Covent Garden, where she thought to find
Madam Brightly, a relation of hers, with whom she designed to continue for about half a year undiscovered, if possible, by her friends in
the country; and ordered therefore her trunk, with her clothes, and
most of her money and jewels, to be brought after her to Madam
Brightly's by a strange porter, whom she spoke to in the street as she
was taking coach, being utterly unacquainted with the neat practices
of this fine city. When she came to Bridges Street, where indeed her
cousin had lodged near three or four years since, she was strangely
surprised that she could not learn anything of her; no, nor so much as
meet with anyone that had ever heard of her cousin's name; till, at
last, describing Madam Brightly to one of the housekeepers in that
place, he told her, that there was such a kind of lady, whom he had
sometimes seen there about a year and a half ago, but that he believed
she was married and removed towards Soho. In this perplexity she
quite forgot her trunk and money, etc, and wandered in her hackney
coach all over St Anne's parish, inquiring for Madam Brightly, still
describing her person, but in vain, for no soul could give her any tale
or tidings of such a lady. After she had thus fruitlessly rambled, till
she, the coachman, and the very horses were even tired, by good fortune for her, she happened on a private house where lived a good, discreet, ancient gentlewoman, who was fallen to decay, and forced to
let lodgings for the best part of her livelihood; from whom she understood, that there was such a kind of lady, who had lain there somewhat more than a twelvemonth, being near three months after she was
married; but that she was now gone abroad with the gentleman her
husband, either to the play, or to take the fresh air; and she believed
would not return till night. This discourse of the good gentlewoman's
so elevated Bellamora's drooping spirits that after she had begged the
liberty of staying there till they came home, she discharged the coachman in all haste, still forgetting her trunk, and the more valuable furniture of it.

When they were alone, Bellamora desired she might be permitted
the freedom to send for a pint of sack, which, with some little difficulty, was at last allowed her. They began then to chat for a matter of
half an hour of things indifferent; and at length the ancient gentlewoman asked the fair innocent (I must not say foolish) one, of what
country, and what her name was: to both which she answered directly

and truly, though it might have proved not discreetly. She then enquired of Bellamora if her parents were living, and the occasion of her coming to town. The fair unthinking creature replied, that her father and mother were both dead, and that she had escaped from her uncle, under the pretence of making a visit to a young lady, her cousin, who was lately married, and lived above twenty miles from her uncle's, in the road to London, and that the cause of her quitting the country was to avoid the hated importunities of a gentleman, whose pretended love to her she feared had been her eternal ruin. At which she wept and sighed most extravagantly. The discreet gentlewoman endeavoured to comfort her by all the softest and most powerful arguments in her capacity, promising her all the friendly assistance that she could expect from her, during Bellamora's stay in town; which she did with so much earnestness, and visible integrity, that the pretty innocent creature was going to make her a full and real discovery of her imaginary insupportable misfortunes; and (doubtless) had done it, had she not been prevented by the return of the lady, whom she hoped to have found her cousin Brightly. The gentleman, her husband, just saw her within doors, and ordered the coach to drive to some of his bottle companions, which gave the women the better opportunity of entertaining one another, which happened to be with some surprise on all sides. As the lady was going up into her apartment, the gentlewoman of the house told her there was a young lady in the parlour, who came out of the country that very day on purpose to visit her; the lady stepped immediately to see who it was, and Bellamora approaching to receive her hoped-for cousin, stopped on the sudden just as she came to her, and sighed out aloud, 'Ah, madam! I am lost – it is not your ladyship I seek'. 'No, madam,' returned the other, 'I am apt to think you did not intend me this honour. But you are as welcome to me, as you could be to the dearest of your acquaintance. Have you forgot me, Madam Bellamora?' continued she. That name startled the other. However, it was with a kind of joy. 'Alas! Madam,' replied the young one, 'I now remember that I have been so happy to have seen you, but where and when, my memory can't tell me'. ''Tis indeed some years since,' return'd the lady, 'but of that another time. Meanwhile, if you are unprovided of a lodging, I dare undertake, you shall be welcome to this gentlewoman.' The unfortunate returned her thanks; and whilst a chamber was preparing for her, the lady entertained her in her own. About ten o'clock they parted, Bellamora being conducted to her lodging by the mistress of the house, who then left her to take what rest she could amidst her so many misfortunes, returning to the other lady, who desired her to search into the cause of Bellamora's retreat to town.

The next morning the good gentlewoman of the house, coming up to her, found Bellamora almost drowned in tears, which by many kind and sweet words she at last stopped; and, asking whence so great signs of sorrow should proceed, vowed a most profound secrecy if she would discover to her their occasion; which, after some little reluctancy, she did, in this manner.

'I was courted,' said she, 'above three years ago, when my mother was yet living, by one Mr Fondlove, a gentleman of good estate, and true worth; and one who, I dare believe, did then really love me. He continued his passion for me, with all the earnest and honest solicitations imaginable, till some months before my mother's death, who, at that time, was most desirous to see me disposed of in marriage to another gentleman, of much better estate than Mr Fondlove, but one whose person and humour did by no means hit with my inclinations; and this gave Fondlove the unhappy advantage over me. For, finding me one day all alone in my chamber, and lying on my bed, in as mournful and wretched a condition to my then foolish apprehension, as now I am, he urged his passion with such violence and accursed success for me, with reiterated promises of marriage whensoever I pleased to challenge them, which he bound with the most sacred oaths, and most dreadful execrations that, partly with my aversion to the other, and partly with my inclinations to pity him, I ruined myself. Here she relapsed into a greater extravagance of grief than before, which was so extreme that it did not continue long. When therefore she was pretty well come to herself, the ancient gentlewoman asked her, why she imagined herself ruined. To which she answered, 'I am great with child by him, madam, and wonder you did not perceive it last night. Alas! I have not a month to go. I am ashamed, ruined, and damned, I fear, for ever lost.' 'Oh! fie, madam, think not so,' said the other, 'for the gentleman may yet prove true, and marry you.' 'Ay, madam,' replied Bellamora, 'I doubt not that he would marry me; for soon after my mother's death, when I came to be at my own disposal, which happened about two months after, he offered, nay most earnestly solicited me to it, which still he perseveres to do.' 'This is strange!' returned the other, 'and it appears to me to be your own fault that you are yet miserable. Why did you not or why will you not consent to your own happiness?' 'Alas!' cried Bellamora, ''tis the only thing I dread in this world. For, I am certain, he can never love me after. Besides, ever since I have abhorred the sight of him, and this is the only cause that obliges me to forsake my uncle, and all my friends and relations in the country, hoping in this populous and public place to be most private, especially, madam, in your house, and in your fidelity and discretion.' 'Of the last you may assure yourself, madam,' said the other, 'but what provision have you made for the reception of the young stranger that you carry about you?' 'Ah, madam!' cried Bellamora, 'you have brought to my mind another misfortune.' Then she acquainted her with the supposed loss of her money and jewels, telling her withal, that she had but three guineas and some silver left, and the rings she wore, in her present possession. The good gentlewoman of the house told her she would send to enquire at the inn where she lay the first night she came to town; for, haply, they might give some account of the porter to whom she had entrusted her trunk; and withal repeated her promise of all the help in her power, and for that time left her much more composed than she found her. The good gentlewoman went directly to the other lady, her lodger, to whom she recounted Bellamora's mournful confession; at which the lady appeared mightily concerned: and at last she told her landlady, that she would take care that Bellamora should lie in according to her quality. 'For,' added she, 'the child, it seems, is my own brother's.'

As soon as she had dined, she went to the Exchange, and brought childbed linen, but desired that Bellamora might not have the least notice of it. And at her return dispatched a letter to her brother Fondlove in Hampshire, with an account of every particular; which soon brought him up to town, without satisfying any of his or her friends with the reason of his sudden departure. Meanwhile, the good gentlewoman of the house had sent to the Star Inn on Fish Street Hill, to demand the trunk, which she rightly supposed to have been carried back thither. For, by good luck, it was a fellow that plied thereabouts who brought it to Bellamora's lodgings that very night, but unknown to her. Fondlove no sooner got to London, but he posts to his sister's lodgings, where he was advised not to be seen of Bellamora till they had worked farther upon her, which the landlady began in this manner. She told her that her things were miscarried and, she feared, lost; that she had but a little money herself, and if the overseers of the poor (justly so called from their over-looking them) should have the least suspicion of a stranger and unmarried person who was entertained in her house big with child, and so near her time as Bellamora was, she should be troubled, if they could not give security to the parish of twenty or thirty pounds that they should not suffer by her, which she could not; or otherwise she must be sent to the house of correction, and her child to a parish nurse. This discourse, one may imagine, was very dreadful to a person of her youth, beauty, education, family and estate. However, she resolutely protested that she had rather undergo all this than be exposed to the scorn of her friends and relations in the country. The other told her then that she must write down to her uncle a farewell letter, as if she were just going aboard the packet-boat for Holland, that he might not send to enquire for her in town, when he should understand she was not at her new-married cousin's in the country; which accordingly she did, keeping herself close prisoner to her chamber, where she was daily visited by Fondlove's sister and the landlady, but by no soul else, the first dissembling the knowledge she had of her misfortunes.

Thus she continued for above three weeks, not a servant being suffered to enter her chamber, so much as to make her bed, lest they should take notice of her great belly; but for all this caution, the secret had taken wind, by the means of an attendant of the other lady below, who had overhead her speaking of it to her husband. This soon got out of doors, and spread abroad, till it reached the long ears of the wolves of the parish, who, next day, designed to pay her a visit. But Fondlove, by good providence, prevented it; who, the night before, was ushered in Bellamora's chamber by his sister, his brother-in-law, and the landlady. At the sight of him she had like to have swooned away, but he, taking her in his arms, began again, as he was wont to do, with tears in his eyes, to beg that she would marry him ere she was delivered; if not for his, nor her own, yet for the child's sake, which she hourly expected, that it might not be born out of wedlock, and so be made uncapable of inheriting either of their estates; with a great many more pressing arguments on all sides, to which at last she consented; and an honest officious gentleman, whom they had before provided, was called up, who made an end of the dispute. So to bed they went together that night; next day to the Exchange, for several pretty businesses that ladies in her condition want. Whilst they were abroad, came the vermin of the parish (I mean, the overseers of the poor, who eat the bread from them) to search for a young blackhaired lady (for so was Bellamora) who was either brought to bed, or just ready to lie down. The landlady showed them all the rooms in her house, but no such lady could be found. At last she bethought herself, and led them into her parlour, where she opened a little closet door, and showed them a black cat that had just kittened, assuring them that she should never trouble the parish as long as she had rats or mice in the house; and so dismissed them like loggerheads as they came.

MARY WEBB

'In Affection and Esteem'

Mary Webb (1881-1927) was born in Shropshire, the eldest in a family of six children. She spent most of her life in Shropshire, moving to London in 1921. She had a close relationship with her father and, after his death, transferred her dependence to her husband, though her marriage was deteriorating at the time of her death. She contracted a disfiguring thyroid illness in her youth. Her mysticism and her affinity with nature are apparent in many of her books. She wrote poetry, essays and novels, including Gone to Earth *(1917) and* Precious Bane *(1924), which became a bestseller only after her death, and turned to short stories at the end of her life when she was short of money.*

Miss Myrtle Brown had never, since she unwillingly began her earthly course, received the gift of a box or a bouquet of flowers. She used to think, as she trudged away to the underground station every day, to go and stitch buttonholes in a big London shop, that it would have been nice if, on one of her late returns, she had found a bunch of roses – red, with thick, lustrous petals, deeply sweet, or white, with their rare fragrance – awaiting her on her table. It was, of course, an impossible dream. She ought to be glad enough to have a table at all, and a loaf to put on it. She ought to be grateful to those above for letting her have a roof over her head.

'You might,' she apostrophised herself, as she lit her gas ring and put on the kettle, 'not *have* a penny for this slot. You might, Myrtle Brown, not *have* a spoonful of tea to put in this pot. Be thankful!'

And she was thankful to Providence, to her landlady, to her employer, who sweated his workers, to the baker for bringing her loaf, to the milkman for leaving her half a pint of milk on Sundays, to the landlady's cat for refraining from drinking it.

To all these, in her anxious and sincere heart, she gave thanks. She had enough to keep body and soul together. How dared she, then, desire anything so inordinate as a bouquet?

'You might,' she remarked, holding up the teapot to get the last drop, 'be sleeping on the Embankment. Others as good as you, as industrious as you, sleep there every night, poor souls.'

Yet she could not help thinking, when she put out her light and lay down, of the wonderful moment if she ever *did* receive a bouquet.

Think of unpacking the box! Think of seeing on the outside, 'Cut Flowers Immediate,' undoing the string, taking off the paper, lifting the lid!

What then? Ah, violets, perhaps, or roses; lilies of the valley, whiter than belief in their startling bright leaves; lilac or pale pink peonies or mimosa with its benignant warm sweetness.

The little room would be like a greenhouse – like one of the beautiful greenhouses at Kew – with the passionate purity of tall lilies; with pansies, softly creased; with cowslips in tight bunches, and primroses edged with dark leaves, and daffodils with immense frail cups. She would borrow jampots from the landlady, and it would take all evening to arrange them. And the room would be wonderful – like heaven. The flowers would pour out incense, defeating the mustiness of the house and the permanent faint scent of cabbage.

To wake, slowly and luxuriously, on a Sunday morning, into that company – what bliss!

Red roses at the bed's head, white roses at the foot. On the table, pinks. Not a *few* flowers; not just a small box. Many, many flowers – all the sweetness the world owed her.

She dimly felt that it owed her something. All those buttonholes! Yes. There was a debt of beauty. She was the world's creditor for so much of colour and perfume, golden petals, veined mauve chalices, velvet purples, passion flower, flower of the orange. She was its creditor for small daisies and immense sunflowers; for pink water-lilies acquainted with liquid deeps; for nameless blooms, rich, streaked with strange fantastic hues, plucked in Elfland; for starred branches dripping with the honeys of Paradise.

'Dr. to Myrtle Brown, the World. Item, love and beauty. Item, leisure. Item, sunlight, laughter and the heart's desire.'

She might, of course, out of her weekly wage, buy a bunch of flowers. She did occasionally. But that was not quite the perfect thing, not quite what she desired. The centre of all the wonder was to be the little bit of pasteboard with her name on it, and the sender's name, and perhaps a few words of greeting. She had heard that this was the custom in sending a bouquet to anyone – a great actress or prima donna. And on birthdays it was customary, and at funerals.

Birthdays! Suppose, now, she received such a parcel on her birthday. She had had so many birthdays, and they had all been so very much alike. A tomato with her tea, perhaps, and a cinema afterwards. Once it had been a pantomime, the landlady having been given a ticket, and having passed it on in consideration of some help with needlework.

Miss Brown liked the Transformation Scene. She liked the easy way in which the ladies who had been reclining on sharp, green peaks of ice in a snowbound country were suddenly, at the ringing of a bell, changed into languid, rosy summer nymphs with as many blossoms about them as even she could desire. She supposed they were only paper flowers and trees of cardboard, but still it would be pleasant to recline in a warm rosy light and see rows and rows of pleased faces. Yes. If she had been younger, she might have become a transformation fairy. She mentioned this when thanking the landlady for a pleasant evening.

'What? Go as one of those brazen girls? Dear me, Miss Brown, what next?'

'They only just lie there in a nice dress to be looked at,' said Miss Brown, with spirit.

'There's some,' replied the landlady darkly, 'as do more harm, just lying still to be looked at, than respectable people would do in a thousand miles.'

'I'm not young enough, anyway.'

'No. You don't get any younger. Time soon passes.'

She minced the meat for the first-floor dinners as if Time and Death were on the chopping-board.

Myrtle Brown was depressed at the idea of Time and Death marching upon her. She realised that there would come a time when she could not make any more buttonholes. She knew she ought to be saving every penny against the rainy day which, once it came, would go on. Even a bunch of snowdrops would not do.

'There'll come a day,' she said, as she washed her cup and saucer after a frugal tea, 'when you'll *want* a penny, when a penny may be life or death. Save, and be thankful!'

Yet always in her heart was the longing for some great pageant, some splendid gift of radiance. How she could enjoy it! With what zest she would tell over every smallest bit of it! Nothing that they could give her would go unnoticed. Every petal, every leaf would be told over like a rosary.

But nobody seemed anxious to inaugurate any pageant. Nobody wanted to light a candle at Miss Brown's shrine. And at last, on a bleak winter day when everything had gone wrong and she had been quite unable to be grateful to anybody, she made a reckless decision. She would provide a pageant for herself. Before she began to save up for the rainy day, she would save up for the pageant.

'After that,' she remarked, carefully putting crumbs on the window-sill for the birds, 'you'll be quiet. You'll be truly thankful, Myrtle Brown.'

She began to scrimp and save. Week by week the little hoard increased. A halfpenny here and a penny there – it was wonderful how soon she amassed a shilling. So great was her determination that, before her next birthday, she had got together two pounds.

'It's a wild and wicked thing to spend two pounds on what neither feeds nor clothes,' she said. She knew it would be impossible to tell the landlady. She would never hear the last of it. No! It must be a dead secret. Nobody must know where those flowers came from. What was the word people used when you were not to know the name?

'Anon' – something. Yes. The flowers must be 'anon.' There was a little shop at Covent Garden where they would sell retail. Tuberoses, they sometimes had. Wonderful things were heaped in hampers. She would go there on the day before her birthday.

'You ought,' she said, as she drank her cup of cocoa at five o'clock on a winter morning, 'to be downright ashamed of what you're going to do this morning. Spending forty shillings on the lust of the eye!'

But this rather enhanced the enjoyment, and she was radiant as she surveyed early London from the bus.

Tomorrow morning, not much later than this, it would arrive – the alabaster box of precious nard.

She descended at Covent Garden, walking through the piled crates of greenstuff, the casks of fruit, the bursting sacks of potatoes, the large flat frails of early narcissi, exhaling fragrance. She came to her Mecca.

The shopkeeper was busy. He saw a shabby little woman with an expression of mingled rapture and anxiety.

'Well, ma'am, what is it?' he asked. 'Cabbage?'

Cabbage! And she had come for the stored wealth of a hundred flower-gardens!

'No, sir!' she replied with some asperity. 'I want some flowers. Good flowers. They are to be packed and sent to a lady I know, to-night.'

'Vi'lets?'

'Yes. Vi'lets and tuberoses and lilies and pheasant-eye, and maidenhair and mimosa and a few dozen roses, and some of those early polyanthus and gilly-flowers.'

'Wait a minute! Wait a minute! I suppose you know they'll cost a pretty penny?'

'I can pay for what I order,' said Miss Brown with hauteur. 'Write down what I say, add it up as you go on, put down box and postage, and I'll pay.'

The shopkeeper did as he was told.

Miss Brown went from flower to flower, like a sad-coloured butterfly, softly touching a petal, softly sniffing a rose. She was bliss incarnate. The shopkeeper, realising that something unusual was afoot, gave generous measure. At last the order was complete, the address given, the money – all the two pounds – paid.

'Any card enclosed?' queried the shopman.

Triumphantly Miss Brown produced one.

'In affection and esteem.'

'A good friend, likely?' queried the shopman.

'Almost my only friend,' replied Miss Brown.

Through Covent Garden's peculiarly glutinous mud she went in a beatitude, worked in a beatitude, went home in a dream.

She slept brokenly, as children do on Christmas Eve, and woke early, listening for the postman's ring.

Hark! Yes! A ring.

But the landlady did not come up. It must have been only the milkman. Another wait. Another ring. No footsteps. The baker, she surmised.

Where was the postman? He was very late. If he only knew, how quick he would have been!

Another pause. An hour. Nothing. It was long past his time. She went down.

'Postman?' said the landlady, 'why, the postman's been gone above an hour! Parcel? No, nothing for you. There did a parcel come for Miss Brown, but it was a great expensive box with 'Cut Flowers' on it, so I knew it wasn't for you and I sent it straight to Miss Elvira Brown the actress, who was used to lodge here. *She* was always getting stacks of flowers so I knew it was for her.'

MARY DELARIVIERE MANLEY

The Physician's Stratagem

Mary Delarivière Manley (1672?-1724) was born in Jersey, where her father, a royalist, had been appointed Lieutenant-Governor by Charles II. Her life is sporadically documented, but she wrote about herself in The Adventures of Rivella *(1714), a favourably slanted account, and included autobiographical material in* The New Atalantis *(1709). Her mother died when she was a child, and she and her two sisters were sternly educated by a governess. After her father's death, she became a ward of her cousin, John Manley, who persuaded her into a bigamous marriage. He kept her a prisoner in his house to prevent her from discovering that his first wife was still alive, but eventually told her. As she was now pregnant, she remained with him for three years, bitterly resenting that the social blame of the bigamy was directed at her, not at him, while he spent her fortune in drinking and gambling. When she left him, she became a companion to the Duchess of Cleveland for a while. She started her literary career by writing plays, later turning to fiction, in letter form, then secret histories, which were novels of amorous and political intrigue, based on real people and events, intended to satirize members of the Whig party. As a printed key, identifying the characters, was also available, the disguise was thin, and her books provoked hostile attack (which Eliza Haywood was later to experience for writing the same sort of book). When* The New Atalantis *was published, she was arrested with her printer and publishers, and held prisoner illegally until released on a writ of habeas corpus. She was tried but the prosecution was dropped. She had a love affair with John Tilly, warden of Fleet Prison, but when his wife died, she generously encouraged him to make a financially advantageous second marriage. She herself lived with her printer, John Barber, until her death. 'The Physician's Stratagem' from* The Power of Love *(1720) has been edited to half its original length and the spelling and punctuation have been modernized.*

In the reign of Louis XIII of France, the Count de St Severin, being a known enemy of the Cardinal Richelieu, was, upon the Queen Mother's disgrace, dismissed the Court, which caused him to retire to his Château de Brion, within a league of Nîmes in Languedoc. He took along with him his family, designing to return no more to Paris till the death of the Cardinal. Madam the countess was a lady of good understanding, and an agreeable companion; she had acquired in her youth the reputation of a great beauty, which descended to Mademoisel Mariana her daughter, who, to her charms, had the addition of being sole heir to the house of St Severin, for it was not expected monsieur the count, who was already very old and infirm, would have any more children.

As monsieur the count desired nothing more than her establishment, he was highly satisfied to see that the person whom he presented to her as his choice seemed not disagreeable to hers; this was Louis Marquis de Fonteray. Louis had more love for Mariana than it was then the fashion to profess. Persons began to think and speak less respectively of that passion than in the days of their forefathers. The marquis had made so considerable a progress in her heart that monsieur the count intended not to delay his happiness, when the change happened at Court. The Marquis de Fonteray parted with his mistress in all the agony that can be imagined from a passionate lover, who is just upon the point of enjoying a prodigious beauty with great possessions. Their adieu was unspeakably tender, and he promised in a little time to come and find her at Brion, whither the count was going to retire.

Imagine this family settled in their retreat, and tasting more satisfaction than could be found in the hurry and cabals of the Court. Mademoisel Mariana had a young demoisel to attend her, the daughter of a bourgeoise of Paris, whom she was so fond of as to make her bedfellow and companion. The girl was handsome and amorous, which last quality she concealed in a family like that of madam the countess, who was infinitely regular. As Mariana was entirely virtuous, Katherine de Lune, whom they called Caton, was to wear the same appearance, and to dissemble her vicious inclinations, or she must not have remained a moment in that family.

The Count de St Severin had in his youth, even to old age, preserved an intimate friendship with Monsieur Fauxgarde, Counsellor of Parliament at Nîmes; he was lately dead, and had left several children with no large estate. The second, Henry du Fauxgarde, was brought up to the study of physick, he had already taken his degrees, and commenced doctor before his father died. Returning from Paris to Nîmes, to take possession of that small inheritance the Counsellor had left him, he thought it his duty to wait upon monsieur the count, and endeavour to preserve some degree of that favour which he had always shown the counsellor's family. Accordingly he rid over to Castle Brion, where he was extremely well received by all the house. Fauxgarde had wit and pleasantry, was a very good scholar, inclined to libertinism; he had rather, if fortune had so pleased, been a rake than a doctor; his face and person were remarkably handsome. He coveted a large estate without the toil of getting it, and foreseeing, according to custom, he must plod on a great while in the physician's dull road before he could come to be easy, much more eminent, he beat his brains for other methods than the ordinary; hating the drudgery of his profession, he was resolved to lose no opportunity to advance himself.

Whilst Fauxgarde seemed to be infinitely at his ease, and always in good humour, he felt a fire at his heart, lighted by the fair eyes of Mademoisel Mariana, which, nor day, nor night, allowed him any repose. That familiarity with which she treated him had a thousand charms unrevealed to others, for she was generally thought a stately beauty; but considering the doctor as a man of no consequence, she laid aside her reservedness. In those intimacies he discovered a million of charms; her sweetness, her air, her manner, by which her beauties were embellished left him no longer a free agent, and he must either possess her or despair. It is hard to conceive how a person of his gay temper could love so seriously; but whether he were truly attracted by her charms, or that the large inheritance, to which she had an undoubted title, had added the flame of ambition to the fire of love, certain it is, that no desires were ever more ardent. He knew, to his misfortune, the engagement she was under to the Marquis de Fonteray; he foresaw his absence was not likely to be of any long continuance. Therefore the doctor thought what was to be done, must be effected before his return.

Since his first intimacy at Castle Brion, he took care to oblige the chief domestics by his great courtesy and civility, and oftentimes by his generosity, but more especial Caton, who being naturally lovesome, put herself in his way at every opportunity, so that he could not help saying soft things to her, as she was young and pretty. But as he had formed greater designs, in which he knew she could undoubtedly be of service to him, he took care to improve the good spirit in her, and therefore never squandered away the happy minutes she so officiously gave him without kissing, and saying such fine things to her, as she had never heard from anyone before. Those large gardens and covered walks were commodious scenes for love and intrigue. Whilst Mariana would be amusing herself with old philosophers and historians, Caton was treading the grassy paths, and pressing the flowery banks with the young physician, who, making her easily believe he had, by his art, an antidote against pregnancy, by his undeniable practice, put her into the very condition she would have avoided, and which gave her entirely into the power of the person who had occasioned her misfortune.

Things proceeded according to the doctor's mind, who was daily solicited by Caton, to administer wherewith to procure an abortion, or take her from a place whence she must shortly expect to be dismissed with infamy should her growing bigness chance to be discovered, which would expose her to the taunts of that proud minx her mistress, who valued herself upon being virtuous, because she was so ugly nobody would make her otherways. The doctor, seeing her in this excellent cue, flattered her to the height of her own wish, and told her, if she would be advised by him, they would be both revenged upon that proud piece of beauty to the confusion of her pretended virtue, and great hopes of being a marchioness; they might soon put her into a condition below contempt, and worse than Caton's, who had a father for her child, that would make it heir to his estate: but as to Mariana, she might in vain look for anyone to protect her unlucky offspring, for she should never know the hand that struck her. Caton pricked up her ears at this prospect, and after a good decent time of enquiry, was told by Fauxgarde, he had her ill treatment so much at heart that cost what it would, he must be revenged on her lady; which he could no way better effect than by getting her with child also, without her knowing anything of the matter, which might be done by giving her something that he would prepare to cast her into a deep sleep, and Caton being her bedfellow, the doctor would take her place, and try to put her in a condition to mortify her pride, and forever prevent her from reproaching others.

Caton had not delicacy enough to separate the sweet from the bitter. She desired only to be revenged in kind, and did not scruple bestowing her lover for one night upon another if she might but have her desired end. In short, she gave in to all the doctor required, and was impatient till the operation began. They took their measures so well that by means of a soporiferous powder, which Caton administered to Mariana in chocolate, she fell into a deep sleep, of which Caton advertised the doctor, who was too near at hand; he threw himself into that perditious creature's place so to satiate his own wicked passion, and ruin an innocent and virtuous lady.

His guilty design being to make Mariana pregnant, he wasted the night in his endeavours to render her so; though surely with an imperfect taste of happiness to himself, because the charmer was insensible to his embrace; but as he had farther views, he rose from her bed in a full belief that nature would not be deficient, and he should see the good effects of his villainous strategem.

Mademoisel Mariana slept far into the next day, and was so imperfect in her senses when she did awake as alarmed Monsieur and Madam St Severin. The favourite doctor was consulted, who seemed to think it a propensity to an apoplexy; but having taken what he prescribed her, and been let blood, which is sovereign against abortion, the malignity of the drug being evaporated, she returned to herself, and Fauxgarde found he was caressed by the whole family for his art and success, at the same time when he should rather have been hanged for his villainy.

Caton bore herself insufferably insolent upon the knowledge of this secret. Pretending to yield to her desires of removing her to Paris, where Fauxgarde was going to practise, and her father's death giving her a pretence of returning thither, to see what he had been able to do for her, she took her leave of a family who were very glad to be quit of her.

The doctor had taken proper measures with Caton, by which she might without suspicion be carried to Marseilles, where he would meet her, from whence they were to go incognito to Paris, proposing, from the pleasure of the season, to coast it along the shore by sea, to the nearest port of the Isle of France. Caton understood no geography but what had been taught her, to her cost, in the country of love, whence Fauxgarde might unsuspectedly betray her to his wish. They both embarked in a ship outward-bound to the West Indies, though unknown to her. The doctor pretending he had forgot something of consequence on shore, which he would fetch and immediately return, went on board a boat that followed him for that purpose. The ship's crew knowing his intent, having taken a good piece of money of him to carry Caton to the plantation and sell her for a slave, crowded all their sail, the wind favouring their design, whilst the doctor wished her the bonne voyage, made what haste he could to shore, and from thence took post for Paris.

You need not ask if the Marquis of Fonteray made all possible haste to see his dear Mariana, whom he had so long been separated from. After some short refreshment at Paris, he took post for Nîmes, and arrived at Castle Brion, after a tedious absence, with that satisfaction which only true lovers can know.

After the marquis had paid his compliment to monsieur the count and madam the countess, he asked impatiently for his dear mademoisel; earnestly desiring that his marriage might be no longer deferred, which the iniquity of the times had been the occasion of. He was told, with a sigh, by Madam St Severin, that her daughter had for some time been very much indisposed, and now kept her chamber.

When the marquis was brought to Mariana he scarce knew her to be the same, but by the faint remains of that flourishing beauty which had so powerfully enslaved his soul; he was equally surprised and grieved to see her in this condition, her eyes dull and hollow, her lips livid, her face lean and pale: all her words spoke an inward and settled discontent of mind. The count and his lady had consulted all the eminent physicians concerning her distemper, and which way they could hope to cure it. They all agreed she was with child, and her disease no other than the natural infirmity of women in such cases, some in their breeding being much more sick than others.

'Though we heard this judgment of the doctor's,' cried the countess, 'with horror and amazement, we knew not how to credit it, Mariana having always had a behaviour most unexceptionable. Her passionate imprecations have induced us to believe that the doctors may be mistaken in their judgment; and we hope that the swelling, which they consider as an argument of her pregnancy, may be occasioned by some other preternatural tumour, which I flatter myself is the real cause of her distemper.'

Meantime the lovely innocent Mariana, with downcast eyes, heard this relation which she could not contradict; she did not attempt upon this occasion to speak one word to the marquis; sometimes drying her tears, and looking upon him but by stealth; whilst he remained lost in sorrow and amazement. He passed the night tumbling without one wink of sleep; before it was day he called his people to get ready his horses, not able to stay any longer in a place where he suffered such variety of tortures, he left the castle, and an excuse for Monsieur and Madam St Severin, and departed unable to wait the explication of that fatal enigma.

It is not to be doubted but that the count and his lady resented this rude behaviour of the marquis. Mariana alone said he was not to be blamed, the whole affair being so unaccountable, it caused him to do as unaccountable things. But all agreed in this point, that his abrupt departure was giving up the cause, and that there was no further expectation to be had from him.

Some time after Fauxgarde returned to Nîmes, and so to Castle Brion, to see the effects of his fatal stratagem; he was received by the count with open arms, and by madam the countess with as much joy as the situation of her soul could admit.

The count asked him if it were possible for a woman to conceive in her sleep. The doctor answered it was possible; and that we might observe it by several persons who walk in their sleep, and do those several acts of which they have no remembrance when they wake. This one argument persuaded them to think their daughter was with child, and at the same time innocent of the guilt, and ignorant of the person, for she oftentimes rose out of her bed, walked about her chamber, and sometimes down into the garden, without remembering anything of it the next morning.

Fauxgarde, to give the *coup de grâce* to all his exploits, told them both that it was true his own birth was no way comparable to mademoisel's; but if, as circumstances stood, they thought him not unworthy their alliance, he would marry her himself, without seeking to know who was the father, since he was inwardly assured her soul was immaculate and pure, though her body was stained.

This was the first gleam of joy that had accosted Monsieur and Madam St Severin, since Mariana's disposition. They both embraced the doctor, assuring him they did not desire a more worthy son-in-law; and only asked a short time to dispose their daughter to the marriage. Mademoisel gave her hand to the doctor, sufficiently mortified at the necessity of so unequal an alliance.

Madam the countess, being an haughty woman, could ill bear the grief of seeing her only daughter so despicably married; she sunk under the misfortune, and soon after died of regret. The count lived to have the title of St Severin settled in reversion to the doctor and his children by the lady Mariana, and having disposed of his estate to the same use, he not long after departed this world.

Some years passed on, and our new monsieur the count revelled in beauty, wealth and titles: he sacrificed liberally to his genius, unbent from care and fear. One day when some of his choicest favourites were with him, his soul exhilarated with the delicacies he had eaten, and the noble wines he had drank, he observed madam the countess shined more than usual.

The count dissolved in ease, and who had never any great talent of secrecy, together with the vanity he felt to have his stratagem applauded, began the recital how he had obtained a vast fortune and so great a beauty. His happiness could not be perfect, unless his artifice and management were known: contemptible vanity! abominable itch of talking, which rather than not tell, will tell to the ruin of themselves and their family. The table repeated their approbation of his project, more out of compliment than real applause; but the fair Mariana, recovered from her first surprise, which almost sunk her to the earth, bit her lips, and by her change of colour discovered the inward anxiety of her thought. Discreet as she was, she could not forbear some passionate expression that she should lie under the great scandal of a whore, lose the person whom she loved and honoured, and to whom she was contracted, to be betrayed into a marriage with so mean and perfidious a wretch.

She retired to her own apartment, where she put up what jewels and money she had. The count sat himself down again to renew his debauchery, talking over the worthy management of that whole affair; at length repeated to his company what he had told in madam the countess's hearing, touching Caton's slavery in the Indies; adding, that after his marriage, no longer fearing the ill effects of that girl's tattling, he had in conscience sent to redeem her and her child from the plantations to which she was sold; and that as he took care of the boy, for such it proved, so he had given a fortune to his mother, by which she was married to a banker, called D'Ampour, who lived in Rue St Honoré.

Poor afflicted Mariana drove away to Nîmes, where the Governor being told of her arrival, hastened himself to meet her. She lost not a moment's time, but throwing herself at his feet, gave him a full relation of her misfortune, at the same time, petitioning his Highness that he would order a post-carriage to carry her to the Queen, who was declared regent upon the death of Louis XIII.

The Queen easily remembered the growing beauties of Mariana. She was touched with her sorrows, and took her into her protection. Mariana commenced a process against the count, to be tried by the Parliament of Paris. Fauxgarde was obliged to attend this affair, and was not a little surprised to hear that his accomplice Caton de Lune was taken into custody, to be produced in evidence against him.

This new and until now unheard of process made a great noise at Court. The Marquis de Fonteray was soon informed of all the particulars; he still adored Mariana, and now cursed his weakness that had made him too easily credit those appearances that were against her.

He knew full well the slow procedure of the Parliament, and thought the time too long. The law knew no name for his transgression, and as by the blindness of the late Count St Severin, he was enrolled amongst the nobility, the marquis judged him not unworthy of his sword.

They met and fought, and victory easily fell on the marquis's side, as he had the better title, and had long practised the use of the sword. The count left his life at his feet, as some reparation for the injuries Mariana and Fonteray had suffered by his means. The marquis presented himself before her, discoloured with the blood of her cruel husband, and from the merit of revenging her cause, would have pleaded a title to her love.

'See madam,' cried the marquis, 'a criminal who durst not appear in your sight without a powerful expiation.'

'Ah! My lord,' interrupted the countess, 'who gave me up to the horrors of my destiny? Who abandoned me to despair, to the tortures of forsaken love, to the hell of doting where I was despised, loathed, forgotten, though I knew myself to be innocent? Oh ever dear, though cruel Fonteray! What pangs, what torments have I endured for thee?'

'They are past, my charming Mariana. Let us forget our former misery, or remember them only to endear the present joy; you are mine and only mine by a long engagement, and though destiny thrust between us for a while, nothing shall part us now.'

'And yet the cruel laws of honour,' interrupted Mariana, 'forbid us to meet on any terms. Ah Fonteray! had you but waited the slow hand of justice, the villain had perished with ignominy, and I had found nothing to withold me from indulging my inclinations, and rewarding our mutual constancy.'

'What a wretched turn is this, madam,' cried the marquis, 'am I made miserable only by myself?'

At these words the marquis, transported with sorrow, fell upon that fatal sword which since the combat he held in his hand unsheathed. The action was so sudden that Mariana could no otherways prevent it than by a great shriek; throwing herself upon Fonteray, she luckily broke the intended stroke, which instead of piercing his heart glanced sideways against his ribs. The marquis fell to the ground, and Mariana in a swoon upon his body.

Her attendants, hearing the outcry she made, came to her assistance; they carried her to her bed, and sent for surgeons to search the marquis's wound. Nothing but Mariana's absolute commands would have induced him to suffer them to approach him. Fonteray recovered after some time, but with the loss of his mistress, whom no persuasions could prevail upon; she refused her hand though she could not expel him from her heart. As he was the murderer of the man who was a parent to her children, her honour could not permit her to make him her husband; but she promised him never to marry another.

Finding she could get no respite from his solicitations, she disposed of all her affairs, and provided with the best advantage for the education of her children; then put herself into the nunnery of the Augustines. After her probation she took the veil, dedicating the rest of her time to heaven. Fonteray renounced the world, and entered himself among the Carthusians, the most rigid order of the religious; where, after a life full of devotion, they went in search of happiness above, which, by a severe decree, was denied them here below.

DOROTHY RICHARDSON

Christmas Eve

Dorothy Richardson (1873-1957) was brought up in Abingdon, Worthing and Barnes, one of four daughters. After her father lost his money and went bankrupt, she left home and supported herself by teaching in Hanover and north London. She then became an assistant in a dental practice in Harley Street, living in a boarding house in Bloomsbury for many years. She had close relationships with H.G. Wells (she became pregnant but miscarried), Benjamin Grad, a Russian expatriate and Veronica Leslie-Jones, a drama student and suffragist. She married off Benjamin and Veronica to one another to avoid the commitment of a long-term relationship, but later married an unknown artist Alan Odle in 1917 when an army doctor had diagnosed TB and given him six months to live. He survived until 1948, and the couple lived alternately in London and Cornwall. Her novel cycle Pilgrimage, *in thirteen parts, was published from 1915 to 1967 (the last part written with difficulty over a number of years and published posthumously). It was a great critical success with disappointing sales.*

I put down my pilgrim basket and went into the office for Miss Barron's welcome. It was Miss Spencer, in one of her older dresses, writing a letter at the office table. It was too late to alter my expression.

'*Well*, dear lady, this is *very* charming.' She kept her pen in her hand as she spoke.

I had been going to say to Miss Brown I wanted to come.

I laughed uneasily and stood waiting halfway between the door and the table. If I could not quickly find something to say she would at least be asking me to read prayers in the morning.

'*Very* charming,' she repeated, putting an elbow on the table and removing her pince-nez.

I muttered shapelessly that I was taking refuge because I had so many invitations, and thought if I had an engagement here nobody would be offended.

'What an excellent plan – *Isn't* it difficult to keep one's friends from being jealous of each other? Isn't it a *problem*. Well, we're charmed to have you here – *Oh*, we've had such a day, dear lady.'

I beamed insincere curiosity and murmured that she didn't look it.

'Well, it's all over now. All's well that ends well. Weren't you surprised to find the front door unlocked?'

I hurriedly agreed, privately inferring it must be later than I thought. Edith would be putting in time in the common room. She would think I had backed out.

'I say, have you had supper? Have you been journeying?'

I had had a meal.

'Right. Well, sit down a moment before you go upstairs. I *must* tell you our story. D'you mind shutting the door . . . Do you remember Fräulein *Braun*? Of course you do. She was here in the summer. Yes, *that's* the lady. Did you? Well, perhaps it's going ahead in Germany more quickly than we think; if many more of the women are like her. You *ought* to have been here about an hour ago; about ten o'clock. Well. I *must* just give you the story in outline. It's so exceptional. I think you'll be interested . . . It all began *yesterday*. I thought there was something wrong with her about tea-time. She looked the picture of dejection. You know there's nothing like a foreigner when they are dejected. Is there? . . . No. Yes, that's it, isn't it extraordinary? Well; it seems she had been counting on the arrival of a little Christmas tree from Germany. Miss Barron tells me she has talked about it for days; and after this morning's post she began to *despair*. *Oh*, we've had such a day with her. She wandered about the house and kept on coming down to the hall and staring out through the vestibule and muttering to herself. I was afraid we should have her ill. Can you imagine – such an intelligent woman and – well – I suppose thirty, shouldn't you say?'

I suggested that they thought a good deal of Christmas.

'*She* does certainly. It was *really awful*. I think any of us would have given up our parcels only too willingly to put an end to her misery. Well, the climax came after this evening's post. The nine o'clock postman came at ten. She was standing silently waiting on the stairs. I assure you I didn't know how to face her empty-handed. I wish you could have been there. It had its funny side, you know. I said I'm afraid your parcel hasn't come Fräulein Braun. She didn't move. She just stood still on the stairs and said in a loud voice – "I go out – to buy a tree." At ten-fifteen; on Christmas Eve. I saw at once it would be perfectly useless to try and stop her. She would have defied me. And I knew she would not come back until she had found one. So I had to fling X.Y. rules to the winds and let her go forth . . . I sent Miss Banks with her. She's pretty level-headed and knows her way about London . . . I've never had such an experience in the whole of my time. Fortunately they're nearly all away.'

I admired the excitement.

'*Excitement*, dear lady – I *was* anxious until they came back. I was never so glad to see anyone in my life.'

'When did they come?'

'At eleven; just before you did. They found a tree in Lisson Grove. – *Lisson Grove*. She came back beaming. Came in here holding it up in the air, poor Bankie at her last gasp in the background. She sáys Fräulein *ran* along the streets *crying*, and rushed into the green-grocers' shops hardly able to speak. Well. That's not the end. I thought we were well over our troubles when I saw her with the tree. But no. She stood over me – you know how tall she is, and said, "I must have matches." She had bought a little box of coloured candles! I tried to dissuade her diplomatically. She simply said, "It is useless: I must have matches." I had to give in. So she's gone off to her cubicle with her matches and I've put off turning-out time until eleven forty-five. Did you ever hear anything like it? I've warned her room not to go to their cubicles till half past and I've asked her to keep the curtains withdrawn. What do you suppose she is doing?'

'Oh, she'll light up and be satisfied. It's rather charming.'

'It'll be *very* charming if she sets the house on fire. I think it's too comic. One person, with a Christmas tree, in a cubicle. Don't say anything in the common-room. There are a few wild spirits not gone home and a good many strangers.'

I recognised only a few faces. The Greens and Eunice were sitting with their workboxes and underlinen in their usual talking row on the settee facing the fire. Little Green had put up her hair. 'Hello, ghost; here's a ghost,' she said. I greeted them vaguely and passed on to the centre of the room. Edith was sitting over a book at the far table be-neath the windows with her back to the room. I paused under the lights with an open letter, to take in the other groups about the fire. Two women, a mother and daughter, the provincial X.Y. type reading bibles. In the largest armchair a tiny Hindu sitting upright, the fire-light gleaming on the gold threads of her striped draperies. She was listening and smiling gently into vacancy. Her tiny hands clasped on her knees looked, social, as if they had never been alone. Near her sat Miss Banks. The heavy scroll of her profile hung over a moirette petticoat; her compressed lips and the eager hunch of her shoulders expressed her satisfaction in the tuck that would make it short enough to wear. Perhaps she had seen me come in, perhaps not. Four or five figures were grouped about the door side of the fireplace, waiting over X.Y. library books for bedtime, numbly waiting for Christmas to come and go.

'Hullo, Winged Victory,' I murmured under cover of the talk on the settee. Edith darted to her feet and stood restraining her welcome as I went wearily forward.

'Why don't you have the table light and aren't you fearfully cold?' I asked.

'No,' she whispered. 'Is it cold? Are you cold?'

'I don't know. I've just heard one of the most pathetic things I ever heard.'

'Shall we go upstairs?'

I looked vaguely about. 'It was a splendid idea of yours,' whispered Edith.

The door opened suddenly on Miss Spencer. Everyone looked round. 'Oh' – she said comprehensively. 'Will you *all* please come up to No 8 for a few minutes. Fräulein Braun wishes us all to gather together for a few minutes. It is a German custom. I think we must all go. Will you all come? Just for a few minutes.'

Cook was the last to come in. She was wearing her ulster and had a piece of red flannel round her neck and her usual winter expression of being in the midst of a bad cold. The curtains were all thrown up over their rails leaving the room clear. Someone had pushed back the beds so that there was space on the linoleum-covered floor for all to stand about the little tree. Its many candles glowed sharply in the cold air. Fräulein Braun stood near the tree as we all gathered in a rough circle.

'What are we to do, Fräulein?' asked Miss Sharp briskly to cover a giggle from little Green.

'All over here?' asked Fräulein in her deep voice.

'Everyone in the house, Fräulein.'

Fräulein drew back into the awkward circle between Edith and the little Hindu who was standing with reverently bent head and her little hands clasped downwards before her. At the end of a moment Fräulein's rich voice rose and filled the large cold room.

Sh—ti—il-le *Nacht*
Hei—li-ge *Nacht* . . .

As she sang the room seemed to grow less cold. The sharp separate rays of the little candles changed to one rosy golden blur.

When Fräulein's voice ceased there was silence. Miss Spencer looked about with a cheerful questioning face. She could be heard urging someone to do something. In a moment she would speak. I was aware of a stirring at my side and felt the flush that made cook's face uniform with her nose. Her impulse had animated more than one, but it was her old unused voice that broke the silence with song in which presently all joined as they could:

While shepherds watched their flocks by night
All seated on the ground
The Angel of the Lord came down,
And glory shone around.

ELIZA LINTON

Two Cousins

Eliza Linton (1822-98), née Lynn, was the daughter of a clergyman, one of twelve children. She was brought up in Cumberland and later Kent, and was self-educated. She settled alone in London at twenty-three, wrote a historical novel Azeth the Egyptian *(1846), and became a journalist, writing reviews and articles for various periodicals, some of which were later collected in* The Girl of the Period *(1868). She had a very large output both as a novelist and journalist. She married the engraver and journalist W.J. Linton, but had no children. She was later separated from him but was never divorced. She had a close friendship over the years with a younger woman whom she regarded as an adopted daughter, Beatrice Sichel. Her attitude to women's emancipation was ambivalent: she opposed legal discrimination against women, but largely defended the status quo she herself did not conform to, and made capital out of her attacks on the modern woman. She saw domesticity and childbearing as the first duty of women.*

'He didn't care much about it,' he said. 'They might marry him, if they liked, and to whom they liked, provided he was not expected to make love. Give him his hookah and a volume of Shelley, and really, wife or no wife, it was almost the same thing to him. By the bye, one thing he must stipulate for – that she should not hunt nor talk slang.'

This Launcelot Chumley said, yawning – although it was only twelve o'clock and he had not long finished breakfast – and after he had said this, sauntering from the drawing-room through the open window on to the lawn, he stretched himself under the shadow of the chestnut trees to dream vague poems all the day after; a mode of existence that seemed to him to fulfil the sacred destiny of his being.

Launcelot Chumley was a spoilt child – a spoilt child full of noble thoughts and generous impulses tarnished by prosperity and choked for want of stimulants to exertion. He was also vain for want of wholesome opposition. Provided people left him alone they might do as they liked, he used to say. Let them not disturb his books, nor cut down the chestnut trees on the lawn, nor break his pipes, nor talk loud, nor make a noise – and he was perfectly satisfied. His indifference and indolence drove his mother to despair. She tried to tempt him to exertion by dazzling visions of distinction. But Launcelot prided himself on his want of ambition, and vowed he would not accept a dukedom if offered to him – it would be such a bore! His mother had indeed done her best to ruin him by unmitigated indulgence; and now she wrung her hands at her own work. But, as something must be done, she bethought herself of marriage; which, woman-like, she fancied would cure everything – indolence, vanity, selfishness at a blow.

Mrs Chumley bethought her of a marriage – but with whom?

There were in London two Chumley cousins, Ella Limple and little Violet Tudor. These two young ladies were great friends after the fashion of young ladies in general. They had mysterious confidences together and wrote wonderful letters of great frequency and appalling length. Ella Limple, being of a pathetic and sentimental temperament, talked of sorrow and sadness, and said there was no more happiness for her on earth, there being something she could never forget; though nobody knew what that something was. Violet Tudor, her bosom friend, laughed at all sentiment, and expressed a supreme contempt for lovers. She vowed also that she would never marry a less man than a Lion-king or a general who had seen severe service and been wounded badly; and then she did not know – perhaps she might. For Violet rode blood horses, and once pronounced an Indian officer a 'muff', because he had never seen a tiger hunt – an expression which caused that gentleman to feel the kind of anger which is, among his own sex, usually assuaged by a duel.

It may be imagined therefore that Mrs Chumley did not place Miss Violet Tudor very high in her scale of feminine graces; although she did not know one half of that curly-headed gipsy's escapades. Consequently she was passed over at once. Ella was, on the contrary, all that Mrs Chumley wished; young, pretty, mild, manageable; with gold, a stainless pedigree and unexceptionable manners. What more could any mother demand for her son? Wherefore, much to Ella's surprise and pleasure Mrs Chumley sent by that day's post an affectionate invitation asking her to pass a week at High Ashgrove; for Cousin Launcelot had long been a kind of heroic myth to that young lady's imagination; and she was glad to be asked to be with him – 'Though dearest Vi knows that nothing could make me forget poor dear Henry all alone in those terrible East Indies!' she said in the letter which communicated the circumstances to her bosom friend. Out of gratitude then and full of poetic fancy, but, without dangerous designs, she accepted the invitation; and, in less than a week's time, she found herself at High Ashgrove, with all her prettiest dresses and her last new bonnet.

Ella's correspondence with Violet Tudor marvellously multiplied during this visit. The early letters were gay, for her; but soon they deepened into a nameless melancholy, and were rife with mysterious hints. Occasionally there burst forth in them the most terrific self-accusings that English words could frame. If she had become the head of a society of coiners, or the high priestess of a heresy, she could not have used stronger expressions of guilt. At first Violet was frightened; but then she remembered that it was Ella's habit to indulge in all sorts of exaggerated self-accusations and so calmed herself and even smiled. At last came a letter which unveiled the mystery; reducing the terrible sphynx which devoured men's bones to a tame dog that stole his neighbour's cream – the usual ending of most young ladies' mysteries. 'I do not know what my dearest Violet will think of her Ella,' she said, 'but if it is to be the death-blow of that long and tender love which has supported my sad heart through so many bitter trials, I must tell her the truth. Violet, I have broken my vows, and am deserving of the fate of Imogen in that dreadful ballad! Poor dear Henry! Violet, love, I am engaged to my cousin Launcelot. My aunt made me the offer so supplicatingly, and Launcelot said so sweetly: "I think you will make me a very nice wife, Miss Limple," that I could not resist. Besides, Cousin Launcelot is very handsome; and that goes a great way. You know I always found fault with poor dear Henry's figure; he was inclined to be too stout. Launcelot's figure is perfect. He is tall – six feet I should think – and with the most graceful manners possible. He is like a picture; has very bright brown hair, all in thick curls, not short and close like poor dear Henry's. He wears them very long, like the portraits of Raphael. Henry's hair, poor darling, was inclined to be red. His eyes are large and dark grey, with *such* a beautiful expression of melancholy in them. They are poems in themselves, Violet. Now Henry's, you know, were hazel; and hazel eyes are unpleasant – they are so quick and fiery. I like such eyes as Launcelot's – melancholy, poetic eyes that seem to feel and think as well as to see. Hazel eyes only see. Don't you know the difference? He is very quiet; lies all day under the trees smoking out of the most exquisite hookah, and reading Shelley. I dote on Shelley and hate Shakespeare. How fond Henry was of Shakespeare! – that wearisome Hamlet! And now her own Ella is going to beg and pray of her dearest Violet to come here as soon as possible. I enclose a note from Aunt Chumley, asking you; and darling Vi, I will never forgive you if you do not come directly. For no lover in the world could ever separate me from my own Violet. If you do not come I shall think you are angry with me for my bad conduct to poor Henry; and indeed I feel how guilty I am. I had such a terrible dream of him last night! I thought he looked so pale and reproachful, just like his favourite Hamlet. Goodbye. I cannot write another word; for aunt wants me to go with her to the village. Do come, dearest Violet, and come immediately.'

This letter delighted Ella's friend. She had never liked the flirtation with Cornet Henry Dampier which she had thought silly and sentimental; while this seemed to offer a real future. She wrote to her aunt – of whom she was considerably afraid; and in a few days she also arrived at High Ashgrove. She was received by Ella with a burst of enthusiasm, which coming from one so calm as his quiet little *fiancée*, quite electrified Launcelot; by Aunt Chumley with no superfluity of kindness; and, by Launcelot himself, with a cold bow. Yet Violet was pretty enough for any man's admiration. The thick raven hair which it was her will and pleasure to wear crowded over her face; her great black eyes that never rested; her tiny hand; her fabulous waist; her light fairy figure; her wide red lips, and her untamable vivacity, made her appear like some wild child of the desert as she alighted on the steps of that still, lazy, gentlemanlike house.

For the first two days Violet behaved herself with perfect propriety. She embroidered more than two square inches of Berlin work and did not make a single allusion to the stables. She fell asleep only twice when Launcelot condescended to read aloud the mistiest parts of Queen Mab; and she tried hard to look as if she understood what Epipsychidion was all about. Poor little woman! She knew as much about either as if Cousin Launce, as she called him, had informed her in its native dialect of the glory of the Anax Andrôn, or as if he had told her how 'arms and the man' were sung at Mantua long ago. But this state of things could not last long. Old habits and old instincts entered their protest, and Violet Tudor felt that she must be natural or she should die. Launcelot said that she was noisy and made his head ache; and he changed his resting-place for one farther off from the house, complaining of Miss Tudor's voice which he declared was like a bird's whistle that penetrated into his brain. This he said to his mother languidly, at the same time asking when she was going away again.

'You don't keep horses, Cousin Launce?' Violet said on the third morning at breakfast, raising her eyelids and fixing her eyes for an instant on him.

'Not for ladies, Miss Tudor,' said Launcelot.

'Why do you call me Miss Tudor?' she asked again. 'I am your own cousin. It is rude!'

'I should think myself impertinent if I called you by any other name,' returned Launcelot still more coldly.

'How odd! Aunt, why is Cousin Launce so strange?'

'I don't know what you mean, Violet,' said Mrs Chumley a little sternly; 'I think *you* are strange – not my son!'

An answer that steadied the eyes for some time; for Violet looked down, feeling rebuked and wondering how she had deserved rebuke. A moment after, Ella asked Launcelot for something in her gentle, quiet, unintoned voice, speaking as if they had been strangers and had met for the first time that day. It was a striking contrast; and not un-noticed by Chumley, who was inwardly thankful that such a quiet wife had been chosen for him – adding a grace of thanks for having escaped Violet Tudor. After breakfast he strolled, as usual, into the garden – Mrs Chumley going about her household concerns. Violet went to the door, turning round for Ella.

'Come with me, Elly darling,' she said; 'let us go and tease Launce. It is really too stupid here! – I cannot endure it much longer. I want to see what that lazy fellow is really made of. I am not engaged to him, so I am not afraid of him. Come!' And with one spring down the whole flight, she dashed on the lawn like a flash of light. Ella descended like a well-bred lady; but Violet skipped and ran and jumped and once she hopped – until she found herself by Launcelot's side as he lay on the grass, darting in between him and the sun like a humming-bird.

'Cousin Launce, how lazy you are!' were her first words. 'Why don't you do something to amuse us? You take no more notice of Ella than if she were a stranger, and you are not even ordinarily polite to me. It is really dreadful! What will you be when you are a man, if you are so idle and selfish now? There will be no living with you in a few years; for I am sure you are almost insupportable as you are!'

Launcelot had not been accustomed to this style of address, and for the first few moments was completely at fault. Ella looked frightened. She touched Violet, and whispered: 'Don't hurt his feelings!' as if he had been a baby and Violet an assassin.

'And what am I to do to please Miss Tudor?' Launcelot asked in an impertinent voice; 'what herculean exertion must I go through to win favour in the eyes of my strong, brave, manly young lady cousin?'

'Be a man yourself, Cousin Launce,' answered Violet; 'don't spend all your time dawdling over stupid poetry, which I am sure you don't understand. Take exercise – good strong exercise. Ride, hunt, shoot, take interest in something and in some one, and don't think yourself too good for everyone's society but your own. You give up your happiness for pride; I am sure you do; yet, you are perfectly unconscious of how ridiculous you make yourself.'

'You are severe, Miss Tudor,' said Launcelot, his face crimson. Though Violet was so small and so pretty he could not help being dreadfully angry with her.

'I tell you the truth,' she persisted; 'and you don't often hear the truth. Better for you if you did. You must not let it be a quarrel between us; for I speak only for your own good; and if you will only condescend to be a little more like other men I will never say a word to you again. Let us go to the stables. I want to see your horses. You have horses?'

'Yes,' said Launcelot coldly; 'but, as I remarked at breakfast, not ladies' horses.'

'I don't care for ladies' horses: men's horses will suit me better!' said Violet, with a toss of her little head that was charming in its assertion of equality. 'I would undertake to ride horses, Cousin Launce, which you dare not mount; for I am sure you cannot be good at riding, lying on the grass all your life!'

Launcelot was excessively piqued. His burning blood made his face tingle, his brows contracted, and he felt humbled and annoyed; but roused. Tears came into Ella's eyes. She went up to her friend and said: 'Oh, Violet, how cruel you are!'

Launcelot saw this little bye-scene. He was a vain man and a spoilt child in one; and he hated pity on the one side as much as interference on the other. So poor Ella did not advance herself much in his eyes by her championship. On the contrary, he felt more humiliated by her tears than by Violet's rebukes; and, drawing himself up proudly, he said to Violet as if he were giving away a kingdom, 'If you please we will ride today.'

'Bravo! bravo, Cousin Launce!' she cried gaily; and then left the lovers together, hoping they would improve the opportunity; but Ella was too well-bred, and Launcelot was too cold for the improvement of opportunities; and they only called each other Miss Limple and Mr

Chumley, and observed that it was very fine weather – which was the general extent of their love-making.

They arrived at the stable in time to hear some of Violet's candid criticisms. 'That cob's off-fetlock wants looking to. The stupid groom! who ever saw a beast's head tied up like that? Why he isn't a crib-biter, is he?' she said; and with a: 'Wo-ho, poor fellow! steady there, steady!' Violet went dauntlessly up to the big carriage horse's head, and loosened the strain of his halter before Launcelot knew what she was about. In the stable she was in her element. She wandered in and out of the stalls, and did not mind how much the horses fidgeted; nor even if they turned themselves sideways as if they meant to crush her against the manger. Launcelot thought all this vulgar beyond words; and he thought Ella Limple, who stood just at the door and looked frightened, infinitely the superior of the two ladies; and he again thanked his good star that had risen on Ella and not on Violet.

Violet chose the biggest and the most spirited horse of the lot for her mount, Ella an old grey that was as steady as a camel; and both went into the house to dress for their ride. When they came back, even Launcelot – disapproving of Amazons in general – could not but confess that they made a beautiful pair – Ella so fair and graceful, and Violet so full of life and beauty! He was obliged to allow that she was beautiful; but of course not so beautiful as Ella. With this thought he threw himself cleverly into the saddle, and off the three started; Ella holding her pummel very tightly.

They ambled down the avenue together; but, when they got a short distance on the road, Violet raised herself in the saddle and, waving her small hand lost in its white gauntlets, darted off; tearing along the road till she became a mere speck in the distance. Launcelot's blood again came up into his face. Something stirred his heart, strung his nerves up to their natural tone, and made him envy and long and hate and admire all in a breath.

He turned to Ella and said hurriedly, 'Shall we ride faster, Miss Limple?'

'If you please,' answered Ella timidly; 'but I cannot ride *very* fast, you know.'

Launcelot bit his lip. 'Oh, I remember – yet I hate to see women riding like jockeys; you are quite right,' he said. All the same he fretted his horse and frowned. Then he observed very loudly, 'Violet Tudor is a very vulgar little girl.'

After a time Violet came back; her black horse foaming, his head well up, his neck arched, his large eyes wild and bright: she, flushed, animated, bright, full of life and health. Launcelot sat negligently on his bay – one hand on the crupper as lazy men do sit on horseback – walking slowly. Ella's dozing grey was hanging down his head half asleep, with the flies settling on his twinkling pink eyelids.

'Dearest Violet, I thought you would have been killed,' said Ella; 'what made you rush off at that dreadful pace?'

'And what makes you both ride as if you were in a procession and were afraid of trampling on the crowd?' retorted Violet. 'Cousin Launcelot, you are something wonderful! A strong man like you to ride in that manner. Are you made of jelly that would break if shaken? For shame! Have a canter. Your bay won't beat my black; although my black is blown and your mare is fresh.'

She gave her cousin's bay a smart cut with her whip which sent it off at a hard gallop. Away they both flew, clattering along the hard road, like dragoons. But Violet beat by a full length; or, as she phrased it, 'she won cleverly', telling Launcelot that he had a great deal to do yet before he could ride against her – which made him hate her as much as if she had been a Frenchman, or a Cossack; and love Ella more than ever. And so he told his *fiancée*, as he lifted her tenderly from her grey, leaving Violet to spring from her black mammoth unassisted.

All that evening he was sulky to Violet and peculiarly affectionate to Ella; making the poor child's heart flutter like a caged bird.

'Cousin,' whispered Violet the next morning, laying her little hand on his shoulder; 'have you a rifle in the house? – or a pair of pistols?' Launcelot was so taken by surprise that he hurriedly confessed to having guns and pistols and rifles and all other murderous weapons necessary for the fit equipment of a gentleman.

'We will have some fun, then,' she said, looking happy and full of mischief.

She and Ella – Ella dragged sorely against her will; for the very sight of a pistol nearly threw her into hysterics – went into the shrubbery; and there Violet challenged Launcelot to shoot with her at a mark at twenty paces; then, as she grew vain, at thirty. Launcelot was too proud to refuse this challenge; believing of course that a little black-eyed girl, whose waist he could span between his thumb and little finger and with hands that could hardly find gloves small enough for them, could not shoot so well as he.

Launcelot was nervous – that must be confessed; and Violet was excited. Launcelot's nervousness helped in his failure but Violet's excitement helped her success. Her bullet hit the mark every time straight in the centre, and Launcelot never hit once; which was not very pleasant in their respective conditions of lord and subject; for so Launcelot classed men and women – especially little women with small waists – in his own magnificent mind.

He had not shot for a long time, he said; and he was out of practice. He drank coffee for breakfast, and that had made his hand unsteady –

'And confess too, Cousin Launce,' said Violet, 'that you were never very good at shooting any time of your life, without coffee or with it. Why, you don't even load properly; how can you shoot if you don't know how to load? We can't read without an alphabet!' In the prettiest manner possible she took the pistol from her cousin's hand and loaded it for him – first drawing his charge. 'Now try again!' she said, speaking as if to a child; 'nothing like perseverance.'

Launcelot was provoked, but subdued. He did as his little instructress bade him; to fail, once more. His bullet went wide of the target, and Violet's lodged in the bull's eye. So Launcelot flung the pistols on the grass and said, 'It is a very unladylike amusement, Miss Tudor; and I was much to blame to encourage you in such nonsense.' Offering his arm to Ella, he walked sulkily away.

Violet looked after them both for some time, watching them through the trees. There was a peculiar expression in her face – a mixture of whimsical humour, of pain, of triumph, and of a wistful kind of longing, of which she was half unconscious. She then turned away; and with a sigh, said softly to herself, 'It is a pity Cousin Launcelot has such a bad temper!'

After this, Launcelot became more and more reserved to Violet and more and more affectionate to Ella; although he often wondered at himself for thinking so much of the one – though only in anger and dislike – and so little of the other. Why should he disturb himself about Violet?

On the other hand Violet was distressed at Launcelot's evident dislike for her. What had she said? What had she done? She was always good-tempered to him, and ready to oblige. To be sure she had told him several rough truths; but was not the truth always to be told? And just see the good that she had done him! Look how much more active and less spoilt he was now than he used to be! It was all owing to her. She wished, for Ella's sake, that he liked her better; for it would be very disagreeable for Ella when she married, if Ella's husband did not like to see her in his house. It was really very distressing. And Violet cried on her pillow that night, thinking over the dark future when she could not stay with Ella, because Ella's husband hated her.

This was after Violet had beaten Cousin Launcelot three games of chess consecutively. Launcelot had been furiously humiliated; for he was accounted the best chess player of the neighbourhood. But Violet was really a good player, and had won the prize at a chess club where she had been admitted by extraordinary courtesy; it not being the custom of that reputable institution to suffer womanhood within its sacred walls. But she was very unhappy about Cousin Launce for all that; and the next day looked quite pale and cast down. Even Launcelot noticed his obnoxious cousin's changed looks and asked her, rather graciously, 'If she were ill?' To which question Violet replied by a blush, a glad smile bursting out like a song and a pretty pout, 'No, I am not ill, thank you,' she said half shyly. Which ended their interchange of civilities for the day.

Lancelot became restless, feverish, melancholy, cross; at times boisterously gay, at times the very echo of despair. He was kind to Ella and confessed to himself how fortunate he was in having chosen her; but he could not understand – knowing how much he loved her – the extraordinary effect that she had on his nerves. Her passiveness irritated him. Her soft and musical voice made him nervous; for he was incessantly watching for a change of intonation or an emphasis which never came. Her manners were certainly the perfection of manners – he desired none other in his wife – but, if she would sometimes move a little quicker, or look interested and pleased when he tried to amuse her, she would make him so much happier! And oh! if she would only do something more than work those eternal slippers, how glad he would be!

'There they are!' he exclaimed aloud as the two cousins passed before his window. 'By Jove, what a foot that Violet has! – and her hair, what a lustrous black it is! – and what eyes! Pshaw! what is it to me what kind of hair or eyes she has?' He closed his window and turned away. But, in a minute after, he was watching the two girls again, seeing only Violet. 'The strange strength of hate,' he said, as he stepped out on the lawn to follow them.

Launcelot's life was very different now from what it had been. He wondered at himself. He had become passionately fond of riding and was looking forward to the hunting season with delight. He rode every day with his two cousins; and he and Violet had races together, which made them sometimes leave Ella and her grey for half an hour in the lanes. He used to shoot too – practising secretly – until one day he astonished Violet by hitting the bull's eye as often as she herself could hit it. He talked a great deal more than before; and he had not opened

Shelley for a fortnight. He was more natural and less vain; and some-times he even condescended to laugh so as to be heard, and to appreci-ate Violet Tudor's fun. But this was very rare; and always had the appearance of a condescension – as when men talk to children. He still hated Violet; and they quarrelled every day regularly, but were seldom apart. They hated each other so much that they could not be happy without bickering; – although, to do Violet justice, it was all on Launcelot's side. Left to herself, she would never have said a cross word to him. But what could she do when he was so impertinent? Thus they rode and shot and played at chess and quarrelled and sulked and became reconciled and quarrelled again; and Ella, still and calm, looked on with her soft blue eyes and often 'wondered why they were such children together.'

One day, the three found themselves together on a bench under a fine old purple beech which bent down its great branches like a bower about them. Ella gathered a few of the most beautiful leaves and placed them in her hair. They did not look very well; her hair was too light; and Launcelot said so.

'Perhaps they will look better on you, Miss Tudor,' he added, pick-ing a broad and ruddy leaf and laying it Bacchante fashion on her curly, thick black bands. His hand touched her cheek. He started and dropped the leaf as suddenly as if that round fresh face had been burning iron. Violet blushed deeply, and felt distressed, ashamed and angry. Trembling, and with a strange difficulty of breathing, she got up and ran away; saying that she was going for her parasol – although she had it in her hand – and would be back immediately. But she stayed away a long time, wondering at Cousin Launcelot's impertin-ence. When she came back no one was to be seen. Ella and Launcelot had gone into the shrubbery to look after a hare that had run across the path; and Violet sat down on the bench waiting for them – and very pleased they had gone. She heard a footstep. It was Launcelot without his cousin. 'Ella had gone into the house,' he said, 'not quite understanding that Miss Tudor was coming back to the seat.'

Violet instantly rose; a kind of terror was in her face, and she trembled more than ever. 'I must go and look for her,' she said, taking up her parasol.

'I am sorry, Miss Tudor, that my presence is so excessively disagree-able to you!' Launcelot said, moving aside to let her pass.

Violet looked full into his face, trembling no more. 'Disagreeable! Your presence disagreeable to me? Why, Cousin Launce, it is *you* who hate *me*!'

'You know the contrary,' said Launcelot hurriedly. 'You detest and despise me: and take no pains to hide your feelings – not ordinary cousinly pains! I know that I am full of faults,' speaking as if a dam had been removed and the waters were rushing over in a torrent – 'but still I am not so bad as you think me! I have done all I could to please you since you have been here. I have altered my former habits. I have adopted your advice and followed your example. If I knew how to make you esteem me, I would try even more than I have already tried. I can endure anything rather than the humiliating contempt that you feel for me!'

Launcelot became suddenly afflicted with a choking sensation; a sense of fullness was in his head, and his limbs shook. Suddenly tears came into his eyes. Yes, man as he was, he wept. Violet flung her arms round his neck; and took his head between her little hands. She bent her face till her breath came warm on his forehead, and spoke a few innocent words which might have been said to a brother. But they conjured up a strange world in both. Violet tried to disengage herself; for it was Launcelot now who held her. She hid her face; but he forced her to look up.

Suddenly, as if conquered by something stronger than herself, she flung her arms round his neck; then with a little cry and a spasmodic effort she tore herself away and darted into the house in a state of excitement and tumult.

An agony of reflection succeeded to this agony of feeling; and Launcelot and Violet both felt as if they had committed or were about to commit some fearful sin. Could Violet betray her friend? Could she, who had always upheld truth and honour, accept Ella's trust only to deprive her of her lover? It was worse than guilt! Poor Violet wept the bitterest tears which her bright eyes had ever shed; for she laboured under a sense of sin that was insupportable. She dared not look at Ella, but feigned a headache and went into her own room to weep. Launcelot was shocked too; but Launcelot was a man; and the sense of a half-developed triumph somewhat deadened his sense of remorse. A certain dim unravelling of the mystery of the past was also pleasant. Without being dishonourable, he was less overcome.

On that dreadful day Launcelot and Violet spoke no more to each other. They did not even look at each other. Ella thought that some new quarrel had burst forth in her absence, and tried to make it up between them, in her amiable way. But ineffectively. Violet rushed away when Launcelot came near her; and she besought of Ella to leave her alone so pathetically, that the poor girl, bewildered, only sighed at her inability to harmonize the two greatest loves of her life.

The day after, Violet received a letter from her mother, in which that poor woman, having had an attack of spasms in her chest and being otherwise out of sorts, expressed her firm belief that she should never see her sweet child again. The dear old lady consequently bade her adieu resignedly. On ordinary days Violet would have known what all this pathos meant; now she was glad to turn it to account and to appear to believe it. She spoke to her aunt and to Ella, and told them that she must absolutely leave by the afternoon train – poor mamma was ill and she could not let her be nursed by servants. There was nothing to oppose this argument, and Mrs Chumley ordered the brougham to take her to the station precisely at two o'clock. Launcelot was not in the room when these arrangements were made; nor did he know anything that was taking place until he came down to luncheon, pale and haggard, to find Violet in her travelling dress standing by her boxes.

'What is all this, Violet?' he cried, taken off his guard and seizing her hands as he spoke.

'I am going away,' said Violet as quietly as she could; but without looking at him.

He started as if an electric shock had passed through him. 'Violet – going!' he cried in a suffocated voice. He was pale; and his hands, clasped on the back of the chair, were white with the strain. 'Going? Why?'

'Mamma is ill,' said Violet. It was all she could say.

'I am sorry we are to lose you,' he then said very slowly – each word as if ground from him, as words are ground out, when they are the masks of intense passion.

His mother looked at him with surprise. Ella turned to Violet. Everyone felt there was a mystery of which they knew nothing. Ella went up to her cousin.

'Dear Violet, what does all this mean?' she asked, her arm round the little one's neck caressingly.

'Nothing,' answered Violet with great difficulty. 'There is nothing.'

Big drops stood on Launcelot's forehead. 'Ought you not to write first to your mother – to give her notice before you go?' he said.

'No,' she answered, her flushed face quivering from brow to lip; 'I must go now.'

At that moment a servant entered hurriedly to say that she must go at once if she wished to catch the train. Adieux were given in all haste. Violet's tears began to gather – but only to gather as yet; not to flow

– kept bravely back for love and pride. 'Goodbye,' she said to Ella, warmly, tenderly, her heart filled with self-reproach. 'Goodbye,' she said to aunt: aunt herself very sad; and then 'Goodbye,' she said to Launcelot. 'Goodbye, Mr Chumley,' she repeated, holding out her hand, but not looking into his face. He could not speak. He tried to bid her adieu; but his lips were dry and his voice would not come. His features expressed such exquisite suffering that Violet for a moment was overcome, and could scarcely draw away her hand. The hour struck; and duty ranked before all with brave Violet. Launcelot stood where she left him. She ran down the lawn; she was almost out of sight, when 'Violet! Violet!' rang from the house like the cry of death.

Violet – a moment irresolute – returned; then almost unconsciously she found herself kneeling beside Launcelot, who lay senseless on the ground, saying: 'Launcelot, I will not leave you!'

The burden of pain was shifted now. From Launcelot and Violet to Ella. But Ella – sentimental and conventional as she might be – was a girl who, like many, can perform great sacrifices with an unruffled brow; who can ice over their lives, and suffer without expression; who can consume their sorrows inwardly – the world the while believing them happy.

Many years after – when her graceful girlhood had waned into a faded womanhood and when Launcelot had become an active country gentleman and Violet a staid wife – Ella lost her sorrows, and came to her peace in the love of a disabled Indian officer whom she had known many years ago – and whose sunset days she made days of warmth and joy; persuading herself, and him too, that the Cornet Dampier, with whom she had flirted when a girl, she had always loved as a woman and had never forgotten for any other fancy.

FRANÇOISE MALLET-JORIS

Marie

Françoise Mallet-Joris was born Françoise Lilar in Antwerp in 1930. Her parents were both lawyers and professionally distinguished. Her education was disrupted by illness and by the war, and she started writing poetry at this time. She later studied in universities in the United States and in Paris. At twenty, she wrote her first novel Le Rempart des Béguines *(published in 1951), the story of a lesbian relationship between a schoolgirl and an older woman, which aroused controversy both because of the author's youth and the book's subject matter. She used the pseudonym Françoise Mallet, chosen at random, later adding the Flemish name Joris. She has written poetry, songs, fiction, non-fiction and autobiography, much of it available in English. She has been married three times and has four children. A fluent writer, she claims that finding time to write is a 'question of organisation'. 'Marie' was written in 1954 and published in a collection two years later.*

When Marie was a little girl, her mother sometimes shut her up, by way of punishment, in a dark little room where all the family's shoes were kept – the boot-closet, as they called it. Gradually these periods of confinement had ceased to be a punishment and became, instead, a habit. The tiny room received a minimal amount of light and air through one very high skylight. Almost all the floor space was taken up by two large racks, on which were ranged an assortment of heavy boots, men's shoes, and beach sandals. A smell of wax and leather filled the air. Between the two racks there was a narrow passage, where Marie found she could squat cross-legged, Turkish fashion.

After a while this dimly-lit cubby-hole came to be her favourite retreat: a kingdom which, however small, at least belonged to her alone. Her own blue-and-white room (a model children's bedroom), her dolls, with their impeccably groomed hair, the yard where she played every morning, the entire house (so warm, so pleasant, so beautifully polished), even her own mother, her devoted, elegant mother, whose behaviour was so demonstrably perfect – all these struck her as singularly lacking in substance and reality. What did she care about a perfection she had neither chosen nor demanded? Even as a small child she would shake with fury when people told her how lucky she was to have the mother (or house, or life) that she did.

The ease surrounding her she saw as a glass wall, set there with deliberate malice in order to keep her from reality. What she could not bear about this way of life, in fact, was its pre-determined, all-too-predictable pattern. The fact that the ordered sequence led to what is known as 'happiness' Marie found of slight importance. She rejected fatalism. She alone must decide her own destiny. Nevertheless, she came unpleasantly close to being caught.

When Marie was sixteen, Gérard appeared on the scene. He was some sort of distant cousin. At first she had no idea what was happening, and let herself be ensnared by the charm of near-perfect features, to which a few freckles added a certain childish appeal. He came round every Sunday, and Marie's mother put on a wide lace collar to receive him, and made a rich *quatre-quarts* cake with red-currant jam inside it. Gérard would talk of his work, and his examinations, and his plans for the future, in an earnest but somewhat affected manner. Marie just gazed at his face, and didn't listen to a word he said. Such perfect beauty, she thought, has something heartbreaking about it. From this point forward things moved very fast indeed. There was the first dance together, in the big provincial ballroom. They went out to the movies. They went for a walk in the rain. One day Marie's mother said, with a rather thin-lipped smile, 'It's time we started on your trousseau, darling.'

Marie wanted to say no, wanted a period of respite in which to make up her mind, to suffer perhaps; but for a moment she forgot her demands, dazzled by this brand-new mirage, the idea of promising another human being possession of oneself.

So sheets piled up in the linen-cupboard, and nightgowns were sewn and trimmed with lace. Her mother informed Marie, with some condescension, that everything was going extremely well, it couldn't have fallen out better, in fact: the two families' fortunes were evenly balanced and – thanks to her own sensible investments – she had been able to buy a perfectly enchanting house on the coast, which the newly-weds could use as a vacation residence.

Marie agreed to all this without really taking it in. She even accepted the idea of having to live in a house that had been bought without her knowledge or consultation. After all, she would be there with Gérard, and he would be hers, and hers alone, and she would be alone there with him, so that at last some sort of reality would exist for her. Things would regain their colour, she would, at last, be able to *see* the faces round her – faces which hitherto, through wilful and childish blindness, she had refused to look at. The happiness which she conjured up in her mind was still a dream, but this dream was the last one. After her marriage she would be able to cope with her life single-handed, and direct its course according to her own desires. She wandered through the garden, her hand caressing the wan, flowerless rose-bushes, and on her face was that vague, dreamy expression which all young fiancées wear.

Then, suddenly, after the whirlwind chaos of the last few days – the flowers, the gleaming silverware, endless rings at the door-bell, congratulations, the church wedding, the vast banquet that took three full hours to get through – it was evening, and there they were in the car outside their new house. The maid had turned every light on to welcome them, so that it shone from top to bottom, like a dolls' house or a Christmas tree. Then came the silence, and an agonising shock that echoed quietly through Marie's mind in retrospect, like a stone falling to the bottom of a very deep well, so that only a faint splash can be heard as it hits the water. It had begun when he came out of the bathroom and bent over his suitcase, searching for something in it. Marie felt as though she had suddenly woken up from a dream. But it's *true*, she told herself. This is Gérard, he's mine, we're married, he belongs to *me*!

And the young girl, so delicate and modest in her lace-trimmed nightgown, the sad-eyed young bride whose air of innocence had aroused such universal admiration among the wedding guests, now called out, in a voice that was suggestive (to say the least), 'Hurry up, Gérard; I'm waiting.'

It was he who had blushed then, his beautiful features suddenly marred by anxiety and embarrassment, his lips trembling. Ah, for a moment, a moment only, she had really believed it was true, that it was *there*, that this body pressed against hers, this child's face which had been, miraculously, reborn in the face of a man belonged to her, Marie, for ever and ever. But she had waited, waited, her heart beating faster, while that faint moaning went interminably on. What high hopes she had as she lay there with Gérard's face hidden in her shoulder; how impatient she was to see what would come of this prolonged agony when, at last, it reached its conclusion! She paid no attention to the slight but persistent pain she felt, the involuntary flinching of her own body. She waited, holding her breath – holding back, too, the barely articulate flow of words that formed itself somewhere deep in her throat, *Have you done it yet, Do you love me, Do you love me?* – waited for Gérard to lift his head and reveal, in those golden eyes of his, some sign of weakness, a sadness perhaps, which she (poor ignorant little combatant!) could comfort. But no, she had screwed her courage up to no purpose, he had no need of it. On the contrary, it was she who had to let herself be comforted, and submit to the tender questioning of this boy whose face remained blank, untouched by experience, whose beauty would never change.

There was only the ghost of a shadow under those laughing eyes, and only the faint swelling of his lower lip hinted at a bite. His voice was the voice of a brother, whispering words that went back unchanged to one's childhood, to the uncomplicated friendship of wide beaches and big secluded gardens. 'Poor Marie,' he murmured, as though he had accidentally scraped her knee. But don't you realise, she thought, that I want *you* to be hurt, hurt and maybe sad? I could have taken anything from you, anything that would have drawn us closer together, even if I suffered in the process. But this gentleness of yours, the way you smile like a child and nibble your split lip, the terrible look of apology in your eyes, as though you'd done something stupid you didn't dare own up to . . .

Later Marie brooded over him as he lay in a deep peaceful sleep, staring at those closed eyelids (it was the first time she had seen them closed) in helpless fury: They promised you to me, she whispered, they gave you to me, why aren't you mine, why? Her anguish moved as it were on tiptoe, a burning progress, needle-sharp feet treading across her heart.

Morning came. Gérard stretched, smiled, jumped out of bed and – casually naked – went to the window, where he stood breathing in the fresh air, flaring his nose like a cat, breathing short and fast. Then he turned and grinned at his wife. He sang in the bathroom, and called out various diverting ideas for spending the day, at the top of his voice. He came back in, went out again, returned once more. Marie's huge pale eyes followed his movements. He was a little embarrassed. When she failed to answer his countless questions, he knelt beside the bed and took her in his arms.

'You just can't imagine,' he said, 'what it's like not to be alone any more.'

She had a sudden resurgence of hope. She knew, too well, what being alone had meant: her mother's indifference, a series of suspicious governesses, the white-faced little girl whose throat was constantly tightening in an absolute determination not to cry, ever. She embraced him passionately and murmured, almost happy now, 'Oh my poor darling—'

But he got up at once, cheerful, laughing. No, she thought, nothing is ended, it makes no difference. He has never experienced the choked-back tears, the hidden desires and rages that filled my entire childhood. He simply finds it very pleasant to be married to a sweet, gentle, charming girl like Marie.

Marie's fleeting hope flickered and went out. It was to be rekindled many times during those first months of marriage, only to be extinguished once more. It flared up every time Gérard took on that worried expression and childish tone of voice, which she expected, hoped, to be able to melt into a flood of tears; every time they were alone together and he spoke to her of his childhood; every time they returned together in the evening, to that delightful house of theirs. She waited; and she was to go on waiting for a very long time.

Her superior education imposed restraints on her for a while. She did not scream or weep or wring those elegant little hands of hers – the hands of a boarding-school miss, fit only for embroidery. But every morning, as she gazed out across the sea she loved so dearly, the greyest, most beautiful sea in the whole world, she found the desire for such excessive gestures growing stronger in her. Gérard would get up, innocently as ever, his beauty an unconscious insult, and go off crabbing. He would emerge from the water laughing and dripping, the embodiment of simple and absolute happiness. How could I make him suffer? she wondered. She dreamed of spectacular suicides, planned last letters in which all would be explained. But *what*?

One day, on the beach, she met a girl who had been in her class at school. Her name was Julia, and she, too, was married. Marie's mother, who had come to spend the day with her dear children, smiled at the sight of Julia's husband, a man of over forty who cut a mildly ridiculous figure in a bathing suit that was much too small for him. 'Poor Julia, she didn't make a very good match, did she? You were much luckier, darling.' *Luckier*? Marie thought. Why? This man might not be over-attractive, but he obviously loved Julia. He never left her side, he was absorbed in her welfare. No doubt he worried about whether she loved him. Perhaps, two or three times a day, he said, 'If only I were younger!' Perhaps he made Julia swear never to leave him. *Happy Julia*, Marie thought, while at her side that bronzed and perfect body, covered with a faint golden bloom, lay stretched out on the sand.

At dinner, while Gérard was busy eating, and praising, the soufflé (not a single ulterior thought in his head), Marie sat brooding over those unhappy couples one sometimes saw at night, through the windows of strange houses, having dinner in total silence. The husbands were plain, exhausted, and often going bald. They sat there in dreadful old slippers, reading the paper, and replying with a mere grunt when their wives offered them a little more fruit salad. But at night, in their shabby bedrooms, where the wallpaper was patterned with huge mauve flowers or bronze fans, they would at last confess to their wives (whose hands smelled from dishwashing) that their employers were fed up with them, that they'd made fools of themselves at the annual railway workers' dinner, or that they often wondered whether, basically, they hadn't failed in life. Then they would fall asleep, feeling that at least they weren't alone.

Gérard, on the other hand, needed no one's help before *he* went to sleep. Being an orphan, he seemed to have developed a natural habit of self-sufficiency. A day came when Marie watched him settle down in bed, and pick up a book, as he always did; only this was the last time she would see it. She moved about the room, brushing one or two objects with the tips of her fingers. He looked up, briefly, and said, 'Anything you need?' Those were the last words she heard him speak, ever.

Marie loved the shabby ugliness of the room. She felt herself mistress of any conceivable situation that might crop up between those four cold white walls, in that bare and silent apartment. She drew the curtains (the landscape of roofs outside had been none of her choosing: she rejected it) and bustled noiselessly to and fro, arranging various ugly, useful objects with a sort of near-cruel precision, her hands imperious, authoritative. She lit the little spirit-lamp, and put the teapot on the table. It was cracked, with a sad Japanese look about it. The man she was waiting for must, at this very moment, be hesitating outside the door or at the street-corner, uncertain whether to impose on her once again the burden of his lassitude, a weak man's despondency. But she knew he would come in the end, overcome by his need for her, convinced that it was his duty to show himself grateful.

Unless, that is, he had actually met with success? A momentary stab of panic shot through her, which the entry of the boy – one couldn't really call him a man – at once dispersed. Those hunched shoulders, that uncertain expression, even the creased line of the cheek – the bitter, futile line so characteristic of failures and old maids – all held such explicit promise of failure, weakness, and surrender that Marie realised how idle her fears had been. He would never escape her. She stood by the window waiting for his long, plaintive sigh, the signal for her to go and take him by the shoulders, and reassure herself that everything was going the way she wanted it.

'All the same,' she said, a little more vehemently than she intended, 'you know quite well that going the rounds like this isn't getting you anywhere. You wear yourself out, and raise a lot of false hopes. Why don't you stop worrying and just stay here – paint when you want, and how you want, without anything to bother you—'

Gently he yielded to her pressure, laid his hand on her all-too-ready shoulder.

'You think I should?'

'Of course you should. I'm lucky enough to have some money of my own, so why shouldn't you have the benefit of it? Don't tell me you *want* to work – or that you're ashamed of taking money from me. You're not, are you?'

'No,' he said, dubiously.

He would never admit it, but in fact it was true. The first time she had given him money, casually, yes, but with a touch of firmness too, he had not been able to stop himself blushing. But he had accepted it, and he sensed that he would go on accepting it, that his efforts to break free would steadily dwindle, that in the end he would – just as she wanted – become helplessly dependent on this easy source of income.

'All the same,' he muttered, 'I'll have another look round tomorrow.'

'Certainly not,' Marie said, placidly, 'I don't want you to tire yourself out. The day after tomorrow – if you're still all that keen on it.'

Once more he yielded, trying to make Marie's embrace, her gentle yet somehow chilly eyes, provide him with the familiar worthless excuse: 'Do you love me?' he asked her.

'Yes,' she said, and could not tell if she was lying or not.

She had suffered; and in this distant room where she sought refuge she continued to suffer. She had told this feeble youth she loved him; but she was still suffering as she cradled his miserable head on her shoulder. She knew, too, that everything she had abandoned was precious to her, and now for ever irreplaceable. But something had come to a head in her that had never been there before, something which demanded unhappiness, imperfection, suffering, something which guaranteed that every minute she now lived was *hers*, completely and utterly. Others might call this element mere egotism; she preferred to think of it as human awareness.

MARGARET CAVENDISH

The Matrimonial Agreement

Margaret Cavendish (1623-73) was born in Colchester, Essex, the youngest of eight children. Her father died when she was two. Her education was rudimentary, having been entrusted, she later explained, to an 'ancient decayed gentlewoman' attached to the household. During the Civil War, she became a maid of honour to Queen Henrietta Maria, following her into exile in Paris. There she married William Cavendish, later Duke of Newcastle, a royalist in exile who was much older than herself. She wondered if he was marrying her chiefly in the hope of having male heirs (despite two sons from a first marriage), though she saw little advantage in childbearing for women, partly because of the dangers and partly because they had to give up their own surnames and sacrifice dynasty. She never had children, but the marriage was successful. The couple lived first in Paris and then in Antwerp, running up large debts. Margaret Cavendish returned to London for eighteen months during the Interregnum, trying to retrieve money from her husband's estates, with no success. During this time, she wrote her first volumes of poetry. Back in Antwerp, she continued her writing, switching from form to form: plays (unperformed and unperformable), verse, orations and short fiction. At the Restoration, she and her husband returned to England and settled in the country. She was interested in natural philosophy and the developing sciences, but her lack of education meant that she did not have the background or discipline to make any serious contribution, and she tried in vain to get her books taught at the Universities of Oxford and Cambridge. Although she regretted that women were not given a proper education, and compared their lives to caged birds, she did not believe them intellectually equal to men. 'The Matrimonial Agreement' is taken from Natures Pictures Drawn by Francies Pencil to the Life, *a collection containing verse and short stories, both fantastic and realistic, and her autobiography. The spelling and punctuation of 'The Matrimonial Agreement' have been modernized.*

A handsome young man fell in love with a fair young lady, insomuch that if he had her not, he was resolved to die. For live without her, he could not: so, wooing her long, at last, although she had no great nor good opinion of married life, being afraid to enter into so strict bonds, observing the discords therein that trouble a quiet life, being raised by a disagreement of humours, and jealousy of rivals: but considering, withal, that marriage gave respect to women, although beauty were gone, and seeing the man personable, and knowing him to have a good fortune, which would help to counterpose the inconveniences and troubles that go along with marriage, she was resolved to consent to his request.

The gentleman coming as he used to, and persuading her to choose him for her husband, she told him she would, but that she found herself of that humour that she could not endure a rival in wedlock; and the fear of having one would cause jealousy, which would make her very unhappy; and the more, because she must be bound to live with her enemy, for so she should account of her husband when he had broken his faith and promise to her.

He, smiling, told her she need not fear; and that death was not more certain to man than he would be constant to her, sealing it with many oaths and solemn protestations; 'nay,' said he, 'where I may be false, I wish you may be so, which is the worst of all ills.'

She told him, words would not serve her turn, but that he should be bound in bond that not only whensoever she could give a proof, but when she had cause of suspicion she might depart from him, with such an allowance out of his estate as she thought fit to maintain her.

He told her he was so confident, and knew himself so well, that he would unmaster himself of all his estate and make her only mistress.

She answered, a part should serve her turn; so the agreement was made and sealed, they married and lived together as if they had but one soul, for whatsoever the one did or said, the other disliked not; nor had they any reasons, for their study was only to please each other.

After two years the wife had a great fit of sickness which made her pale and wan and not so full of lively spirits as she was wont to be, but yet as kind and loving to her husband as could be; and the husband at her first sickness wept, watched and tormented himself beyond all measure: but the continuance made him so dull and heavy that he could take no delight in himself, or anything else.

His occasions calling him abroad, he found himself so refreshed that his spirits revived again; but, returning home, and finding not the mirth in the sick as in the healthy, it grew wearisome to him insomuch that he always would have occasions to be abroad, and thought home his only prison. His wife, mourning for his absence, complained to him at his return and said that she was not only unhappy for her sickness but miserable in that his occasions were more urgent to call him from her when she had most need of his company to comfort her in the loss of, the absence of her health, than in all the time they had been married before. 'And therefore, pray husband,' said she, 'what is this misfortunate business that employs you so much, that makes me see you so seldom?' He told her, the worldly affairs of men, women did not understand and therefore it was folly to recite them. 'Besides,' said he, 'I am so weary in following them that I hate to repeat them.' She, like a good wife, submitted to her husband's affairs, and was content to sit without him.

The husband returning home one day from jolly company, whose discourse was merry and wanton, he met with his wife's maid at the door and asked her how her mistress did. She said, not very well. 'Thou lookest well,' said he, and chucks her under the chin. She, proud of her master's kindness, smirks and smiles upon him, insomuch that the next time he met her, he kissed her. Now she begins to despise her mistress, and only admires herself, and is always the first person or servant that opens her master the door; and through the diligence of the maid, the master's great affairs abroad were ended, and his only employment and busy care is now at home; that whensoever he was abroad, he was in such haste that he could scarce salute anybody by the way; and when his friends spake to him, his head was so full of thoughts that he would answer quite from the question, insomuch that he was thought one of the best and carefullest husbands in the world.

In the meantime his wife grew well, and his maid grew pert and bold towards her mistress; and the mistress wondered at it, began to observe more strictly what made her so, for perceiving that the wench came oftener than accustomed where her husband and she were; also she found her husband had always some excuse to turn his head and eyes to that place where she was; and whensoever the wench came where they were, he would alter his discourse, talking extravagently.

Whereupon not liking it, she examined her husband whether his affections were as strong to her as they ever were. He answered he was the perfectest good husband in the world, and so he should be until he died.

It chanced that he was employed by the state into another country;

where, at the parting, his wife and he lamented most sadly and many tears were shed. But when he was abroad, he being in much company who took their liberty, and had many mistresses, he then considered with himself, he was a most miserable man that must be bound only to one; and begins to consider what promises he made his wife, and what advantages she had on him in his estate, which kept him in good order for a time.

But being persuaded by his companions to fling off all care, and take his pleasure whilst he might, 'for,' said they, 'what do our wives know what we do? Besides,' said they, 'wives are only to keep our house, to bring us children, not to give us laws.' Thus preaching to him, at last he followed their doctrine and improved so well that he became the greatest libertine of them all; like a horse that hath broken his reins, when he finds himself loose, skips over hedges, ditches, pales, or whatsoever is in his way, so wildly he runs about until he hath wearied himself.

But his wife having some intelligence, as most commonly they want none, or maybe out of pure love, comes to see him; he receives her with the greatest joy and makes so much of her, carrying her to see all the country and towns thereabouts, and all the varieties, curiosities and sights that were to be seen. But when she had been there a month, or such a time, he tells her how dangerous it is to leave his house to servants who are negligent and his estate to be entrusted he knows not to whom so that there is no way but to return, both for her and his good, especially if they had children, 'although,' said he, 'I had rather part with my life than be absent from you; but necessity hath no laws.' So she, good woman, goeth home to care and spare, whilst he spends; for in the meantime he follows his humours; and custom making confidence, and confidence carelessness, begins to be less shy and more free; insomuch as when he returned home, his maid, whom he did but eye, and friendly kiss, now he courts in every room; and were it not for his estate he made over, even before his wife's face; but that made him fawn and flatter, and somewhat for quietness' sake.

But his wife being one day in his closet by chance opened a cabinet wherein she found a letter from a mistress of his; whereat she was much amazed; and being startled at it, at last calling herself to herself again, showed it to her husband. He fain would have excused it, but that the plainest of truth would not give him leave; whereupon he craved pardon, promising amendment and swearing he would never do so again; 'no,' said she, 'I never will trust a broken wheel; do you know what is in my power?' said she; 'yes,' said he, 'a great part of my estate.' 'Oh how I adore Dame Nature,' said she, 'that gave me those two eyes, prudence to foresee, and providence to provide; but I have not only your estate but your honour and fame in my power; so that if I please, all that see you shall hiss at you, and condemn whatsoever you do.

'For if you had the beauty of *Paris*, they would say you were but a fair cuckold.

'If you had the courage of *Hector*, they would say you were but a desperate cuckold.

'Had you the wisdom of *Ulysses* or *Solomon*, they would laugh and say, there goes he that is not yet so wise as to keep his wife honest.

'If you had the tongue of *Tully*, and made as eloquent orations, they would say, there is the prating cuckold.

'If you were as fine a poet as *Virgil*, or as sweet as *Ovid*, yet they would laugh and scorn and say, he makes verses while his wife makes him a cuckold.'

Now jealousy and rage are her two bawds to corrupt her chastity; the one persuading her to be revenged, to show her husband she could take delight, and have lovers as well as he. This makes her curl, paint, prune, dress, make feasts, plays, balls, masques, and the like, have merry meetings abroad; whereupon she begins to find as much pleasure as her husband in variety; and now begins to flatter him, and to dissemble with him, that she may play the whore more privately, finding a delight in obscurity, thinking that most sweet which is stolen, so they play like children at bo-peep in adultery; and face it out with fair looks, and smooth it over with sweet words, and live with false hearts, and die with large consciences. But these repenting when they died, made a fair end, etc.

JANET FRAME

The Bedjacket

Janet Frame was born in Dunedin, New Zealand, in 1924. She studied at Dunedin Teachers' Training College and the University of Otago but left teaching after one year to concentrate on her writing. She has written novels, short stories and poetry. Her first novel was Owls Do Cry; *her most recent,* Living in the Maniototo *(1979).* Faces in the Water *(first published in 1961) describes the life of a woman confined in mental institutions. 'The Bedjacket' is taken from her first book,* The Lagoon, *published in 1951, which she wrote while she was working as a housemaid in Dunedin. Janet Frame now lives in Wanganui, New Zealand.*

It was almost Christmas time and everybody in the mental hospital was wanting to go home. Some had homes and some didn't have homes but that made not much difference, they all wanted to go to a place that could be called home, where there were no locked doors and dayrooms and parks and Yards and circumspect little walks in the gardens on a Sunday afternoon, to smell the flowers and see the mag- nolia and the fountain and perhaps go as far as the gates beyond which lay the world. When I get home, the patients said to each other, when I get to my own home, and sometimes when they went shopping down to the store on a Friday afternoon, past the school where the kids gardening in the school garden stopped to stare at the loonies till the master jerked them back to their task with, they're people like you and me, remember, when they weren't at all, they weren't people like anybody in the outside world, they were shut away from streets and houses and fun and theatres and beaches, well when they got to the store they would buy a Christmas card, for the Superintendent they said, then perhaps he will let me go home, because I want to go home, there's no reason for my staying here. They all said the same thing, there's nothing wrong with me really. They looked so sad walking down to the store and buying their Christmas cards for the Superintendent. They had such queer clothes on and their shoes were slipper-slopper and their stockings were twisted at the ankle. The nurse said keep together walk slowly and remember to buy only sensible things. So they walked together, in a herd, and they clutched their five shillings in their hands, and they looked with bright hungry eyes at the road and the sky and the grass and the people walking down the road, the people with homes and lives of their own. And then after going round and round in the little exciting whirlpool that was Friday and shopping day, they would return to the dead still water of hospital life, the dayroom and the park, and the laundry where their faces got hot and red and their eyes streamed in the heat, and the nurses' Home where they scrubbed and polished and tried to smile when the doctor came in with the matron every morning. Their smiles said I'm well aren't I, I can go home for Christmas. And the doctor would smile back at them and whisper something to the matron and then walk away to meet the next patient and the next forced smile. And so every day hopes rose and fell about going home.

But some had no hope of home at all for they had no real home. Of these was Nan. Everybody knew about Nan. She had been in charge of the Child Welfare for years. She had been in a mental hospital up north but she had escaped from that one so they took her to this one. It was safer. It was built after the style of a Norman castle. It had everything but a moat and a drawbridge. But now when Christmas was coming Nan was wishing she had stayed up north for Christmas was better up there, you had silk stockings and cigarettes and the Superintendent himself gave you a present, besides you had a day off every week but here you worked seven days a week, anyway it was nicer up north you were allowed to go for walks and you didn't have to work so hard. You see Nan had spent Christmas in both places so she knew. She had tried to escape too from this hospital, the rat-house they called it, but they had got her and put her in the Yard for punishment, and it isn't pleasant in the Yard, you are liable to get a knock on the head or else go madder yourself. Nan didn't mind however. It was interesting, she said, but I would like to be up north for Christmas.

But in a way I wouldn't. Do you know why? She didn't tell anybody why but some guessed. It was because of Nurse Harper, a charge nurse, small and dark and very kind and very gentle. After work was over at six o'clock every night, Nan, who had parole, would go over to Nurse Harper's room and they would talk about the things girls talk about, and Nan would tell Nurse Harper about what she would do when she was allowed out in the World. She was going to be a cook, not a third cook nor a second one but a first cook in a large hotel. And sometimes they went for walks together round the grounds or up near the pig-sties to see the new little pigs with their transparent ears like petals, and they would come back with their arms full of cherry-blossom, for there were many cherry trees in the garden. It was funny to see the two of them together, Nan awkward and fat and loud-voiced, Nurse Harper gentle and quiet and small. She was like a sister to Nan. She gave her little things, toothpaste and soap and under-clothing that was not stiff and striped like mattress ticking, and dresses that were not print smocks with high waists and sleeves to the elbow. Nan wore her new clothes proudly and she pressed them at night with the old flat iron out of Fours Ward, and she used the lip-stick that Nurse Harper had given her, and the hair-ribbons and the soap. And once the nurse brought back a grey kitten from Twos Ward, a fluffy one for Nan. Nan picked it up and fondled it and tickled its ears, and put her fingers under its chin to feel if it was pur-ring. I'll call it Harold after the doctor, she said. Harold, puss puss.

And when the other patients talked of going home at Christmas, what their home was like and who was waiting eagerly for them to come, when they lay in bed on the long light summer evenings and told tales of mother and father and sister and brother and husband, Nan talked too, about Nurse Harper, and Nurse Harper's sister and mother and father, and how the nurse would be a sub-matron some day and then a matron. Matron Harper. And when the others talked of presents for Christmas, whatever will I give him whatever will I give her, Nan talked too, I wonder what Nurse Harper would like most in all the world.

And then one day after Nan had wondered and wondered about a present for Nurse Harper, the idea of the bedjacket came to her. Knit a bedjacket for Nurse Harper. A blue one to match her fair hair. Now Nan couldn't knit, she had never knitted a garment in her life. But I can learn she thought. Barbara in Ward Two will teach me, Barbara is knitting a bedjacket, a pink one in a shell pattern. I will get the pat-tern. I will knit Nurse Harper a bedjacket.

In the days that followed, Nan was scarcely ever seen without her knitting. Barbara out of Ward Two taught her to knit. Barbara was old now, she had lived in the hospital for years, she was tall and gaunt and the cats followed her and she fed the birds every morning with crumbs from the big kitchen. Barbara was kind to everybody. She wanted Nan to learn to knit and make a bedjacket for Nurse Harper, so she coached her well. At night when the others sat in the dayroom and listened to the wireless or tried to play the old piano with its yellowed keys, or turned over the pages of an old Punch and War Cry, Nan would sit by the fire knitting the bedjacket. Sometimes she pulled it all undone and began again. Sometimes she swore over her knitting. Sometimes she flung it down on the floor and vowed that she would never knit another stitch, she would buy Nurse Harper a cake of soap and a face-cloth wrapped in cellophane, how could Nurse Harper expect you to knit a blue bedjacket with shell pattern when you had never knitted anything in your life, had never had the chance, stuck in rat-houses, cooped up under lock and key, with pictures only every Thursday night and then the machine was broken and they switched the light on all the time because they couldn't trust you to sit in the dark, and sending a brass band out every two months to play hymns on the lawn, and stare at you because you were a loony, and having a man from the city come every week to give you a paper lolly and ask kindly after your health, how could you be expected to knit a blue bedjacket in a shell pattern?

But in spite of all, en tout dépit, Nan continued her labour. And a week before Christmas, blue and soft and beautiful, the bedjacket was finished. It was a thing to be excited about. Nan wrapped it in tissue paper and the whole ward was allowed to unwrap the paper and fondle the jacket and say how lovely, Nan it's lovely. I've never knitted before, she said. And now I've made it I don't want to give it away, because it's mine, I made it. It belongs to me. Nothing's ever belonged to me before. I made it. It belongs to me.

That night Nan was sick. They took her out of the ward and down to a single room where she wouldn't disturb the other patients. She was crying and laughing too and she had the bedjacket clutched under her arm. For four days she was by herself. She wouldn't eat anything and she wouldn't speak to anybody, she held the bedjacket under her arm, and she stroked it and fondled it as if it were a live thing. And when after four days she came back to the ward she was wearing the bedjacket and looking pale and sad. When they all sat down to the table for tea, while they were talking waiting for the matron to come through and the knives to be counted and the order to rise to be given, Nan sat without speaking, staring straight ahead of her. And the next afternoon which was shopping afternoon, Nan who was not allowed to go shopping sent one of the patients to buy something for her, a box of soap and a face-cloth wrapped in cellophane, a Christmas present for Nurse Harper.

ELIZABETH ROBINS

'Gustus Frederick

Elizabeth Robins (1862-1952) was born in Louisville, Kentucky, and had an unsettled childhood as her parents became poorer and moved around the United States. She went to Vassar to study medicine, but left to go on the stage. She became an actress despite her father's disapproval (he walked out of the only play he ever went to see her in) and toured widely before coming to London. She was married briefly to an actor who committed suicide. She had many successes in Ibsen's plays, which she promoted vigorously, and had much sympathy for his women characters. She was an active suffragist, writing and speaking for female suffrage, and worked with, among others, Evelyn Sharp. Her play Votes for Women *was produced in 1907 and the novel version,* The Convert, *was published the same year. The play was a commercial success, and she used the money from the play and the novel to buy a farmhouse in Sussex, which she opened to suffragists and women medical students whom she supported. ''Gustus Frederick' is taken from a collection of 1896, published under the pseudonym C.E. Raimond, which she used to conceal her sex.*

'Goodbye, babies,' she called out from the gate. She waved the end of her boa to the group of curly-headed children crowding at the open door. The pony cart was waiting to take my Lady Bountiful on her weekly round. 'Jump in,' she said to her sister. The two settled themselves, and the elder took up the reins. She glanced behind to see that the well-filled basket was not forgotten, nor the bundle of cast-off clothes.

'Goo'-bye, mammy,' the four-year-old Chrissie called out from the door. 'Goodbye, my angel,' Mrs Wiloughby said, smiling over her shoulder. Then to her sister, while the groom tightened a strap in the harness, 'Just look at those blessed babies, Mary. Did you ever see such darlings?'

Mary Hayward had been watching the children. She turned to look at her sister, smiling a little enigmatically at the radiant satisfaction that illumined the proud mother's face. The noncommittal smile was not lost on Constance Wiloughby. 'Right,' she said briskly to the groom, and the pony started off as though he too were of a charitable nature, eager, impatient even, to visit the haunts of poverty with his burden of good cheer.

'You think I'm foolish about the children?' Mrs Wiloughby said good-humouredly. 'I suppose the ecstasies of an adoring mother are a little trying to a—'

'To an old-maid aunt,' said Mary Hayward.

'Don't be silly; a girl of twenty-seven isn't an old maid in these days.'

'You had three children when you were my age,' said the younger woman.

'Yes, and so might you if only you had been a little reasonable.'

Mary Hayward glanced back at the groom, but that small person had jumped down and was running on before to open a gate.

'This is a new short cut,' said Mrs Wiloughby, pointing down a road marked 'Private'. 'I mustn't be out long, I've promised to get back and read to Willie.'

'How is his throat this afternoon?'

'Oh, nearly well. The doctor said he could get up to tea, but I was afraid to let him. I've promised to come back early and amuse him.'

'What a baby you make of that great boy!'

'I suppose I do,' answered the mother contentedly. 'I can't bear to think of my children getting to the stage when they won't need me. I'd like them always to be little.'

'Well, you can't pretend that young giant of yours is *little* any longer.'

'You mean Willie?'

'Yes. He's fourteen, isn't he?'

'Yes, I suppose he is,' she sighed.

'But still you have the others,' Mary Hayward said. 'It will be a long time before all five of them are—'

'Yes, yes, thank heaven. And besides—'

'Yes?'

The elder woman smiled and looked away. There was such a light of gladness in the half-averted face that Mary stared. The usual alert, rather cynical expression of her sister was softened and changed. Ah, yes, it was something about the children. That look of tenderness and gentle brooding – *that* was the mother look! It was a stranger to the keen humorous face unless it was bent over one of her children, or at times when the intimate, personal sense of motherhood was abroad in her blood. They drove on in silence. They were near another semi-private lane, and again the little groom ran on before.

'You are making a great mistake, Mary,' said the elder woman.

'A new one?'

'Yes, it's old and it's new. As I've told you before, there is nothing so well worth having in the world as a child. There is nothing else very important in a woman's life. *Any* marriage is better than none, just on that account.'

'I sometimes think you're right. It's a pity that marriage is the condition.'

'Well, it *is* the condition,' said Mrs Wiloughby. 'And – and I can't bear to see you throwing away your life. If you knew what it felt like to have a little tender helpless baby in your arms, your own – your very own – ' She looked across the fields with a vague soft smile.

'You see,' said the younger woman, 'you have that instinct very strongly developed; many people are without it.'

'So I've heard childless women say,' said Mrs Wiloughby, as the little groom caught up with the cart again.

On the outskirts of the village they stopped at old Mrs Hill's. Mrs Wiloughby went round to the back of the cart and took out a parcel. The old woman looked out of her window and hobbled to the tiny front door. She stood there with curtsies and toothless smiles, raining blessings, and giving a harrowing description of the last attack of 'rheumatics'. Her visitors allowed themselves to be taken into her stuffy little front room, and Mrs Wiloughby inquired about the grandson out in Australia, and the cow out in the paddock – both of whom had been ill. She recognised, with a delicate comprehension all her own, that the old dame's real anxiety was about the cow. Accordingly she promised a visit from the vet, and departed. Then they went to see a sick child, and here Mrs Wiloughby's tact and kindness came out in fair colours.

'How well you know what to say to these people,' said Mary. 'I haven't been with you on one of these expeditions for so long that I'm filled with a fresh admiration.'

'Nonsense. It's easy enough.'

'I shouldn't find it so.'

'Why not?'

'Do you want me to say why?'

'Of course.'

'Well then, I should feel it was such an impertinence.'

'Oh no, you wouldn't!' laughed the other. 'Not if you took them tea and petticoats.'

'Yes, particularly if I took them tea and petticoats.'

'Would you?'

'Yes; I should feel it so ridiculous that I should be given so much more tea than I could drink, and so many more petticoats than I could wear, that I could take a cartload of things and dole them out from door to door as gifts. *Gifts*! And all their blessings and hideous little curtsies – their loathsome gratitude, too! No, I always say you do this thing to perfection since it has to be done.'

'You're just as mad as ever, Mary. I'm not sure you haven't got worse in the year I've been away.'

'I'm not sure, either.'

'I'm afraid Willie will be restless before I can get back,' said the anxious mother, looking at her watch as they drove on; 'but I must just go over to Moltons Hill and see Mrs Bunce. I haven't been there for ages – not since I got back from abroad. She lives out of my beaten track, too, and she's such an old—'

'Isn't she the woman who had those three pretty daughters?'

'Yes. Anne went as housemaid to one of Algy's aunts in Hertford-shire.'

'You mean Lady Henry Morland? We met one of her boys, you know, at Torquay last year. Don't you remember I wrote you?'

'Oh yes, that was Wilfred. But you can't go anywhere without meeting a Morland. They're as the sands of the sea.'

'Yes; he was always mentioning a brother or sister I hadn't heard of before.'

'Yes; there's a round dozen of them – twelve *living*. I think we'll walk this steep bit,' Mrs Wiloughby said; and they both got out and trudged along the road. 'If it weren't for this hill, I believe I'd come here oftener, in spite of that rude old Bunce woman. Rather one's duty, you know.' She stopped a moment, breathing a little heavily, and turned to look back at the cart, and, for a fraction of a moment, abroad over the wide undulating country, where, for miles and miles, as far as she could see, the land was, and had been for many a long year, Wiloughby property. As the cart caught up with them, she went on with her silent companion towards the Bunce cottage.

'Lady Henry used to say Anne Bunce was the pearl of parlour maids. She so fired Maud Aylward, you know, with stories of Anne's abilities that the Aylwards want me to get Maria to come to them in town. Maria's the eldest girl. Always been at home. But I'm afraid Anne's not so high in favour as she used to be.'

'Oh! Turned out badly after all?'

'Well, you see, she'd gone on for seven years there at the Morlands. They were all used to her and liked her, and then all of a sudden she took it into her head nothing would do but she must marry the butler. It was frightfully upsetting.'

'To the butler?'

'No; to my aunt and the whole family.'

'Oh, I see!'

'Such a good servant, too!'

'But I don't understand. Was the butler obdurate?'

'Absolutely. Wouldn't listen to a word my aunt said.'

'Your aunt? I thought it was Anne—'

'It was Anne who wanted to marry him, stupid!'

'But you said he was obdurate.'

'Yes – wouldn't listen to reason at all. Wanted to throw up his place, and marry the girl, and set up shop, or something foolish. And he'd been with Lady Henry over *fifteen years!*'

'Oh!'

'Still, I suppose people like that *do* want to marry each other: there's no accounting for tastes!' And Mrs Wiloughby laughed in her light satiric way. 'Stop! we'll drive this little bit,' she called to the groom.

'And so they gave up their good situations?' said Mary Hayward, following Mrs Wiloughby into the cart.

'No. My aunt gave in at last, when she found how pig-headed they were, and kept them both in her service. Run on and knock,' she said to the groom.

'Oh! then it all ended happily?'

'No, it didn't altogether. They weren't content with being married: they must needs go and have a child.'

'That was very inconsiderate.'

Mrs Wiloughby laughed too, with the same hard, bright ring. 'Yes; servants in such comfortable quarters oughtn't to make themselves troublesome. However, Lady Henry was an angel to the girl; supplied her place while she was disabled, and took her back the moment she was fit to work. And how do you think she repaid Lady Henry?'

'Can't imagine.'

'By having another child just as quickly as ever she could manage it!'

She flicked the pony with an indignant whip, and the cart rattled smartly along. 'I should think their patience was about exhausted,' she went on. 'I understand that when Lady Henry said something to the girl about it, the creature was quite uppish: said she didn't mean to have as many as some folks, or something of the kind. You can imagine how angry Lady Henry was – the impudence of the creature! Here we are.'

'Bunce got hurt down at the mines a month or two ago,' Mrs Wiloughby whispered as she drew up. 'That's why I must go and see how they're getting on. The youngest girl has been nursemaid to the Hopkinson children for three or four years. Very honest people – only the mother is an old bear. You never get any "loathsome gratitude" out of *her*!' And Mrs Wiloughby got slowly out of the cart, laughing the while as at some vivid recollection.

The Bunce cottage was very decent, and the place wore a prosperous air. The front door was open. A woman was on her knees scrubbing the steps. As the visitors came up the little path the kneeling figure turned. It was the eldest Bunce girl. She got up, threw her cloth into the bucket, and dried her hands on her apron, while she curtsied.

'Oh, is that you, Maria?' said Mrs Wiloughby kindly. 'I haven't seen you for a long time. You never seemed to be about when I called before I went away.' The girl laughed in a pleasant, stupid way, and went on rubbing her fingers. 'How is your father?'

'He's 'bout the same, thank ye.'

'Oh! what a fine baby!' said Mrs Wiloughby, glancing into the entry, where a fat, sturdy little fellow was pulling himself up on his podgy bare legs with the help of a chair.

'Ye-es,' giggled the large young woman, looking at him with interest.

'What's his name?' inquired Mrs Wiloughby genially.

''Gustus Frederick.'

'Oh!' Mrs Wiloughby shot an amused glance at her sister. 'Is that the name of Anne's husband?' 'No'm!' the young woman said, looking surprised. 'Well, you're a very nice baby, 'Gustus Frederick,' said Lady Bountiful, with a shade of resentment in her voice; thinking, doubtless, with a proper family concern, of the inconvenience 'Gustus Frederick had been to Algy's aunt in Hertfordshire.

'Mariar!' some one called from inside. It was a harsh voice, and resonant of authority. The girl moved aside the bucket of soapy water. 'That's moother,' she said; 'won't ye coom in?'

The two ladies followed her. Mrs Bunce stood at the kitchen door.

'Give me the child,' she said, looking past the visitors. 'Will ye coom in?' she added with scant hospitality.

'Oh, I'm afraid you're busy,' began Mrs Wiloughby.

'Yes, on washdays we find soomthin' to do.' She pulled down her rolled-up sleeves and kept her eye on the baby. 'Gustus Frederick was kicking and wriggling in the strong arms of 'Mariar.'

'I called to see how Mr Bunce was doing.'

'He's verra bad. He'll never be the same again.' She held out her arms for the baby, and 'Mariar' brought him nearer, clucking and crowing and beating the air with his doubled fists. 'I'll mind him now. You git on with the scroobin',' the old woman said to her daughter, and she led the way into the kitchen. Mrs Wiloughby followed composedly; she was used to Mrs Bunce's cordiality. It crossed her mind that in the good cause of her husband's Hertfordshire aunt she might beard the old lioness in her den. She would intimate that Anne was endangering her good situation.

'That's a remarkably fine child of Anne's!' she began, by way of mollification, helping herself to a chair.

''Tain't Anne's!' said the woman, dandling the child with a dogged air.

'No? Whose is it?'

'It's Mariar's.'

'Oh, indeed! I hadn't heard Maria was married.'

'No more she is.'

'Not married?' There was an awkward pause. Mrs Wiloughby exchanged looks with Mary. 'Who is the father?' she asked at length. Mary made an impulsive gesture, but Mrs Wiloughby waited calmly for her answer. Mary got up and looked out of the window.

'He's a soldier,' said Mrs Bunce discreetly.

'Is he hereabouts?'

'Naa.'

'Couldn't he be made to marry her?' Mary's fingers tightened on the window-frame. She could hear the sound of Mariar's scrubbing brush outside. 'Don't you think he could be got to?' insisted Mrs Wiloughby.

The old woman trotted the baby on her knee, with a wooden expression. 'He's gone to the Cape,' she said briefly, while 'Gustus Frederick cooed and waved his hands like one who signals a scoffing farewell.

'Isn't Maria very unhappy about it?'

'Naa, I doan't think so.'

'Don't you think she ought to be?' said the righteous matron.

'Naa, I doan't – rightly speakin'. Ye see, he warn't good for mooch, an' she's got rid of him.'

'But she's got the child on her hands,' said Prudence, through the mouth of the great lady.

'Ay!' said the woman, with a harsh gladness grating through her voice. 'Ay! *she's got the child!*' And she settled her square shoulders back, and seemed to take a firmer hold on the baby.

'Poor little man!' said Mrs Wiloughby, rising. 'I'm very sorry.'

'Oh! the child's all right! Ain't never been a finer baby hereaboots.'

'Goo! goo!' the infant remarked with an air of indecent triumph. Mrs Wiloughby looked disconcerted. She drew her mantle about her shoulders, and took a step towards the door. 'I can only repeat I'm very sorry. If there is anything I can do for your husband you must let me know. This must be a great blow to him.'

'It ain't *that* blow that's knocked him over – it's what happened down yonder.' She jerked her head towards the mines.

Mrs Wiloughby hastened to add, 'Yes, we were all terribly sorry. I hope he'll soon be better,' and turning to go, she fixed her eye for a moment's cold contemplation on the baby. 'Gustus Frederick gave a derisive gurgle and lolled his tongue. 'Good morning!' she said, and hurried out. Mary Hayward followed, bending backward glances upon the insolent and cheerful young person who sprawled at his ease in his grandmother's lap. He returned the girl's look with the wide, self-possessed 'who-are-you?' stare of healthy babyhood. And the girl smiled and nodded surreptitiously as she hurried after her sister.

'Mariar' was standing outside near the door talking and laughing with a neighbour. 'Shameless creature,' observed Mrs Wiloughby under her breath. 'I really shall have to say something to her, I suppose.'

'No, don't,' whispered Mary, clutching the other's arm.

'I really must. If they think this sort of thing isn't frowned on, there'll soon be an end of all decency, to say nothing of law and order.' She went forward with a grave face. 'Good morning, Mrs Black. Maria, I would like to say a few words to you.' The girl came towards her, and Mary Hayward walked away with lowered eyes. Her attention was arrested by Mrs Bunce's voice from the cottage door, and the sound of the child's crying. She hurried back, drawn to the commonplace little drama more strongly than she fully understood.

'My cousin, Mrs Aylward,' Mrs Wiloughby was saying, 'spoke to me when I was in town last about sending for you in the spring, but of course now—'

'Doan't ye hear me tellin' ye to take the child,' said the old woman harshly, from the doorway.

'Mariar' held out her arms, and the baby curled with delight. The stout young woman's dull face brightened and flushed. She took him into her arms, and he rubbed his round face against her generous breast. She turned away to go indoors, with one hand at the buttons of her print gown. 'No,' she said, 'I can't leave home now, thank ye, ma'am.' But there was no sorrow in her face.

'No,' said Mrs Wiloughby significantly. 'You can't go to Mrs Aylward *now*. Come, Mary,' and she went rapidly towards the cart. 'Take that basket to Mrs Harding,' she said to the groom, 'I can't wait.' She took her place and gathered up the reins. 'Never in my life saw anything so cool!' she said, when they had driven on some distance. 'This is the third event of the kind in and about Northley within a year or two.'

'You see,' said Mary, in the pause, 'there are others besides you who think there's nothing so well worth having as a child.'

Mrs Wiloughby looked sharply at the girl and touched the pony with the whip. 'You know as well as I do that you're talking nonsense.'

'I am only quoting you.'

'I didn't mean a child was worth having at that price.'

'I see. It's when you've counted the cost and made sure of it's being a good investment – it's then that it's worthwhile!'

'My dear, you and I can't reconstruct society,' said Mrs Wiloughby a little sharply. 'As the world is constituted it *isn't* worthwhile – except under approved conditions.'

'I wonder,' said the girl under her breath.

'Good heavens, Mary Hayward, are you mad?' The keen eyes flashed their search-light into the girl's face. 'I hope you don't let other people hear you saying such things.'

'Why?'

'Well, it's excessively bad taste, for one thing; and it might come to Arthur's ears.'

'And what then?' said the girl, but she flushed uncomfortably.

'Well, even his patience might find that a little too—'

'I wish I'd had the courage to say as much to him long ago,' the girl interrupted. Constance Wiloughby compressed her lips, and held the pony in as he sidled down hill. 'If long ago,' the girl went on with quiet self-scorn – 'If *long* ago I'd said, "My good Arthur, I don't love you and I never shall love you. But if you keep for ever tormenting me, I don't promise I won't end by marrying you, just because – just because—'''

'Well?'

Mary laughed uncertainly. 'But you see *he* mightn't go to the Cape – and then where'd I be!'

They were rounding a bend in the road, and, before her sister had time to answer, a high T-cart dashed into view. 'Why, it's Algy and Arthur,' said Mrs Wiloughby, signalling with her whip. Her husband, sitting very high, and looking rather like an overfed coachman, was driving the new greys – driving recklessly, it might seem to one ignorant of his skill. As the cart dashed by, almost grazing their wheel, two billycock hats flew off in a kind of spasmodic greeting. 'Can't stop!' called out the man who was driving – 'got to meet the 5.10 – Baldwin's coming!' and the T-cart vanished in a cloud of dust.

'How alike those two brothers are growing,' said Mary.

'Oh, do you think so? Arthur is much more like what Algy was years and years ago.'

'Was Algy like *that* when you married him?' said the girl absently. The unconscious criticism in her tone was not lost.

'Yes,' said Mrs Wiloughby. 'They're excellent specimens of the burly Briton. Not very romantic, perhaps, but men of substance.' She smiled, and looked abroad over her lord and master's lands. 'Men who live well, ride hard, sleep o' nights, and make good husbands and fathers. I only wish you might have such a man to stand between you and the world, my little sister.' Her voice was very kind. The girl sat silent. 'If you don't make up your mind soon to marry Arthur,' Constance began again, the softness leaving her manner—

'Tell me,' Mary interrupted, 'tell me honestly, which do you care for most, your husband or Willie?'

Mrs Wiloughby looked far down the straight brown road.

'If you had to give up one or other of them,' insisted the girl, 'which would it be?'

'I couldn't give up Willie.' The mother's face showed the quick anguish of the thought.

'And you *could* live, and you know you could live, without your husband? But why do I ask you? Don't I know quite well you could? Algy has come to be "the children's father" in more senses than one.'

'Come, come, let us get out of the clouds, you impossible person! Don't make the mistake of supposing I'm a disappointed woman. I'm much fonder of Algy than I was when I married him, and my life has been altogether delightful. He would say the same of his. It's because

I've *proved* the wisdom of what I'm advising you, that I go back to it again and again. You are wasting your youth, waiting for an unimportant and even embarrassing detail. Marry some good man. The rest will come.' The girl said nothing. 'No woman,' the elder went on after a moment, in a lower tone, 'not one of us can find out what life means till she holds her child in her arms.' The whimsical look faded utterly out of the high-bred features, and the old brooding settled softly in Constance Wiloughby's face. 'Mary—'

'Yes.'

'I'm glad you can stay with us so long this year.'

'So am I, dear,' said the other wearily.

'I want you to be here when – when – about Christmas—' And her shadowed look followed the roadside as they hurried past.

'You don't mean—' said the girl, rousing herself with a start. They turned and met each other's eyes.

'Yes,' said the older woman, smiling a little.

The girl sat up and caught her breath in ever so slightly. 'And yet you grudged that girl her 'Gustus Frederick!' she said.

'That girl! You're not comparing!' The look of delicate scorn rounded the sentence eloquently.

'And *she* didn't have a son of fourteen either,' the girl went on a little incoherently, 'nor many another good thing that's fallen to you. And yet you grudged her 'Gustus Frederick!' she smiled a little fiercely. 'You mean to *punish* her, too, for *having* 'Gustus Frederick; most of all for not being ashamed of him! And yet *you* – there's Willie looking out of the playroom window!'

'Oh! he'll catch his death!'

'No, he's dressed. What a man he looks! What are you going to do about Willie?'

'About Willie?'

'Yes; when – when – I don't think I'll stay for Christmas, after all.'

'Why not, for heaven's sake?'

'It makes me feel a little shy – doesn't it you?' she said hurriedly, with an upward glance at the playroom window. 'Almost ashamed—'

'It makes me quite ashamed to have such a crackbrained sister. I think you'll develop into a hopeless crank unless you can induce some sensible man to marry you.'

'Perhaps!' said the girl, jumping out of the cart with a bound.

'It's a little discouraging,' Mrs Wiloughby observed, following her cautiously. 'This is such an old bone of contention between us – But you seem to forget there's this to be said in Arthur's favour—'

'My dear!' said the girl, turning suddenly and facing her sister as they stood together on the bottom step. 'Listen to me. I'm not going to marry Arthur – but for all that—'

'Well?' said the elder woman, cocking her head humorously and smiling again.

'For all that – I envy "Mariar" her 'Gustus Frederick.'

'You're a disgrace to your family,' Mrs Wiloughby observed, without much concern, as she opened the door.

'A disgrace to my family?' the girl repeated, smiling vaguely, as she followed her sister. 'I knew there was a bond of some sort between 'Gustus Frederick and me.'

MARGARET OLIPHANT

A Story of a Wedding Tour

Margaret Oliphant (1828-97) was brought up in Scotland and Liverpool by a distant father and an affectionate but reserved mother. She started writing in her teens, and her first three-volume novel was published when she was twenty-two. She continued to be a prolific writer for the next half-century, producing lengthy novels, biographies and miscellaneous works, as well as regular contributions to Blackwood's Magazine. *She wrote in the middle of a busy family life, without apparently feeling the need for a room of her own, claiming that she had never had two hours undisturbed in the whole of her literary life. She married her cousin who died of TB when she was thirty-one, leaving her with three children to support. After her brother lost all his money, she took him into her household with his children, sending her two sons and nephew to Eton and her nieces to Germany to be educated. She managed to support this large family by means of her enormous literary output, but it was always a struggle. Her tightly-knit family life was marred by many losses: two children as babies, then her husband, and a few years later her small daughter. Her nephew died in India, and both her sons, whom she was close to, died before she did. She found time, in her busy life, to pursue long unbroken friendships with her women friends and to travel widely on the Continent.* Miss Marjoribanks, *first published in 1866, is still re-issued from time to time. 'A Story of a Wedding Tour' was published posthumously in 1898 in* A Widow's Tale.

They had been married exactly a week when this incident occurred.

It was not a love marriage. The man, indeed, had been universally described as 'very much in love,' but the girl was not by any one supposed to be in that desirable condition. She was a very lonely little girl, without parents, almost without relations. Her guardian was a man who had been engaged in business relations with her father, and who had accepted the charge of the little orphan as his duty. But neither he nor his wife had any love to expend upon her, and they did not feel that such visionary sentiments came within the line of duty. He was a very honourable man, and took charge of her small – very small – property with unimpeachable care.

If anything, he wronged himself rather than Janey, charging her nothing for the transfers which he made of her farthing's worth of stock from time to time, to get a scarcely appreciable rise of interest and income for her. The whole thing was scarcely appreciable, and to a large-handed man like Mr Midhurst, dealing with hundreds of thousands, it was almost ridiculous to give a moment's attention to what a few hundreds might produce. But he did so; and if there is any angel who has to do with trade affairs, I hope it was carefully put to his account to balance some of the occasions on which he was not perhaps so particular. Nor did Mrs Midhurst shrink from her duty in all substantial and real good offices to the girl. She, who spent hundreds at the dressmaker's every year on account of her many daughters, did not disdain to get Janey's serge frocks at a cheaper shop, and to have them made by an inexpensive workwoman, so that the girl should have the very utmost she could get for her poor little money.

Was not this real goodness, real honesty, and devotion to their duty? But to love a little thing like that with no real claim upon them, and nothing that could be called specially attractive about her, who could be expected to do it? They had plenty – almost more than enough – of children of their own. These children were big boys and girls, gradually growing, in relays, into manhood and womanhood, when this child came upon their hands. There was no room for her in the full and noisy house. When she was grown up most of the Midhurst children were married, but there was one son at home, who, in the well known contradictiousness of young people – it being a very wrong and indeed, impossible thing – was quite capable of falling in love with Janey – and one daughter, with whom it was also possible that Janey might come into competition.

The young Midhursts were nice-looking young people enough; but Janey was very pretty. If Providence did but fully consider all the circumstances, it cannot but be felt that Providence would not carry out, as often is done, such ridiculous arrangements. Janey was very pretty. Could anything more inconvenient, more inappropriate, be conceived?

The poor little girl had, accordingly, spent most of her life at school, where she had, let it not be doubted, made many friendships and little loves; but these were broken up by holidays, by the returning home of the other pupils, while she stayed for ever at school: and not at one school, but several – for in his extreme conscientiousness her guardian desired to do her 'every justice,' as he said, and prepare her fully for the life – probably that of a governess – which lay before her. Therefore, when she had become proficient in one part of her education she was carried on to another, with the highest devotion to her commercial value no doubt, but a sublime indifference to her little feelings. Thus, she had been in France for two years, and in Germany for two years, so as to be able to state that French and German acquired in these countries were among the list of her accomplishments. English, of course, was the foundation of all; and Janey had spent some time at a famous academy of music – her guardian adding something out of his own pocket to her scanty means, that she might be fully equipped for her profession. And then she was brought, I will not say home: Janey fondly said home, but she knew very well it did not mean home. And it was while Mrs Midhurst was actually writing out the advertisement for *The Times*, and the *Morning Post*, and the *Guardian*, which was to announce to all the world that a young lady desired an engagement as governess that her husband burst in with the extraordinary news that Mr Rosendale, who had chanced to travel with Janey from Flushing, on her return, and who had afterwards, by a still greater chance, met her when asked to lunch at the Midhursts', and stared very much at her, as they all remarked – had fallen in love with, and wanted to marry, this humble little girl.

'Fallen in love with Janey!' Mrs Midhurst cried. 'Fallen in love with you, Janey!' said Agnes Midhurst, with a little emphasis on the pronoun. He was not, indeed, quite good enough to have permitted himself the luxury of falling in love with Mr Midhurst's daughter, but he was an astonishing match for Janey. He was a man who was very well off: he could afford himself such a caprice as that. He was not handsome. He was a thick set little man, and did not dress or talk in perfect taste; but – in love! These two words made all the difference. Nobody had ever loved her, much less been 'in love' with her. Janey consented willingly enough for the magic of these two words. She felt that she was going to be like the best of women at last – to have some one who loved her, some one who was in love with her. He might not be 'joli, joli,' as they say in France. She might not feel any very strong impulse on her own part towards him; but if he was in love with her – in love! Romeo was no more than that with Juliet. The thought went to Janey's head. She married him quite willingly for the sake of this.

I am afraid that Janey, being young and shy, and strange, was a good deal frightened, horrified, and even revolted, by her first discoveries of what it meant to be in love. She had made tremendous discoveries in the course of a week. She had found out that Mr Rosendale, her husband, was in love with her beauty, but as indifferent to herself as any of the persons she had quitted to give herself to him. He did not care at all what she thought, how she felt, what she liked or disliked. He did not care even for her comfort, or that she should be pleased and happy, which, in the first moment even of such a union, and out of pure self-regard to make a woman more agreeable to himself, a man – even the most brutal – generally regards more or less. He was, perhaps, not aware that he did not regard it. He took it for granted that, being his wife, she would naturally be pleased with what pleased him, and his mind went no further than this.

Therefore, as far as Janey liked the things he liked, all went well enough. She had these, but no other. Her wishes were not consulted further nor did he know that he failed in any way towards her. He had little to say to her, except expressions of admiration. When he was not telling her that she was a little beauty, or admiring her pretty hair, her pretty eyes, the softness of her skin, and the smallness of her waist, he had nothing to say. He read his paper, disappearing behind it in the morning; he went to sleep after his midday meal (for the weather was warm); he played billiards in the evening in the hotels to which he took her on their wedding journey; or he overwhelmed her with caresses from which she shrank in disgust, almost in terror. That was all that being in love meant, she found; and to say that she was disappointed cruelly was to express in the very mildest way the dreadful downfall of all her expectations and hopes which happened to Janey before she had been seven days a wife. It is not disagreeable to be told that you are a little beauty, prettier than any one else. Janey would have been very well pleased to put up with that; but to be petted like a little lapdog and then left as a lapdog is – to be quiet and not to trouble in the intervals of petting – was to the poor little girl, unaccustomed to love and athirst for it, who had hoped to be loved, and to find a companion to whom she would be truly dear, a disenchantment and disappointment which was almost more than flesh and blood could bear.

She was in the full bitterness of these discoveries when the strange incident occurred which was of so much importance in her life. They were travelling through France in one of those long night journeys to which we are all accustomed nowadays; and Janey, pale and tired, had been contemplating for some time the figure of her husband thrown back in the corner opposite, snoring complacently with his mouth open, and looking the worst that a middle-aged man can look in the utter abandonment of self-indulgence and rude comfort, when the train began to slacken its speed, and to prepare to enter one of those large stations which look so ghastly in the desertion of the night.

Rosendale jumped up instinctively, only half awake, as the train stopped. The other people in the carriage were leaving it, having attained the end of their journey, but he pushed through them and their baggage to get out, with the impatience which some men show at any pause of the kind, and determination to stretch their legs, or get something to drink, which mark the breaks in the journey. He did not even say anything to Janey as he forced his way out, but she was so familiar with his ways by this time that she took no notice. She did take notice, however, when, her fellow-passengers and their packages having all been cleared away, she suddenly became sensible that the train was getting slowly into motion again without any sign of her husband.

She thought she caught a glimpse of him strolling about on the opposite platform before she was quite sure of what was happening. And then there was a scurry of hurrying feet, a slamming of doors, and as she rose and ran to the window bewildered, she saw him, along with some other men, running at full speed, but quite hopelessly, to catch the train. The last she saw was his face, fully revealed by the light of the lamp, convulsed with rage and astonishment, evidently with a yell of denunciation on the lips. Janey trembled at the sight. There was that in him, too, though as yet in her submissiveness she had never called it forth, a temper as unrestrained as his love-making, and as little touched by any thought save that of his own gratification. Her first sensation was fright, a terror that she was in fault and was about to be crushed to pieces in his rage: and then Janey sank back in her corner, and a flood of feeling of quite another kind took possession of her breast.

Was it possible that she was alone? Was it possible that for the first time since that terrible moment of her marriage she was more safely by herself than any locked door or even watchful guardian could keep her, quite unapproachable in the isolation of the train? Alone!

'Safe!' Janey ventured to say to herself, clasping her hands together with a mingled sensation of excitement and terror and tremulous delight which words could not tell.

She did not know what to think at first. The sound of the train plunging along through the darkness, through the unknown country, filled her mind as if someone was talking to her. And she was fluttered by the strangeness of the incident and disturbed by alarms. There was a fearful joy in thus being alone, in having a few hours, perhaps a whole long tranquil night to herself: whatever came of it, that was always so much gained. But then she seemed to see him in the morning coming in upon her heated and angry. She has always felt that the moment would come when he would be angry, and more terrible to confront than any governess, or even principal of a ladies' college. He would come in furious, accusing her of being the cause of the accident, of doing something to set the train in motion; or else he would come in fatigued and dusty, claiming her services as if she were his valet – a thing which had, more or less, happened already and against which Janey's pride and her sense of what was fit had risen in arms. She thought of this for a little time with trouble, and of the difficulties she would have in arriving, and where she would go to, and what she would say. It was an absurd story to tell, not to his advantage, 'I lost my husband at Montbard.' How could she say it? The hotel people would think she was a deceiver. Perhaps they would not take her in. And how would he know where to find her when he arrived? He would feel that he had lost her, as much as she had lost him.

Just as this idea rose in her mind, like a new thing full of strange suggestions, the train began to shorten speed again, and presently stopped once more. She felt it to do so with a pang of horror. No doubt he had climbed up somewhere, at the end or upon the engine, and was now to be restored to his legitimate place, to fall upon her either in fondness or in rage, delighted to get back to her, or angry with her for leaving him behind: she did not know which would be the worst. Her heart began to beat with fright and anticipation. But to her great relief it was only the guard who came to the door. He wanted to know if madame was the lady whose husband had been left behind; and to offer a hundred apologies and explanations. One of those fools at Montbard had proclaimed twenty minutes' pause when there were but five. If he had but heard he would have put it right, but he was at the other end of the train. But madame must not be too much distressed; a few hours would put it all right.

'Then there is another train?' said Janey, her poor little head buzzing between excitement and relief.

'Not for some hours,' said the guard. 'Madame will understand that there is not more than one *rapide* in the middle of the night; but in the morning quite early there is the train omnibus. Oh, very early, at five o'clock. Before madame is ready for her dinner monsieur will be at her side.

'Not till evening, then?' said Janey, with again a sudden accelera-
tion of the movement of her heart.

The guard was desolated. 'Not before evening. But if madame will
remain quietly in the carriage when the train arrives at the station, I
will find the omnibus of the hotel for her – I will see to everything!
Madame, no doubt, knows which hotel to go to?'

Janey, as a matter of fact, did not know. Her husband had told her
none of the details of the journey; but she said with a quick breath of
excitement, 'I will go to the one that is nearest, the one at the Gare.
There will be no need for any omnibus.'

'And the baggage? Madame has her ticket?'

'I have nothing,' cried Janey, 'except my travelling bag. You must
explain that for me. But otherwise – otherwise, I think I can manage.'

'Madame speaks French so well,' the man said, with admiration. It
was, indeed, a piece of good fortune that she had been made to ac-
quire the language in the country: that she was not frightened to find
herself in a foreign place, and surrounded by people speaking a
strange tongue, as many a young English bride would have been.
There was a moment of tremendous excitement and noise at the station while all was explained to a serious *chef de Gare*, and a gesticulating band of porters and attendants, whose loud voices, as they all
spoke together, would have frightened an ordinary English girl out of
her wits. But Janey, in the strange excitement which had taken possession of her, and in her fortunate acquaintance with the language,
stood still as a little rock amid all the confusion. 'I will wait at the
hotel till my husband comes,' she said, taking out the travelling bag
and her wraps, and maintaining a composure worthy of all admiration. Not a tear, not an outcry. How astonishing are these English,
cried the little crowd, with that swift classification which the Frenchman loves.

Janey walked into the hotel with her little belongings, not knowing
whether she was indeed walking upon her feet or floating upon wings.
She was quite composed. But if any one could only have seen the
commotion within that youthful bosom! She locked the door of the
little delightful solitary room in which she was placed. It was not delightful at all; but to Janey it was a haven of peace, as sweet, as secluded from everything alarming and terrible, as any bower. Not till
evening could he by any possibility arrive – the man who had caused
such a revolution in her life. She had some ten hours of divine quiet
before her, of blessed solitude, of thought. She did not refuse to take
the little meal that was brought to her, the breakfast of which she

stood in need; and she was glad to be able to bathe her face, to take off her dusty dress, and put on the soft and fresh one, which, happily, had folded into very small space, and therefore could be put into her bag. Her head still buzzed with the strangeness of the position, yet began to settle a little. When she had made all these little arrangements she sat down to consider. Perhaps you will think there was very little to consider, nothing but how to wait till the next train brought him, which, after all, was not a very great thing to do. Appalling, perhaps, to a little inexperienced bride; but not to Janey, who had travelled alone so often, and knew the language, and all that.

But whoever had been able to look into Janey's mind would have seen that something more was there, – a very, very different thing from the question of how best to await his coming back. Oh, if he had loved her, Janey would have put up with many things! She would have schooled herself out of all her private repugnances; she would have been so grateful to him, so touched by the affection which nobody had ever bestowed upon her before! But he did not love her. He cared nothing about herself, Janey; did not even know her, or want to know her, or take into consideration her ways or her wishes. He was in love with her pretty face, her fresh little beauty, her power of pleasing him. If ever that power ceased, which it was sure to do, sooner or later, she would be to him less than nothing, the dreary little wife whom everybody has seen attached to a careless man: Janey felt that this was what was in store for her. She felt the horror of him, and his kind of loving, which had been such a miserable revelation to her. She felt the relief, the happiness, ah, the bliss, of having lost him for a moment, of being alone.

She took out her purse from her pocket, which was full of the change she had got in Paris of one of the ten pound notes which her guardian had given her when she left his house on her wedding morning. She took out the clumsy pocketbook, an old one, in which there were still nine ten pound notes. It was all her fortune, except a very, very small investment which brought her in some seven pounds a year. This was the remainder of another small investment which had been withdrawn in order to provide her with her simple trousseau, leaving this sum of a hundred pounds which her guardian had given her, advising her to place it at once for security in her husband's hands. Janey had not done this, she scarcely could tell why. She spread them on the table – the nine notes, the twelve napoleons of shining French money. A hundred pounds: she had still the twelve francs which made up the sum. She had spent nothing. There were even the few coppers over for the *agio*. She spread them all out, and counted them from right to left, and again from left to right. Nine ten pound notes, twelve-and-a-half French napoleons – or louis, as people call them nowadays – making a hundred pounds. A hundred pounds is a large sum in the eyes of a girl. It may not be much to you and me, who know that it means only ten times ten pounds, and that ten pounds goes like the wind as soon as you begin to spend it. But to Janey! Why, she could live upon a hundred pounds for – certainly for two years: for two long delightful years, with nobody to trouble her, nobody to scold, nobody to interfere. Something mounted to her head like the fumes of wine. Everything began to buzz again, to turn round, to sweep her away as on a rapidly mounting current. She put back all the money in the pocketbook – her fortune, the great sum that made her independent; and she put back her things into the bag. A sudden energy of resolution seized her. She put on her hat again, and as she looked at herself in the glass encountered the vision of a little face which was new to her. It was not that of Janey, the little governess-pupil; it was not young Mrs Rosendale. It was full of life, and meaning, and energy, and strength. Who was it? Janey? Janey herself, the real woman, whom nobody had ever seen before.

It is astonishing how many things can be done in sudden excitement and passion which could not be possible under any other circumstances. Janey was by nature a shy girl and easily frightened, accustomed indeed to do many things for herself, and to move quietly without attracting observation through the midst of a crowd; but she had never taken any initiative, and since her marriage had been reduced to such a state of complete dependence on her husband's wishes and plans that she had not attempted the smallest step on her own impulse.

Now, however, she moved about with a quiet assurance and decision which astonished herself. She carried her few possessions back again to the railway station, leaving the small gold piece of ten francs to pay, and much overpay, her hour's shelter and entertainment at the hotel.

Nobody noticed her as she went through the bustle of the place and back to the crowded station, where a little leisurely local train was about starting – a slow train occupied by peasants and country folk, and which stopped at every station along the line. English people abound in that place at all hours, except at this particular moment, when the *rapide* going towards Italy had but newly left and the little country train was preparing in peace. Nobody seemed to notice Janey as she moved about with her bag on her arm. She took her ticket in her irreproachable French 'acquired in the country', which attracted no attention. She got into a second-class carriage in which there were already various country people, and especially a young mother with a baby, and its nurse in a white round cap with long streaming ribbons. Janey's heart went out to these people. She wondered if the young woman was happy, if her husband loved her, if it was not very sweet to have a child – a child must love you; it would not mind whether your cheeks were rosy or pale, whether you were pretty or not, whether you had accomplishments or languages acquired in the country.

Looking at this baby, Janey almost forgot that she was going out upon the world alone, and did not know where. It is a tremendous thing to do this, to separate from all the world you are acquainted with, to plunge into the unknown. Men do it often enough, though seldom without some clue, some link of connection with the past and way of return. Janey was about to cut herself off as by the Fury's shears from everything. She would never join her husband again. She would never fear her guardian again. She must drop out of sight like a stone into the sea. There was no longing love to search for her, no pardon to be offered, no one who would be heart-struck at the thought of the little girl lost and unhappy. Only anger would be excited by her running away, and a desire to punish, to shake her little fragile person to pieces, to make her suffer. She knew that if she did it at all, it must be final. But this did not overwhelm her. What troubled Janey a great deal more than the act of severance which she was about to accomplish, was the inevitable fib or fibs she must tell in order to account for her appearance in the unknown. She did not like to tell a fib, even a justifiable one. It was against all her traditions, against her nature. She felt that she could never do it anything but badly, never without exciting suspicions; and she must needs have some story, some way of accounting for herself.

This occupied her mind while the slow train crawled from station to station. It was the most friendly, idle, gossiping little train. It seemed to stop at the merest signal-box to have a talk, to drink as it were a social glass administered through that black hose, with a friend; it stopped wherever there were a few houses, it carried little parcels, it took up a leisurely passenger going next door, and the little electric bell went on tingling, and the guard cried 'En voiture!' and the little bugle sounded. Janey was amused by all these little sounds and sights, and the country all flooded with sunshine, and the flowers every-where, though it was only March, and dark black weather when she had left home.

Left home! and she had no home now, anywhere, no place to take refuge in, nobody to write to, to appeal to, to tell if she was happy or unhappy. But Janey did not care! She felt a strange elation of ease and relief. All alone, but everybody smiling upon her, the young mother opposite beginning to chatter, the baby to crow to her, the nurse to smile and approve of the *bonne petite dame* who took so much notice of the child. Her head was swimming, but with pleasure, and the blessed sensation of freedom – pleasure tinctured with the exhilara-tion of escape, and the thrill of fright which added to the excitement. Yet at that moment she was certainly in no danger. He was toiling along, no doubt, fuming and perhaps swearing, on another slow train on the other side of Marseilles. Janey laughed to herself a little guiltily at the thought.

And she had escaped! It was not her doing primarily. She might have gone on all her life till she had died, but for that accident which was none of her doing. It was destiny that had done it, fate. The cage door had been opened and the bird had flown away. And how nice it would be to settle down, with this little mother, just about her own age, for a neighbour, and to help to bring the baby up! The kind, sweet faces they all had, mother and baby and *bonne* all smiling upon her! When Janey looked out on the other side she saw the sea flashing in the sunshine, the red porphyry rocks reflecting themselves in the brilliant blue, and village after village perched upon a promontory or in the hollow of a bay. She had never in all her life before felt that sen-sation of blessedness, of being able to do what she liked, of having no one to call her to account. She did not know where she was going, but that was part of the pleasure. She did not want to know where she was going.

Then suddenly this sentiment changed, and she saw in a moment a place that smiled at her like the smiling of the mother and baby. It was one of those villages in a bay: a range of blue mountains threw forth a protecting arm into the sea to shield it: the roofs were red, the houses were white, they were all blazing in the sun. Soft olives and palms fringed the deep green of the pines that rolled back in waves of ver-dure over the country behind, and strayed down in groups and scat-tered files to the shore below. Oh, what a cheerful, delightsome place! and this was where the little group with the baby was preparing to get out. 'I will go too,' said Janey to herself; and her heart gave a little bound of pleasure. She was delighted to reach the place where she was going to stay – just as she had been delighted to go on in the little pottering train, not knowing where she was going, and not wishing to know.

This was how Janey settled herself on the day of her flight from the world. She scarcely knew what story it was she told to the young woman whose face had so charmed her, and whom she asked whether she would be likely to find lodgings anywhere, lodgings that would not be too expensive.

'My husband is – at sea,' Janey heard herself saying. She could scarcely tell what it was that put those words into her head.

'Oh, but yes,' the other young woman cried with rapture. Nothing was more easy to get than a lodging in St Honorat, which was beginning to try to be a winter resort, and was eager to attract strangers. Janey had dreamed of a cottage and a garden, but she was not dissatisfied when she found herself in a sun-bright room on the second floor of a tall white house facing the sea. It had a little balcony all to itself. The water rippled on the shore just over the road, the curve of the blue mountains was before her eyes.

I do not say that when she had settled down, when the thrill of movement was no longer in her brain, Janey was not without a shiver at the thought of what she had done. When the sun set, and that little chill which comes into the air of the south at the moment of its setting breathed a momentary cold about her, and when the woman of the house carefully closed the shutters and shut out the shining of the bay, and she was left alone with her candle, something sank in Janey's heart – something of the unreasonable elation, the fantastic happiness, of the day. She thought of 'Mr Rosendale' (she had never got so near her husband as to call him by any other name) arriving, of the fuss there would be about her and the inquiries.

Was it rash to have come to a place so near as this – within an hour or two of where he was? Was there a danger that some one might have seen her? that it might be found out that she had taken her ticket? But then she had taken her ticket for a place much further along the coast. She thought she could see him arrive all flaming with anger and eagerness, and the group that would gather round him, and how he would be betrayed by his bad French, and the rage he would get into! Again she laughed guiltily; but then got very grave again trying to count up all the chances – how some porter might have noticed and might betray her, how he might yet come down upon her furiously, to wreak upon her all the fury of his discomfiture. Janey knew by instinct that though it was in no way her fault, her husband would wreak his vengenance upon her even for being left behind by the train. She became desperate as she sat and thought it all over. It would be better for her to leap from the window, to throw herself into the sea, than to fall into his hands. There would be no forgiveness for her if he once laid hands upon her. Now that she had taken this desperate step, she must stand by it to the death.

Ten years had passed away since the time of that wedding tour.

Ten years! It is a very long time in a life. It makes a young man middle-aged, and a middle-aged man old. It takes away the bloom of youth, and the ignorance of the most inexperienced; and yet what a little while it is! – no more than a day when you look back upon it. The train from Marseilles to Nice, which is called the *rapide*, goes every day, and most people one time or another have travelled by it.

One day last winter one of the passengers in this train, established very comfortably in the best corner of a sleeping carriage in which he had passed the night luxuriously, and from which he was now looking out upon the shining sea, the red rocks, the many bays and headlands of the coast, suddenly received such a shock and sensation as seldom occurs to any one. He was a man of middle-age and not of engaging aspect. His face was red, and his eyes were dull yet fiery. He had the air of a man who had indulged himself much and all his inclinations, had loved good living and all the joys of the flesh, had denied himself nothing – and was now paying the penalties. Such men, to tell the truth, are not at all unusual apparitions on that beautiful coast or in the train *rapide*. No doubt appearances are deceitful, and it is not always a bad man who bears that aspect or who pays those penalties: but in this case few people would have doubted.

His eyes were bloodshot, he had a scowl upon his brow, his foot was supported upon a cushion. He had a servant with him to whom he rarely spoke but with an insult. Not an agreeable man – and the life he was now leading, whatever it had been, was not an agreeable life. He was staring out the window upon the curves of the coast, sometimes putting up the collar of his fur coat over his ears, though it was a warm morning, and the sun had all the force of April. What he was thinking of it would be difficult to divine – perhaps of the good dinner that awaited him at Monte Carlo when he got there, perhaps of his good luck in being out of England when the east winds began to blow, perhaps of something quite different – some recollection of his past. The *rapide* does not stop at such small places as St Honorat, which indeed had not succeeded in making itself a winter resort. It was still a very small place. There were a few people on the platform when the train rushed through. It seemed to pass like a whirlwind, yet notwithstanding, in that moment two things happened. The gentleman in the corner of the carriage started in his seat, and flung himself half out of the window, with a sudden roar which lost itself in the tunnel into which the train plunged. There was an awful minute in that tunnel: for the servant thought his master had taken a fit, and there was no light to see what convulsions he might have fallen into, while at the same time he fought furiously against the man's efforts to loose his wrappings and place him in a recumbent position, exclaiming furiously all the time. He had not taken a fit, but when the train emerged into the light he was as near to it as possible – purple-red in his face, and shouting with rage and pain.

'Stop the train! stop the train!' he shouted. 'Do you hear, you fool? stop the train! Ring the bell or whatever it is! break the—thing! Stop the train!'

'Sir, sir! if you will only be quiet, I will get your medicine in a moment!'

'Medicine, indeed!' cried the master, indignantly, and every furious name that he could think of mounted to his lips – fool, idiot, ass, swine – there was no end to his epithets. 'I tell you I saw her, I saw her!' he shouted. 'Stop the train! Stop the train!'

On the other hand, among the few insignificant persons, peasants and others, who had been standing on the platform at St Honorat when the *rapide* dashed past, there had been a woman and child. The woman was not a peasant: she was very simply dressed in black, with one of the small bonnets which were a few years ago so distinctively English, and with an air which corresponded to that simple coiffure. She was young, and yet had the air of responsibility and motherhood which marks a woman who is no longer in the first chapter of life. The child, a boy of nine or ten, standing close by her side, had seized her hand just as the train appeared impatiently to call her attention to something else; but, by some strange spell of attraction or coincidence, her eyes fixed upon that window out of which the gouty traveller was looking. She saw him as he saw her, and fell back dragging the boy with her as if she would have sunk into the ground. It was only a moment and the *rapide* was gone, screaming and roaring into the tunnel, making too much noise with the rush and sweep of its going to permit the shout of the passenger to be heard.

Ten years, ten long years, during which life had undergone so many changes! They all seemed to fly away in a moment, and the girl who had arrived at the little station of St Honorat alone, a fugitive, elated and intoxicated with her freedom, suddenly felt herself again the little Janey who had emancipated herself so strangely – though she had for a long time been frightened by every train that passed and every stranger who came near.

In the course of these long years all this had changed. Her baby had been born, her forlorn state had called forth great pity, great remark and criticism, in the village where she had found refuge, – great censure also, for the fact of her marriage was not believed by everybody. But she was so lonely, so modest, and so friendly, that the poor little English stranger was soon forgiven. Perhaps her simple neighbours were glad to find that a prim Englishwoman, supposed to stand so fierce on her virtue, was in reality so fallible – or perhaps pity put all other sentiments out of court. She told her real story to the priest when the boy was baptised, and though he tried to persuade her to return to her husband, he only half believed in that husband, since the story was told not under any seal of confession. Janey never became absolutely one of his flock. She was a prim little Protestant in her heart, standing strong against the saints, but devoutly attending church, believing with simple religiousness that to go to church was better than not to go to church, whatever the rites might be, and reading her little English service steadily through all the prayers of the Mass, which she never learned to follow. But her boy was like the other children of St Honorat, and learned his catechism and said his lessons with the rest.

There were various things which she did to get a living, and got it very innocently and sufficiently, though in the humblest way. She taught English to the children of some of the richer people in the village: she taught them music. She had so much credit in this latter branch, that she often held the organ in church on a holiday and pleased everybody. Then she worked very well with her needle, and would help on an emergency at first for pure kindness, and then, as her faculties and her powers of service became known, for pay, with diligence and readiness. She found a niche in the little place which she filled perfectly, though only accident seemed to have made it for her. She had fifty pounds of her little fortune laid by for the boy. She had a share of a cottage in a garden – not an English cottage indeed, but the upper floor of a two-storeyed French house; and she and her boy did much in the garden, cultivating prettinesses which do not commend themselves much to the villagers of St Honorat. Whether she ever regretted the step she had taken nobody ever knew. She might have been a lady with a larger house than any in St Honorat, and servants at her call. Perhaps she sometimes thought of that; perhaps she felt herself happier as she was; sometimes, I think, she felt that if she had known the boy was coming she might have possessed her soul in patience, and borne even with Mr Rosendale. But then at the time the decisive step was taken she did not know.

She hurried home in a great fright, not knowing what to do; then calmed herself with the thought that even if he had recognised her, there were many chances against his following her, or at least finding her, with no clue, and after so many years. And then a dreadful panic seized her at the thought that he might take her boy from her. He had known nothing about the boy: but if he discovered that fact it would make a great difference. He could not compel Janey to return to him, but he could take the boy. When this occurred to her she started up again, having just sat down, and put on her bonnet and called the child.

'Are you going out again, mother?' he cried.

'Yes, directly, directly: come, John, come, come!' she said putting his cap upon his head and seizing him by the hand. She led him straight to the presbytery, and asked for the *curé*, and went in to the good priest in great agitation, leaving the boy with his housekeeper.

'M. l'Abbé,' she said, with what the village called her English directness, 'I have just seen my husband go past in the train!'

'Not possible!' said M. l'Abbé, who only half believed there was a husband at all.

'And he saw me. He will come back, and I am afraid he will find me. I want you to do something for me.'

'With pleasure,' said the priest; 'I will come and meet Monsieur your husband, and I will explain—'

'That is not what I want you to do. I want you to let John stay with you, to keep him here till – till – He will want to take him away from me!' she cried.

'He will want to take you both away, *chère petite dame*. He has a right to do so.'

'No, no! but I do not ask you what is his right. I ask you to keep John safe; to keep him here – till the danger has passed away!'

The priest tried to reason, to entreat, to persuade her that a father, not to say a husband, had his rights. But Janey would hear no reason: had she heard reason either from herself or another, she would not have been at St Honorat now. And he gave at last a reluctant consent.

There was perhaps no harm in it after all. If a man came to claim his rights, he would not certainly go away again without some appeal to the authorities – which was a thing it must come to sooner or later – if there was indeed a husband at all, and the story was true.

Janey then went back to her home. She thought she could await him there and defy him. 'I will not go with you,' she would say. 'I may be your wife, but I am not your slave. You have left me alone for ten years. I will not go with you now!' She repeated this to herself many times, but it did not subdue the commotion in her being. She went out again when it became too much for her, locking her door with a strange sense that she might never come back again. She walked along the sea shore, repeating these words to herself, and then she walked up and down the streets, and went into the church and made the round of it, passing all the altars and wondering if the saints did pay any attention to the poor women who were there, as always, telling St Joseph or the Blessed Mary all about it. She sank down in a dark corner, and said—

'Oh, my God! oh, my God!'

She could not tell Him about it in her agitation, with her heart beating so, but only call His attention, as the woman in the Bible touched the Redeemer's robe. And then she went out and walked up and down again. I cannot tell what drew her back to the station – what fascination, what dreadful spell. Before she knew what she was doing she found herself there, walking up and down, up and down.

As if she were waiting for someone! 'You have come to meet a friend?' someone said to her, with an air of suspicion. And she first nodded and then shook her head; but still continued in spite of herself to walk up and down. Then she said to herself that it was best so – that to get it over would be a great thing, now John was out of the way; he would be sure to find her sooner or later – far better to get it over! When the train came in, the slow local train, coming from the side of Italy, she drew herself back a little to watch. There was a great commotion when it drew up at the platform. A man got out and called all the loungers about to help to lift out a gentleman who was ill – who had had a bad attack in the train.

'Is there anywhere here we can take him to? Is there any decent hotel? Is there a room fit to put my master in?' he cried.

He was English with not much French at his command, and in great distress. Janey, forgetting herself and her terrors, and strong in the relief of the moment that he whom she feared had not come, went up to offer her help. She answered the man's questions; she called the right people to help him; she summoned the *chef de Gare* to make some provision for carrying the stricken man to the hotel.

'I will go with you,' she said to the servant, who felt as if an angel speaking English had suddenly come to his help. She stood by full of pity, as they lifted that great inert mass out of the carriage. Then she gave a great cry and fell back against the wall.

It was a dreadful sight the men said afterwards, enough to over-come the tender heart of any lady, especially of one so kind as Madame Jeanne. A huge man, helpless, unconscious, with a purple countenance, staring eyes, breathing so that you could hear him a mile off. No wonder that she covered her eyes with her hands not to see him; and then covered her ears with her hands not to hear him: but finally she hurried away to the hotel to prepare for him, and to call the doctor, that no time should be lost. Janey felt as if she was restored for the moment to life when there was something she could do. The questions were all postponed. She did not think of flight or conceal-ment, or even of John at the presbytery. 'He is my husband,' she said, with awe in her heart.

This was how the train brought back to Janey the man whom the train had separated from her ten years before. The whole tragedy was of the railway, the noisy carriages, the snorting locomotives. He was taken to the hotel, but he never came to himself again, and died there next day, without being able to say what his object was, or why he had got out of the *rapide*, though unable to walk, and insisted on return-ing to St Honorat. It cost him his life; but then his life was not worth a day's purchase, all the doctors said, in the condition in which he was.

Friends had to be summoned, and men of business, and it was im-possible but that Janey's secret should be made known. When she found herself and her son recognised, and that there could be no doubt that the boy was his father's heir, she was struck with a great horror which she never quite got over all her life. She had not blamed herself before; but now seemed to herself no less than the murderer of her husband: and could not forgive herself, nor get out of her eyes the face she had seen, nor out of her ears the dreadful sound of that lab-ouring breath.

KATE CHOPIN

A Pair of Silk Stockings

Kate Chopin (1850-1904) was born in St Louis. Her father was an Irish immigrant, a successful merchant; her mother was from a distinguished French Creole family who had been among the first settlers of St Louis. Kate, one of four children, was educated at a convent school, and except for her father's death when she was twelve, her childhood was happy and privileged, with access to contemporary and older literature. In 1868 she was launched into society which was not always congenial to her rather private character. She married Oscar Chopin, also a French Creole, and they lived for nine years in New Orleans, a culturally progressive and lively city. Despite her large family – six children eventually – she developed the habit of wandering around the city alone. When Oscar's business failed, they moved up country to north-western Louisiana where he managed part of the family plantations and owned a general store. In 1883, Oscar died of swamp fever and Kate managed the estate for a year before moving to St Louis. She now started writing, encouraged by her doctor as a form of therapy, beginning with short stories and an early, shaky novel At Fault *(1890). She wrote fast and fluently, seldom revising her first drafts, and working in the family living-room so that she would always be available to her children. Her stories were published in periodicals and two collections appeared in the next decade,* Bayou Folk *(1894) and* A Night in Acadie *(1897), both popular and well received but seen more as cosy examples of the American 'local colour' tradition than as fiction influenced by the abrasive realism of nineteenth-century French literature, with which she was familiar (she had translated some of Maupassant's work). She was eager for national recognition when her novel* The Awakening *was published in 1899. Her portrait of a married woman discovering independence and her own identity outraged critics: the book was censured and banned from libraries. Kate Chopin had relied on sympathetic support from critics, as well as needing a market, and she wrote very little after this. She died in 1904 of a brain haemorrhage, her literary career broken by the hostility of her critics.*

Little Mrs Sommers one day found herself the unexpected possessor of fifteen dollars. It seemed to her a very large amount of money, and the way in which it stuffed and bulged her worn old *porte-monnaie* gave her a feeling of importance such as she had not enjoyed for years.

The question of investment was one that occupied her greatly. For a day or two she walked about apparently in a dreamy state, but really absorbed in speculation and calculation. She did not wish to act hastily, to do anything she might afterwards regret. But it was during the still hours of the night when she lay awake revolving plans in her mind that she seemed to see her way clearly toward a proper and judicious use of the money.

A dollar or two should be added to the price usually paid for Janie's shoes, which would insure their lasting an appreciable time longer than they usually did. She would buy so and so many yards of percale for new shirt waists for the boys and Janie and Mag. She had intended to make the old ones do by skilful patching. Mag should have another gown. She had seen some beautiful patterns, veritable bargains in the shop windows. And still there would be left enough for new stockings – two pairs apiece – and what darning that would save for a while! She would get caps for the boys and sailor hats for the girls. The vision of her little brood looking fresh and dainty and new for once in their lives excited her and made her restless and wakeful with anticipation.

The neighbours sometimes talked of certain 'better days' that little Mrs Sommers had known before she had ever thought of being Mrs Sommers. She herself indulged in no such morbid retrospection. She had no time – no second of time to devote to the past. The needs of the present absorbed her every faculty. A vision of the future like some dim, gaunt monster sometimes appalled her, but luckily tomorrow never comes.

Mrs Sommers was one who knew the value of bargains; who could stand for hours making her way inch by inch toward the desired object that was selling below cost. She could elbow her way if need be; she had learned to clutch a piece of goods and hold it and stick to it with persistence and determination till her turn came to be served, no matter when it came.

But that day she was a little faint and tired. She had swallowed a light luncheon – no! when she came to think of it, between getting the children fed and the place righted, and preparing herself for the shopping bout, she had actually forgotten to eat any luncheon at all!

She sat herself upon a revolving stool before a counter that was comparatively deserted, trying to gather strength and courage to charge through an eager multitude that was besieging breast-works of shirting and figured lawn. An all-gone limp feeling had come over her and she rested her hand aimlessly upon the counter. She wore no gloves. By degrees she grew aware that her hand had encountered something very soothing, very pleasant to touch. She looked down to see that her hand lay upon a pile of silk stockings. A placard near by announced that they had been reduced in price from two dollars and fifty cents to one dollar and ninety-eight cents; and a young girl who stood behind the counter asked her if she wished to examine their line of silk hosiery. She smiled just as if she had been asked to inspect a tiara of diamonds with the ultimate view of purchasing it. But she went on feeling the soft, sheeny luxurious things – with both hands now, holding them up to see them glisten, and to feel them glide serpent-like through her fingers.

Two hectic blotches came suddenly into her pale cheeks. She looked up at the girl.

'Do you think there are any eights-and-a-half among these?'

There were any number of eights-and-a-half. In fact, there were more of that size than any other. Here was a light blue pair; there were some lavender, some all black and various shades of tan and gray. Mrs Sommers selected a black pair and looked at them very long and closely. She pretended to be examining their texture, which the clerk assured her was excellent.

'A dollar and ninety-eight cents,' she mused aloud. 'Well, I'll take this pair.' She handed the girl a five dollar bill and waited for her change and for her parcel. What a very small parcel it was! It seemed lost in the depths of her shabby old shopping bag.

Mrs Sommers after that did not move in the direction of the bargain counter. She took the elevator, which carried her to an upper floor into the region of the ladies' waiting-rooms. Here, in a retired corner, she exchanged her cotton stockings for the new silk ones which she had just bought. She was not going through any acute mental process or reasoning with herself, nor was she striving to explain to her satisfaction the motive of her action. She was not thinking at all. She seemed for the time to be taking a rest from that laborious and fatiguing function and to have abandoned herself to some mechanical impulse that directed her actions and freed her of responsibility.

How good was the touch of the raw silk to her flesh! She felt like lying back in the cushioned chair and revelling for a while in the luxury of it. She did for a little while. Then she replaced her shoes, rolled the cotton stockings together and thrust them into her bag. After doing this she crossed straight over to the shoe department and took her seat to be fitted.

She was fastidious. The clerk could not make her out; he could not reconcile her shoes with her stockings, and she was not too easily pleased. She held back her skirts and turned her feet one way and her head another way as she glanced down at the polished, pointed-tipped boots. Her foot and ankle looked very pretty. She could not realize that they belonged to her and were a part of herself. She wanted an excellent and stylish fit, she told the young fellow who served her, and she did not mind the difference of a dollar or two more in the price so long as she got what she desired.

It was a long time since Mrs Sommers had been fitted with gloves. On rare occasions when she had bought a pair they were always 'bargains,' so cheap that it would have been preposterous and unreasonable to have expected them to be fitted to the hand.

Now she rested her elbow on the cushion of the glove counter, and a pretty, pleasant young creature, delicate and deft of touch, drew a long-wristed 'kid' over Mrs Sommers' hand. She smoothed it down over the wrist and buttoned it neatly, and both lost themselves for a second or two in admiring contemplation of the little symmetrical gloved hand. But there were other places where money might be spent.

There were books and magazines piled up in the window of a stall a few paces down the street. Mrs Sommers bought two high-priced magazines such as she had been accustomed to read in the days when she had been accustomed to other pleasant things. She carried them without wrappings. As well as she could she lifted her skirts at the crossings. Her stockings and boots and well fitted gloves had worked marvels in her bearing – had given her a feeling of assurance, a sense of belonging to the well-dressed multitude.

She was very hungry. Another time she would have stilled the cravings for food until reaching her own home, where she would have brewed herself a cup of tea and taken a snack of anything that was available. But the impulse that was guiding her would not suffer her to entertain any such thought.

There was a restaurant at the corner. She had never entered its doors; from the outside she had sometimes caught glimpses of spotless damask and shining crystal, and soft-stepping waiters serving people of fashion.

When she entered her appearance created no surprise, no consternation, as she had half feared it might. She seated herself at a small table alone, and an attentive waiter at once approached to take her order. She did not want a profusion; she craved a nice and tasty bite – a half dozen blue-points, a plump chop with cress, a something sweet – a crème-frappée, for instance; a glass of Rhine wine, and after all a small cup of black coffee.

While waiting to be served she removed her gloves very leisurely and laid them beside her. Then she picked up a magazine and glanced through it, cutting the pages with a blunt edge of her knife. It was all very agreeable. The damask was even more spotless than it had seemed through the window, and the crystal more sparkling. There were quiet ladies and gentlemen, who did not notice her, lunching at the small tables like her own. A soft, pleasing strain of music could be heard, and a gentle breeze was blowing through the window. She tasted a bite, and she read a word or two, and she sipped the amber wine and wiggled her toes in the silk stockings. The price of it made no difference. She counted the money out to the waiter and left an extra coin on his tray, whereupon he bowed before her as before a princess of royal blood.

There was still money in her purse, and her next temptation presented itself in the shape of a matinée poster.

It was a little later when she entered the theatre, the play had begun and the house seemed to her to be packed. But there were vacant seats here and there, and into one of them she was ushered, between brilliantly dressed women who had gone there to kill time and eat candy and display their gaudy attire. There were many others who were there solely for the play and acting. It is safe to say there was no one present who bore quite the attitude which Mrs Sommers did to her surroundings. She gathered in the whole stage and players and people in one wide impression, and absorbed it and enjoyed it. She laughed at the comedy and wept – she and the gaudy woman next to her wept over the tragedy. And they talked a little together over it. And the gaudy woman wiped her eyes and sniffled on a tiny square of filmy, perfumed lace and passed little Mrs Sommers her box of candy.

The play was over, the music ceased, the crowd filed out. It was like a dream ended. People scattered in all directions. Mrs Sommers went to the corner and waited for the cable car.

A man with keen eyes, who sat opposite to her, seemed to like the study of her small, pale face. It puzzled him to decipher what he saw there. In truth, he saw nothing – unless he were wizard enough to detect a poignant wish, a powerful longing that the cable car would never stop anywhere, but go on and on with her forever.

MARY WILKINS

A New England Nun

Mary Wilkins (1852-1930) was born in Randolph, Massachusetts and moved later to Vermont where she was educated in a local high school. Her family declined financially and socially and, after the death of her parents and only sister within a brief period, she returned to Randolph to live with her childhood friend Mary Wales, with whom she spent the next twenty years. She was now established as a writer of short stories for adults and children, and serial novels. At the age of fifty she married Dr Charles Freeman after an engagement last- ing three years which she had broken off once. After her marriage, Mary Wilkins dropped her maiden name and started to write under her married name, Mary Wilkins Freeman. The marriage eventually ended in legal separation, after Freeman had spent periods in hospital for alcoholism. Her early collections of stories, A Humble Romance *(1887) and* A New England Nun *(1891), contain interesting portraits of women in New England in a period of depression and rural depop- ulation, when single men left for the cities and single women remained behind.*

It was late in the afternoon, and the light was waning. There was a dif- ference in the look of the tree shadows out in the yard. Somewhere in the distance cows were lowing and a little bell was tinkling; now and then a farm wagon tilted by, and the dust flew; some blue-shirted labourers with shovels over their shoulders plodded past; little swarms of flies were dancing up and down before the peoples' faces in the soft air. There seemed to be a gentle stir arising over everything for the mere sake of subsidence – a very premonition of rest and hush and night.

This soft diurnal commotion was over Louisa Ellis also. She had been peacefully sewing at her sitting-room window all the afternoon. Now she quilted her needle carefully into her work, which she folded precisely, and laid in a basket with her thimble and thread and scissors. Louisa Ellis could not remember that ever in her life she had mislaid one of these little feminine appurtenances, which had become, from long use and constant association, a very part of her personality.

Louisa tied a green apron round her waist, and got out a flat straw hat with a green ribbon. Then she went into the garden with a little blue crockery bowl, to pick some currants for her tea. After the currants were picked she sat on the back doorstep and stemmed them, collecting the stems carefully in her apron, and afterwards throwing them in the hen coop. She looked sharply at the grass beside the step to see if any had fallen there.

Louisa was slow and still in her movements; it took her a long time to prepare her tea; but when ready it was set forth with as much grace as if she had been a veritable guest to her own self. The little square table stood exactly in the centre of the kitchen, and was covered with a starched linen cloth whose border pattern of flowers glistened. Louisa had a damask napkin on her tea-tray, where were arranged a cut-glass tumbler full of teaspoons, a silver cream pitcher, a china sugar bowl, and one pink china cup and saucer. Louisa used china every day – something which none of her neighbours did. They whispered about it among themselves. Their daily tables were laid with common crockery, their sets of best china stayed in the parlour closet, and Louisa Ellis was no richer nor better bred than they. Still she would use the china. She had for her supper a glass dish full of sugared currants, a plate of little cakes, and one of light white biscuits. Also a leaf or two of lettuce, which she cut up daintily. Louisa was very fond of lettuce, which she raised to perfection in her little garden. She ate quite heartily, though in a delicate, pecking way; it seemed almost surprising that any considerable bulk of food should vanish.

After tea she filled a plate with nicely baked thin corn-cakes and carried them out into the back-yard.

'Caesar!' she called. 'Caesar! Caesar!'

There was a little rush, and the clank of a chain, and a large yellow and white dog appeared at the door of his tiny hut, which was half hidden among the tall grasses and flowers. Louisa patted him and gave him the corn-cakes. Then she returned to the house and washed the tea things, polishing the china carefully. The twilight had deepened: the chorus of the frogs floated in at the open window wonderfully loud and shrill, and once in a while a long sharp drone from a tree-toad pierced it. Louisa took off her green gingham apron, disclosing a shorter one of pink and white print. She lighted her lamp, and sat down again with her sewing.

In about half an hour Joe Dagget came. She heard his heavy step on the walk, and rose and took off her pink and white apron. Under that was still another – white linen with a little cambric edging on the bottom; that was Louisa's company apron. She never wore it without her calico sewing apron over it unless she had a guest. She had barely folded the pink and white one with methodical haste and laid it in a table-drawer when the door opened and Joe Dagget entered.

He seemed to fill up the whole room. A little yellow canary that had been asleep in his green cage at the south window woke up and fluttered wildly, beating his little yellow wings against the wires. He always did so when Joe Dagget came into the room.

'Good evening,' said Louisa. She extended her hand with a kind of solemn cordiality.

'Good evening, Louisa,' returned the man, in a loud voice.

She placed a chair for him, and they sat facing each other, with the table between them. He sat bolt upright, toeing out his heavy feet squarely, glancing with a good humoured uneasiness around the room. She sat gently erect, folding her slender hands in her white linen lap.

'Been a pleasant day,' remarked Dagget.

'Real pleasant,' Louisa assented, softly. 'Have you been haying?' she asked, after a little while.

'Yes, I've been haying all day, down in the ten acre lot. Pretty hot work.'

'It must be.'

'Yes, it's pretty hot work in the sun.'

'Is your mother well today?'

'Yes, mother's pretty well.'

'I suppose Lily Dyer's with her now?'

Dagget coloured. 'Yes, she's with her,' he answered, slowly.

He was not very young, but there was a boyish look about his large face. Louisa was not quite as old as he, her face was fairer and smoother, but she gave people the impression of being older.

'I suppose she's a good deal of help to your mother,' she said further.

'I guess she is; I don't know how mother'd get along without her,' said Dagget, with a sort of embarrassed warmth.

'She looks like a real capable girl. She's pretty-looking too,' remarked Louisa.

'Yes, she is pretty fair looking.'

Presently Dagget began fingering the books on the table. There was a square red autograph album, and a Young Lady's Gift Book which had belonged to Louisa's mother. He took them up one after the other and opened them; then laid them down again, the album on the Gift Book.

Louisa kept eyeing them with mild uneasiness. Finally she rose and changed the position of the books, putting the album underneath. That was the way they had been arranged in the first place.

Dagget gave an awkward little laugh. 'Now what difference did it make which book was on top?' said he.

Louisa looked at him with a deprecating smile. 'I always keep them that way,' murmured she.

'You do beat everything,' said Dagget, trying to laugh again. His large face was flushed.

He remained about an hour longer, then rose to take leave. Going out, he stumbled over a rug, and trying to recover himself, hit Louisa's work basket on the table, and knocked it on the floor.

He looked at Louisa, then at the rolling spools; he ducked himself awkwardly toward them, but she stopped him. 'Never mind,' said she; 'I'll pick them up after you're gone.'

She spoke with a mild stiffness. Either she was a little disturbed, or his nervousness affected her, and made her seem constrained in her effort to reassure him.

When Joe Dagget was outside he drew in the sweet evening air with a sigh, and felt much as an innocent and perfectly well intentioned bear might after his exit from a china shop.

She tied on the pink, then the green apron, picked up all the scattered treasures and replaced them in her work basket, and straightened the rug. Then she set the lamp on the floor, and began sharply examining the carpet. She even rubbed her fingers over it, and looked at them.

'He's tracked in a good deal of dust,' she murmured. 'I thought he must have.'

Louisa got a dustpan and brush, and swept Joe Dagget's track carefully.

If he could have known it, it would have increased his perplexity and uneasiness, although it would not have disturbed his loyalty in the least. He came twice a week to see Louisa Ellis and every time, sitting there in her delicately sweet room, he felt as if surrounded by a hedge of lace. He was afraid to stir lest he should put a clumsy foot or hand through the fairy web, and he had always the consciousness that Louisa was watching fearfully lest he should.

Still the lace and Louisa commanded perforce his perfect respect and patience and loyalty. They were to be married in a month, after a singular courtship which had lasted for a matter of fifteen years. For fourteen out of the fifteen years the two had not once seen each other, and they had seldom exchanged letters. Joe had been all those years in Australia, where he had gone to make his fortune, and where he had stayed until he made it. He would have stayed fifty years if it had taken so long, and come home feeble and tottering, or never come home at all, to marry Louisa.

But the fortune had been made in the fourteen years, and he had come home now to marry the woman who had been patiently and unquestioningly waiting for him all that time.

Shortly after they were engaged he had announced to Louisa his determination to strike out into new fields, and secure a competency before they should be married. She had listened and assented with the sweet serenity which never failed her, not even when her lover set forth on that long and uncertain journey. Joe, buoyed up as he was by his sturdy determination, broke down a little at the last, but Louisa kissed him with a mild blush, and said goodbye.

'It won't be for long,' poor Joe had said, huskily; but it was for fourteen years.

In that length of time much had happened. Louisa's mother and brother had died, and she was all alone in the world. But the greatest happening of all – a subtle happening which both were too simple to understand – Louisa's feet had turned into a path, smooth maybe under a calm, serene sky, but so straight and unswerving that it could only meet a check at her grave, and so narrow that there was no room for any one at her side.

Louisa's first emotion when Joe Dagget came home (he had not apprised her of his coming) was consternation, although she would not admit it to herself, and he never dreamed of it. Fifteen years ago she had been in love with him – at least she considered herself to be. Just at that time, gently acquiescing with and falling into the natural drift of girlhood, she had seen marriage ahead as a reasonable feature and a probable desirability of life. She had listened with calm docility to her mother's views upon the subject. Her mother was remarkable for her cool sense and sweet, even temperament. She talked wisely to her daughter when Joe Dagget presented himself, and Louisa accepted him with no hesitation. He was the first lover she had ever had.

She had been faithful to him all these years. She had never dreamed of the possibility of marrying anyone else. Her life, especially for the last seven years, had been full of a pleasant peace, she had never felt discontented nor impatient over her lover's absence; still she had always looked forward to his return and their marriage as the inevitable conclusion of things. However, she had fallen into a way of placing it so far in the future that it was almost equal to placing it over the boundaries of another life.

When Joe came she had been expecting him, and expecting to be married for fourteen years, but she was as much surprised and taken aback as if she had never thought of it.

Joe's consternation came later. He eyed Louisa with an instant confirmation of his old admiration. She had changed but little. She still kept her pretty manner and soft grace and was, he considered, every wit as attractive as ever. As for himself, his stint was done; he had turned his face away from fortune-seeking, and the old winds of romance whistled as loud and sweet as ever through his ears. All the song which he had been wont to hear in them was Louisa; he had for a long time a loyal belief that he heard it still, but finally it seemed to him that although the winds sang always that one song, it had another name. But for Louisa the wind had never more than murmured; now it had gone down, and everything was still. She listened for a little while with half-wistful attention; then she turned quietly away and went to work on her wedding clothes.

Joe had made some extensive and quite magnificent alterations in his house. It was the old homestead; the newly-married couple would live there, for Joe could not desert his mother, who refused to leave her old home. So Louisa must leave hers. Every morning, rising and going about among her neat maidenly possessions, she felt as one looking her last upon the faces of dear friends. It was true that in a measure she could take them with her, but, robbed of their old environments, they would appear in such new guises that they would almost cease to be themselves. Then there were some peculiar features of her happy solitary life which she would probably be obliged to relinquish altogether. Sterner tasks than these graceful but half-needless ones would probably devolve upon her. There would be a large house to care for; there would be company to entertain; there would be Joe's rigorous and feeble old mother to wait upon; and it would be contrary to all thrifty village traditions for her to keep more than one servant. Louisa had a little still, and she used to occupy herself pleasantly in summer weather with distilling the sweet and aromatic essences from roses and peppermint and spearmint. By-and-by her still must be laid away. Her store of essences was already considerable, and there would be no time for her to distil for the mere pleasure of it. Then Joe's mother would think it foolishness, she had already hinted her opinion in the matter. Louisa dearly loved to sew a linen seam, not always for use, but for the simple, mild pleasure which she took in it. She would have been loath to confess how more than once she had ripped a seam for the mere delight of sewing it together again. Sitting at her window during long sweet afternoons, drawing her needle gently through the dainty fabric, she was peace itself. But there was small chance of such foolish comfort in the future. Joe's mother, domineering, shrewd old matron that she was even in her old age, and very likely even Joe himself, with his honest masculine rudeness, would laugh and frown down all these pretty but senseless old maiden ways.

Louisa had almost the enthusiasm of an artist over the mere order and cleanliness of her solitary home. She had throbs of genuine triumph at the sight of the window panes which she had polished until they shone like jewels. She gloated gently over her orderly bureau drawers, with their exquisitely folded contents redolent with lavender and sweet clover and very purity. Could she be sure of the endurance of even this? She had visions, so startling that she half repudiated them as indelicate, of coarse masculine belongings strewn about in endless litter; of dust and disorder arising necessarily from a coarse masculine presence in the midst of all this delicate harmony.

Among her forebodings of disturbance, not the least was with regard to Caesar. Caesar was a veritable hermit of a dog. For the greater part of his life he had dwelt in his secluded hut, shut out from the society of his kind and all innocent canine joys. Never had Caesar since his early youth watched at a woodchuck's hole; never had he known the delights of a stray bone at a neighbour's kitchen door. And it was all on account of a sin committed when hardly out of his puppyhood. No one knew the possible depth of remorse of which this mild visaged, altogether innocent-looking old dog might be capable; but whether or not he had encountered remorse, he had encountered a full measure of righteous retribution. Old Caesar seldom lifted up his voice in a growl or a bark; he was fat and sleepy; there were yellow rings which looked like spectacles around his dim old eyes; but there was a neighbour who bore on his hand the imprint of several of Caesar's sharp white youthful teeth, and for that he had lived at the end of a chain, all alone in a little hut, for fourteen years. The neighbour, who was choleric and smarting with the pain of his wound, had demanded either Caesar's death or complete ostracism. So Louisa's brother, to whom the dog had belonged, had built him his little kennel and tied him up. It was now fourteen years since, in a flood of youthful spirits, he had inflicted that memorable bite, and with the exception of short excursions, always at the end of the chain, under the strict guardianship of his master or Louisa, the old dog had remained a close prisoner. It is doubtful if, with his limited ambition, he took much pride in the fact, but it is certain that he was possessed of considerable cheap fame. He was regarded by all the children in the village and by many adults as a very monster of ferocity. St George's dragon could hardly have surpassed in evil repute Louisa Ellis's old yellow dog. Mothers charged their children with solemn emphasis not to go too near to him, and the children listened and believed greedily, with a fascinated appetite for terror, and ran by Louisa's house stealthily, with many sidelong and backward glances at the terrible dog. If per chance he sounded a hoarse bark, there was a panic. Wayfarers chancing into Louisa's yard eyed him with respect, and inquired if the chain were stout. Caesar at large might have seemed a very ordinary dog, and excited no comment whatever; chained, his reputation overshadowed him, so that he lost his own proper outlines and looked darkly vague and enormous. Joe Dagget, however, with his good humoured sense and shrewdness, saw him as he was. He strode valiantly up to him and patted him on the head, in spite of Louisa's clamour of warning, and even attempted to set him loose. Louisa grew so alarmed that he desisted, but kept announcing his opinion in the matter quite forcibly at intervals. 'There ain't a better-natured dog in town,' he would say, 'and it's down-right cruel to keep him tied up there. Some day I'm going to take him out.'

Louisa had very little hope that he would not, one of these days, when their interests and possessions should be more completely fused in one. She pictured to herself Caesar on the rampage through the quiet and unguarded village. She saw innocent children bleeding in his path. She was herself very fond of the old dog, because he had belonged to her dead brother, and he was always very gentle with her; still she had great faith in his ferocity. She always warned people not to go too near him. She fed him on ascetic fare of corn-mush and cakes, and never fired his dangerous temper with heating and sanguinary diet of flesh and bones. Louisa looked at the old dog munching his simple fare, and thought of her approaching marriage and trembled. Still no anticipation of disorder and confusion in lieu of sweet peace and harmony, no forebodings of Caesar on the rampage, no wild fluttering of her little yellow canary, were sufficient to turn her a hair's-breadth. Joe Dagget had been fond of her and working for her all these years. It was not for her, whatever came to pass, to prove untrue and break his heart. She put the exquisite little stitches into her wedding-garments, and the time went on until it was only a week before her wedding-day. It was a Tuesday evening, and the wedding was to be a week from Wednesday.

There was a full moon that night. About nine o'clock Louisa strolled down the road a little way. There were harvest fields on either hand, bordered by low stone walls. Luxuriant clumps of bushes grew beside the wall, and trees – wild cherry and old apple trees – at intervals. Presently Louisa sat down on the wall and looked about her with mildly sorrowful reflectiveness. Tall shrubs of blueberry and meadow-sweet, all woven together and tangled with blackberry vines and horsebriars, shut her in on either side. She had a little clear space between them. Opposite her, on the other side of the road, was a spreading tree; the moon shone between its boughs, and the leaves twinkled like silver. The road was bespread with a beautiful shifting dapple of silver and shadow; the air was full of a mysterious sweetness. 'I wonder if it's wild grapes?' murmured Louisa. She sat there some time. She was just thinking of rising, when she heard footsteps and low voices, and remained quiet. It was a lonely place, and she felt a little timid. She thought she would keep still in the shadow and let the persons, whoever they might be, pass her.

But just before they reached her the voices ceased, and the footsteps. She understood that their owners had also found seats upon the stone wall. She was wondering if she could not steal away unobserved, when the voice broke the stillness. It was Joe Dagget's. She sat still and listened.

The voice was announced by a loud sigh, which was as familiar as itself. 'Well,' said Dagget, 'you've made up your mind, then, I suppose?'

'Yes,' returned another voice; 'I'm going day after tomorrow.'

'That's Lily Dyer,' thought Louisa to herself. The voice embodied itself in her mind. She saw a girl tall and full-figured, with a firm, fair face, looking fairer and firmer in the moonlight, her strong yellow hair braided in a close knot. A girl full of a calm rustic strength and bloom, with a masterful way which might have beseemed a princess. Lily Dyer was a favourite with the village folk; she had just the qualities to arouse the admiration. She was good and handsome and smart. Louisa had often heard her praises sounded.

'Well,' said Joe Dagget, 'I ain't got a word to say.'

'I don't know what you could say,' returned Lily Dyer.

'Not a word to say,' repeated Joe, drawing out the words heavily. Then there was a silence. 'I ain't sorry,' he began at last, 'that that happened yesterday – that we kind of let on how we felt to each other. I guess it's just as well we knew. Of course I can't do anything any different. I'm going right on an' get married next week. I ain't going back on a woman that's waited for me fourteen years, an' break her heart.'

'If you should jilt her tomorrow, I wouldn't have you,' spoke up the girl, with sudden vehemence.

'Well, I ain't going to give you the chance,' said he; 'but I don't believe you would either.'

'You'd see I wouldn't. Honour's honour, an' right's right. An' I'd never think anything of any man that went against 'em for me or any other girl; you'd find that out, Joe Dagget.'

'Well, you'll find out fast enough that I ain't going against 'em for you or any other girl,' returned he. Their voices sounded almost as if they were angry with each other. Louisa was listening eagerly.

'I'm sorry you feel as if you must go away,' said Joe, 'but I don't know but it's best.'

'Of course it's best. I hope you and I have got commonsense.'

'Well, I suppose you're right.' Suddenly Joe's voice got an undertone of tenderness. 'Say, Lily,' said he, 'I'll get along well enough myself, but I can't bear to think – You don't suppose you're going to fret much over it?'

'I guess you'll find out I shan't fret much over a married man.'

'Well, I hope you won't – I hope you won't, Lily. God knows I do. And – I hope – one of these days – you'll – come across somebody else—'

'I don't see any reason why I shouldn't.' Suddenly her tone changed. She spoke in a sweet, clear voice, so loud that she could have been heard across the street. 'No, Joe Dagget,' said she, 'I'll never marry any other man as long as I live. I've got good sense, an' I ain't going to break my heart nor make a fool of myself; but I'm never going to be married, you can be sure of that. I ain't that sort of a girl to feel this way twice.'

Louisa heard an exclamation and a soft commotion behind the bushes; then Lily spoke again – the voice sounded as if she had risen. 'This must be put a stop to,' said she. 'We've stayed here long enough. I'm going home.'

Louisa sat there in a daze, listening to their retreating steps. After a while she got up and slunk softly home herself. The next day she did her housework methodically; that was as much a matter of course as breathing; but she did not sew on her wedding clothes. She sat at her window and meditated. In the evening Joe came. Louisa Ellis had never known that she had any diplomacy in her but when she came to look for it that night she found it, although meek of its kind, among her little feminine weapons. Even now she could hardly believe that she had heard aright, and that she would not do Joe a terrible injury should she break her troth plight. She wanted to sound him without betraying too soon her own inclinations in the matter. She did it successfully, and they finally came to an understanding; but it was a difficult thing, for he was as afraid of betraying himself as she.

She never mentioned Lily Dyer. She simply said that while she had no cause of complaint against him, she had lived so long in one way that she shrank from making a change.

'Well, I never shrank, Louisa,' said Dagget. 'I'm going to be honest enough to say that I think maybe it's better this way; but if you'd wanted to keep on, I'd have stuck to you till my dying day. I hope you know that.'

'Yes, I do,' said she.

That night she and Joe parted more tenderly than they had done for a long time. Standing in the door, holding each other's hands, a last great wave of regretful memory swept over him.

'Well, this ain't the way we've thought it was all going to end, is it Louisa?' said Joe.

She shook her head. There was a little quiver on her placid face.

'You let me know if there's ever anything I can do for you,' said he. 'I ain't ever going to forget you, Louisa.' Then he kissed her, and went down the path.

Louisa, all alone by herself that night, wept a little, she hardly knew why; but the next morning, on waking, she felt like a queen who, after fearing lest her domain be wrested away from her, sees it firmly insured in her possession.

Now the tall weeds and grasses might cluster around Caesar's little hermit hut, the snow might fall on its roof year in and year out, but he never would go on a rampage through the unguarded village. Now the little canary might turn itself into a peaceful yellow ball night after night, and have no need to wake and flutter with wild terror against its bars. Louisa could sew linen seams, and distil roses, and dust and polish and fold away in lavender, as long as she listed. That afternoon she sat with her needlework at the window, and felt fairly steeped in peace. Lily Dyer, tall and erect and blooming, went past; but she felt no qualm. If Louisa Ellis had sold her birthright she did not know it, the taste of the potage was so delicious, and had been her sole satisfaction for so long. Serenity and placid narrowness had become to her as the birthright itself. She gazed ahead through a long reach of future days strung together like pearls in a rosary, every one like the others, and all smooth and flawless and innocent, and her heart went up in thankfulness. Outside was the fervid summer afternoon; the air was filled with the sounds of the busy harvest of men and birds and bees; there were halloos, metallic clatterings, sweet calls, and long hummings. Louisa sat, prayerfully numbering her days like an uncloistered nun.

JUNE ARNOLD

From, Sister Gin

June Arnold is an American who was born in the South, where she spent her childhood, mostly in Houston, Texas. She took her master's degree at Rice University. She has four children and supported them by working as a teacher, while writing at the same time. She has been active in the women's liberation movement since 1969. She is a co-founder of Daughters Inc, one of the first American feminist publishing houses which built a list of original fiction by feminist writers. In her work as writer and publisher June Arnold has consistently innovated with form and subject matter, freeing women's writing from its traditional constraints. She has written four novels. Her first, Applesauce, *written in the early 60s, was first published in 1966 and reissued by Daughters in 1977.* The Cook and the Carpenter *(1973) was followed by* Sister Gin *(1975). Her most recently completed novel is* Baby Houston *(forthcoming); its theme is mother and daughter love. June Arnold is a member of PEN, the international organization of writers, and also of the Texas Institute of Letters. After some years in Vermont and New York, she has returned to Houston, Texas.*

With a late September sunset of lavender-gold behind her and the smell of fish and seawater making her hungry all over, Su stepped into the inside of her love's house for the first time. The flat straw rug made the soles of her feet ache through sandals and longed to be kissed. Mamie Carter kissed her on the cheek after the custom. Seizing that proximate cheek's smell with her nostrils, Su inhaled her reward and knew better than to kiss back.

They sat on the back porch and watched the sun set over Wrightsville Sound, on that old weathered porch of an old two-storey beach house where Mamie Carter had spent her summers as a child (and subsequently her children and then her grandchildren), one of the few houses to withstand all the hurricanes – sat listening to the leftover summer sounds of children's water games and deploring the increasing number of motored boats each season replacing the elegant sails. The martini threw a skin over Su's brain wiping out the city as they sat in the gentle decay of the day, the house softly decaying behind them, the summer itself mature and used and gracefully marked, letting out its last few days with the dignity of a menopausal woman releasing her last few eggs, knowing that they were for form only, that the season was over but there was no hurry about slipping over into the next, it will come in its season and here, these my last are as worthy as my first.

Su felt ashamed that she had been afraid . . . of Mamie Carter who was as legal in all her tentacles as old Wilmington itself; of her own passion which, here on this clan-protected porch, could be sublimated into charm as if she were a real member of that impeccable clan.

Shaking her olive free from its gregarious ice, Su heard Mamie Carter's voice off her left ear asking her to fetch them each a refill, because Captain wasn't here, because she was alone, expecting no one but Su this evening. Su took each glass in a grip firm enough to break them – someone could still drop in, would come visit, seeing the lights, her car, could drop by for hours yet, this being the tradition of the beach, the gregariousness of ice and an island.

They talked of the town's recent rapes and the bizarre circumstances of the two rapists' being laid out, tied to a board, one on the steps of the old folks' home, one in the front yard of the councilman who pulled the largest vote and was therefore mayor. Both rapists were white, short-haired, in their middle thirties, and were found nether-naked and tied outstretched to a piece of plywood in the shape of an x. Since the first rape had been of a sixty-five-year-old woman of colour, it was thought that the first man's punishment was the work of a Black Klan group. The rapist had hysterically insisted that the old woman sent five old women spirits after him but no one paid him any mind. The second rape victim had been a junior high school girl, forced at stranglehold to suck off her attacker; since she was white and since in this case too the rapist had babbled of five grannies who, though masked, had white hands, some of the townspeople wondered if there were witches still afoot.

'Posh,' Mamie Carter said. 'What kind of talk is that? Black Klans and witches. Next thing they'll say the free-booters are back haunting the Cape Fear.'

'What do you think?' Su asked.

'I think the rapists are getting a big fuss made over them. They're not the victims.'

166   *June Arnold*

'Do you think it was really ... women who did it?'

'*Old women*?' Mamie Carter's black eyes glinted with laughter. She stood up. 'You know, I can't wear flat-heel shoes any more,' she said, looking at her medium-heeled sandals below white sharkskin slacks. 'I wore high heels so long my Achilles' tendon is permanently shortened.'

'Do you?'

Su followed her strong slightly-humped back into the house. 'These slacks are from before the war. Would you feel bad if a real shark had given his skin for them?'

The inside of the house was dark after the bright twilight reflections of the porch. Mamie Carter led Su to the kitchen and flicked on the light.

'You've painted it yellow!' Su remembered to speak loud. 'Yellow is my favourite colour.'

'Mine too.' Mamie Carter's smile was a caress. 'Have you ever thought of wearing a bright yellow wig? Now don't try to talk to me while I'm fixing dinner. You know I can't hear you when my back is turned.'

'Now that streak there,' Mamie Carter said, nodding at a white swath across the middle of the dining-room table, 'was made by the yankees. They came to my grandmother's house and took everything they could. Since they didn't have any way to carry off the table, the yankee officer sent to the kitchen for some vinegar and poured it across there. It won't come off. Have some more shrimp, Su.' Mamie Carter wiped her mouth delicately and smiled. 'Old tables tell old tales.'

'Mamie Carter,' Su said, her fingers holding the ancient heavy lace of her napkin, her other fingers resting on the heavy stem of the gold-leaf wine glass, her eyes staring at that bright elfin face leaning toward her through the candlelight. 'I've never eaten such delicious shrimp.'

'It wasn't too hot, was it?' Mamie Carter had cooked the tiny North Carolina shrimp with sour cream, wine, onions, mushrooms, and a lot of cayenne. 'I don't taste anything without cayenne any more. Besides, it's the only way I can keep my grandchildren from eating every meal with me.'

'It made all other shrimp seem bland, diluted, incomplete, wan, and colourless. Unworthy of notice.' All unmarked tables, unlined faces, modern clothes, new napkins, streamlined wine glasses, all young or middle-aged things were thrown into a heap of inconsequentiality which, like herself, Su felt to be unfinished, unseasoned, green and smooth and callow. 'I think I am in love with you, Mamie Carter.'

The bright elfin face smiled broadly and did not answer.

Had she heard? In this pocket of the past, within dark wood and the dark saltiness of a September tide coming in and the faint rust smell of old screens and occasional sound of wind flapping the awnings, Su felt herself suddenly dead. She doubted that she had spoken. She had been switched into afterlife where words did not need to be spoken. She had left her amorphous dully-young fifty-year-old body behind and drifted through the definite world of the dead, the epitomized grave, the capsule of self which carried in its concentrate all the love she had ever sought. Mamie Carter did not need to hear; she would know.

A spare hand marbled with a bulging network of veins reached for Su's. 'I know.'

'Of course you do,' Su said, laughing, unable to move her own hand caught in a cave beneath that perfect antique one.

'I've known for a while.'

'Of course you have!' Su's smile was as stiff as her body balanced off the touch of that hand. 'I should have known you'd know.'

'Mamie Carter?' She held that final face taut on a thread of sight. Her hand closed across the silk bones that were Mamie Carter's hand, curled up-reaching on a free patch of sheet in the middle of a Queen Anne bed. Memory was already claiming the sight of her dimpled flesh, infinite dimples winking in their softness, skin so old it had lost all abrasives, rid itself of everything that can shield the body against the world; skin vulnerable, non-resilient, soft forever – Su's fingers had to resist the longing to take some of that flesh and mold it.

'Yes, perfect?'

Su sunk her face into the ageless curve of her love's shoulder and smothered a giggle. 'There is one extraordinary thing about us that I have to say, even here on these romantic rainswept sheets, even at the risk of hearing your "posh" ... your silk is matched only by our exquisite ability to prolong swallowing, our mutual toothlessness allowing for such a long balance on the tip of flavour: I just never imagined that the delights of age would include the fact of endlessly drawn-out orgasms. Did you always know?'

'You like it, too?'

'Without leaving us with a mouthful of cotton wadding. Without wearing down flavour. Without diminishment. With the loss of nothing at all, in fact, except fear.'

'I always thought, if old age could be beautiful, life would hold no more terrors. Now if you'll stop talking a minute, Su, I want to get up and put on my negligee.'

Mamie Carter swung her legs out of sight, turned her beautiful back, and slipped into a charcoal-red robe – really slipped, but then she had had sixty years' practice. Su saw in her mind her coveted breasts, bound flat to her chest when she was in her twenties to produce a flapper fashion, hanging now from the base of the breastbone like soft toys, too small to rest a head upon, fit for a hand to cuddle very gently like the floppy ears of a puppy.

Memory moved her hand to Mamie Carter's belly – skin white as milk, finely pucked like sugar-sprinkled clabber; memory dropped her hand to Mamie Carter's sparse hair curling like steel – there was strength between her legs and no dough there where the flesh was fluid enough to slip away from the bone and leave that tensed grain hard as granite and her upright violent part like an animal nose against Su's palm. The impact of memory bruised. Su said, to the back that could not hear, 'Don't you dare die, Mamie Carter Wilkerson.'

Now, as Su was feeling wicked lying in bed while Mamie Carter sat up in her little armchair with the rose-coloured skirt, a flash began in a tiny prickling over her upper skin. Last night, just as she had reached to kiss Mamie Carter the second time, reached towards those lips as to a dandelion, she had felt this same beginning prickle and a tear had dropped down each cheek, pre-wetting the flash with despair.

'You're flashing, Su,' Mamie Carter had said.

Tears streamed as if they would flood out the flash and Su had said helplessly, 'Why now? Why why why *now*?'

'Why not now?' Mamie Carter had said gently, laying Su back down on the bed, circling her shoulder, stroking her cheek and neck and breasts. 'Why not now?' she had said, kissing the shame from Su's flushed lips, sliding her cheek over the sweat of Su's doubly-wet cheek and slippery forehead. Her arm had reached through Su's legs and she had held her in an infant curve, whispering again, 'Why not now?' as Su slipped down into the abandon of hotly wetting herself and the flash had raged, burst, and slowly subsided.

Now, lying wickedly in bed, Su ducked under the prickles and welcomed the flash which centred her whole extraordinary body in a fever of change.

'What about Bettina?' Mamie Carter said and Bettina's voice echoed in the room, her blue quilted robe accusing.

I'll always love you, Bettina had said twenty years ago, when always had been forever. Now, with always cut in half, it seemed she had exchanged her mobility for a foundation of quicksand which would suck the house in after it. But still Bettina said it, and even now the words made her feel safe inside their sucking sound.

'*I'll* always love you, Su,' Mamie Carter said with a small dry laugh like a kick. 'Now Bettina's old enough to know better than to compare her "always" with mine . . . certainly old enough to know better than that and I naturally know exactly how old she is since her mother and I had our daughters the same month.' Mamie Carter held Su's flailing head. 'When I say always, perfect, it's an underbid.'

'Mamie,' Su said to feel the impertinence of using that bare name. 'Did you really fall in love with me?'

'No. I just wanted to get you in bed where I could hear you.'

'Now you sit among the yellow and read the paper. I'll fix breakfast,' Su said, wishing Mamie Carter were fragile so she could perch her on the breakfast table in a vase. Her hand met an upper arm as muscular as her own.

'That's yesterday's paper.'

'Well, I didn't read it. I was out all day. Doesn't news keep?'

'You didn't read the paper yesterday?'

Su put coffee on to perk and squeezed two glasses of orange juice as if this kitchen were her own. 'Why, what's in the paper? How do you like your eggs?'

'Quietly in the icebox.'

A bumping along the boardwalk and cry of *o-cree! o-cree! fresh tomatoes and o-o-o-creeeee!* came into the morning. Su sat down with a temporary cup of instant coffee and pulled the paper over. 'What's in the paper?'

'What we were talking about last night. There.'

BOUND SOCIALITE LEFT ON CORNWALLIS STEPS

Clayton Everett Eagle III, Wilmington socialite, was found tied to a board early this morning by a fish merchant, Rowland Livers. Mr Livers called the police, who reached the scene at approximately seven o'clock.

Mr Eagle, who declined to comment, was apparently the victim of the same person or persons responsible for similar incidents in the past month. He was tied, partially nude, to a piece of plywood and had been placed in the side yard by the steps leading up to the Cornwallis house sometime early this morning.

The most puzzling clue was a note pinned to his shirt reading,

Shirley Temples Emeritae. When a reporter asked the police if this might indicate that the gang responsible included some members of the fair sex, Lieutenant Francis Colleton, who described himself as an amateur Shakesperian, replied, 'If fair is foul and foul is fair.'

The question still unanswered is the reason for Mr Eagle's pillorying. The previous victims of the gang had been an alleged rapist and an alleged sodomite. The choice of the Cornwallis house might be connected to the fact that Mr Eagle recently moved to this area from New England.

'Isn't he related to you?' Su asked.

'Connected. Or was. He's kin only to Lucifer.'

'Who do you think . . . ?' A non-North Carolinian herself by birth, Su felt the reflex of an outsider who would never be able to say *ho-oose* (house) giving the word its full Chaucerian diphthong like a native. Although she was not a yankee, she wondered if Clayton Eagle had gotten himself labelled 'outside agitator' and prepared to draw in her liberal skirts against this Temple gang.

'Now that's just damned nonsense, Su. We're not still fighting the War Between the States here. You know we'd already voted not to secede, but when they opened fire on our cousins, then we had to. South Carolina was family – we weren't even separated until 1729. No, I think Mr Eagle has more to answer for than his misfortune of a birthplace. The Temple Gang. I like that.'

Driving back across the causeway that separated land from land, Su threw her words wide so they could skip across the gray glass of Wrightsville Sound: 'Change of life by definition refers to the future; one life is finishing therefore another life must be beginning. The menopausal armies mass on the brink of every city and suburb; everything that was is over and there is nothing left there to keep our sights lowered. See the rifles raised? This army doesn't travel on its uterus any more. Bettina, you must see that to stay back in that young section with you when I can reach out to age itself, lust after a final different dry silken life and so much grace and elegance from all that knowledge of days . . . There is no more beautiful word in the language than withered.'

WILLA CATHER

A Wagner Matinée

Willa Cather (1873-1947) was born in Virginia, one of seven children, and moved to Nebraska with her family at the age of nine. She was brought up among farming people and had an unusually free childhood. She did not go to school until quite late, having been educated at first by her two grandmothers. She went to the University of Nebraska and while she was still a student started to write theatre reviews for the Nebraska State Journal *in order to help support herself. After she graduated, she lived in Pittsburg, working first for a women's magazine and then for a daily newspaper, later switching to teaching so that she would have the long summer holidays free for writing. At this period she was writing poetry and short stories (including 'A Wagner Matinée'), which were published in magazines and then in book form, and in 1906 she moved to New York and started to work for* McClure's Magazine. *Her first novel (*Alexander Bridge*) was published in 1912 and* O Pioneers! *a year later, and with this second novel, she achieved critical success. She was able to support herself by her writing and was a popular as well as a critically acclaimed success.* One of Ours *won the Pulitzer prize and she was awarded several honorary degrees. She lived permanently in New York with Edith Lewis, who wrote an informal biography of her after her death.*

I received one morning a letter, written in pale ink on glassy, blue-lined notepaper, and bearing the postmark of a little Nebraska village. This communication, worn and rubbed, looking as if it had been carried for some days in a coat pocket that was none too clean, was from my uncle Howard, and informed me that his wife had been left a small legacy by a bachelor relative, and that it would be necessary for her to go to Boston to attend to the settling of the estate. He requested me to meet her at the station and render her whatever services might be necessary. On examining the date indicated as that of her arrival, I found it to be no later than tomorrow. He had characteristically delayed writing until, had I been away from home for a day, I must have missed my aunt altogether.

The name of my Aunt Georgiana opened before me a gulf of recollection so wide and deep that, as the letter dropped from my hand, I felt suddenly a stranger to all the present conditions of my existence, wholly ill at ease and out of place amid the familiar surroundings of my study. I became, in short, the gangling farmer-boy my aunt had known, scourged with chilblains and bashfulness, my hands cracked and sore from the corn husking. I sat again before her parlour organ, fumbling the scales with my stiff, red fingers, while she, beside me, made canvas mittens for the huskers.

The next morning, after preparing my landlady for a visitor, I set out for the station. When the train arrived I had some difficulty in finding my aunt. She was the last of the passengers to alight, and it was not until I got her into the carriage that she seemed really to recognize me. She had come all the way in a day coach; her linen duster had become black with soot and her black bonnet grey with dust during the journey. When we arrived at my boarding-house the landlady put her to bed at once and I did not see her again until the next morning.

Whatever shock Mrs Springer experienced at my aunt's appearance, she considerately concealed. As for myself, I saw my aunt's battered figure with that feeling of awe and respect with which we behold explorers who have left their ears and fingers north of Franz-Joseph-Land, or their health somewhere along the Upper Congo. My Aunt Georgiana had been a music teacher at the Boston Conservatory, somewhere back in the latter sixties. One summer, while visiting in the little village among the Green Mountains where her ancestors had dwelt for generations, she had kindled the callow fancy of my uncle, Howard Carpenter, then an idle, shiftless boy of twenty-one. When she returned to her duties in Boston, Howard followed her, and the upshot of this infatuation was that she eloped with him, eluding the reproaches of her family and the criticism of her friends by going with him to the Nebraska frontier. Carpenter, who, of course, had no money, took up a homestead in Red Willow County, fifty miles from the railroad. There they had measured off their land themselves, driving across the prairie in a wagon, to the wheel of which they had tied a red cotton handkerchief, and counting its revolutions. They built a dug-out in the red hillside, one of those cave dwellings whose inmates so often reverted to primitive conditions. Their water they got from the lagoons where the buffalo drank, and their slender stock of provisions was always at the mercy of bands of roving Indians. For thirty years my aunt had not been farther than fifty miles from the homestead.

I owed to this woman most of the good that ever came my way in my boyhood, and had a reverential affection for her. During the years when I was riding herd for my uncle, my aunt, after cooking the three meals – the first of which was ready at six o'clock in the morning – and putting the six children to bed, would often stand until midnight at her ironing-board, with me at the kitchen table beside her, hearing me recite Latin declensions and conjugations, gently shaking me when my drowsy head sank down over a page of irregular verbs. It was to her, at her ironing or mending, that I read my first Shakespeare, and her old text book on mythology was the first that ever came into my empty hands. She taught me my scales and exercises on the little parlour organ which her husband had bought her after fifteen years during which she had not so much as seen a musical instrument. She would sit beside me by the hour, darning and counting, while I struggled with the 'Joyous Farmer'. She seldom talked to me about music, and I understood why. Once when I had been doggedly beating out some easy passages from an old score of *Euryanthe* I had found among her music books, she came up to me and, putting her hands over my eyes, gently drew my head back upon her shoulder, saying tremulously, 'Don't love it so well, Clark, or it may be taken from you.'

When my aunt appeared on the morning after her arrival in Boston, she was still in a semi-somnambulant state. She seemed not to realize that she was in the city where she had spent her youth, the place longed for hungrily half a lifetime. She had been so wretchedly train-sick throughout the journey that she had no recollection of anything but her discomfort and, to all intents and purposes, there were but a few hours of nightmare between the farm in Red Willow County and my study on Newbury Street. I had planned a little pleasure for her that afternoon, to repay her for some of the glorious moments she had given me when we used to milk together in the straw-thatched cowshed and she, because I was more than usually tired, or because her husband had spoken sharply to me, would tell me of the splendid performance of the *Huguenots* she had seen in Paris, in her youth.

At two o'clock the Symphony Orchestra was to give a Wagner programme, and I intended to take my aunt; though as I conversed with her, I grew doubtful about her enjoyment of it. I suggested our visiting the Conservatory and the Common before lunch, but she seemed altogether too timid to wish to venture out. She questioned me absently about various changes in the city, but she was chiefly concerned that she had forgotten to leave instructions about feeding half-skimmed milk to a certain weakling calf, 'old Maggie's calf, you know, Clark,' she explained, evidently having forgotten how long I had been away. She was further troubled because she had neglected to tell her daughter about the freshly-opened kit of mackerel in the cellar, which would spoil if it were not used directly.

I asked her whether she had ever heard any of the Wagnerian operas, and found that she had not, though she was perfectly familiar with their respective situations, and had once possessed the piano score of the *The Flying Dutchman*. I began to think it would be best to get her back to Red Willow County without waking her, and regretted having suggested the concert.

From the time we entered the concert hall, however, she was a trifle less passive and inert, and for the first time seemed to perceive her surroundings. I had felt some trepidation lest she might become aware of her queer, country clothes, or might experience some painful embarrassment at stepping suddenly into the world to which she had been dead for a quarter of a century. But, again, I found how superficially I had judged her. She sat looking about her with eyes as impersonal, almost as stony, as those with which the granite Rameses in a museum watches the froth and fret that ebbs and flows about his pedestal. I have seen this same aloofness in old miners who drift into the Brown hotel at Denver, their pockets full of bullion, their linen soiled, their haggard faces unshaven; standing in the thronged corridors as solitary as though they were still in a frozen camp on the Yukon.

The matinée audience was made up chiefly of women. One lost the contour of faces and figures, indeed any effect of line whatever, and there was only the colour of bodices past counting, the shimmer of fabrics soft and firm, silky and sheer; red, mauve, pink, blue, lilac, purple, écru, rose, yellow, cream, and white, all the colours that an impressionist finds in a sunlit landscape, with here and there the dead shadow of a frock coat. My Aunt Georgiana regarded them as though they had been so many daubs of tube paint on a palette.

When the musicians came out and took their places, she gave a little stir of anticipation, and looked with quickening interest down over the rail at that invariable grouping, perhaps the first wholly familiar thing that had greeted her eye since she had left old Maggie and her weakling calf. I could feel how all those details sank into her soul, for

I had not forgotten how they had sunk into mine when I came fresh from ploughing forever and forever between green aisles of corn, where, as in a treadmill, one might walk from daybreak to dusk without perceiving a shadow of change. The clean profiles of the musicians, the gloss of their linen, the dull black of their coats, the beloved shapes of the instruments, the patches of yellow light on the smooth, varnished bellies of the 'cellos and the bass viols in the rear, the restless, wind-tossed forest of fiddle necks and bows – I recalled how, in the first orchestra I ever heard, those long bow-strokes seemed to draw the heart out of me, as a conjurer's stick reels out yards of paper ribbon from a hat.

The first number was the *Tannhäuser* overture. When the horns drew out the first strain of the Pilgrim's chorus, Aunt Georgiana clutched my coat sleeve. Then it was I first realized that for her this broke a silence of thirty years. With the battle between the two motives, with the frenzy of the Venusberg theme and its ripping of strings, there came to me an overwhelming sense of the waste and wear we are so powerless to combat; and I saw again the tall, naked house on the prairie, black and grim as a wooden fortress; the black pond where I had learned to swim, its margin pitted with sun-dried cattle tracks; the rain gullied clay banks about the naked house, the four dwarf ash seedlings where the dishcloths were always hung to dry before the kitchen door. The world there was the flat world of the ancients; to the east, a cornfield that stretched to daybreak; to the west, a corral that reached to sunset; between, the conquests of peace, dearer-bought than those of war.

The overture closed, my aunt released my coat sleeve, but she said nothing. She sat staring dully at the orchestra. What, I wondered, did she get from it? She had been a good pianist in her day, I knew, and her musical education had been broader than that of most music teachers of a quarter of a century ago. She had often told me of Mozart's operas and Meyerbeer's, and I could remember hearing her sing, years ago, certain melodies of Verdi. When I had fallen ill with a fever in her house she used to sit by my cot in the evening – when the cool, night wind blew in through the faded mosquito netting tacked over the window and I lay watching a certain bright star that burned red above the cornfield – and sing 'Home to our mountains, O, let us return!' in a way fit to break the heart of a Vermont boy near dead of homesickness already.

I watched her closely through the prelude to *Tristan and Isolde*, trying vainly to conjecture what that seething turmoil of strings and winds might mean to her, but she sat mutely staring at the violin bows that drove obliquely downward, like the pelting streaks of rain in a summer shower. Had this music any message for her? Had she enough left to at all comprehend this power which had kindled the world since she had left it? I was in a fever of curiosity, but Aunt Georgiana sat silent upon her peak in Darien. She preserved this utter immobility throughout the number from *The Flying Dutchman*, though her fingers worked mechanically upon her black dress, as if, of themselves, they were recalling the piano score they had once played. Poor hands! They had been stretched and twisted into mere tentacles to hold and lift and knead with – on one of them a thin, worn band that had once been a wedding ring. As I pressed and gently quieted one of those groping hands, I remembered with quivering eyelids their services for me in other days.

Soon after the tenor began the 'Prize Song', I heard a quick drawn breath and turned to my aunt. Her eyes were closed, but the tears were glistening on her cheeks, and I think, in a moment more, they were in my eyes as well. It never really died, then – the soul which can suffer so excruciatingly and so interminably; it withers to the outward eye only; like that strange moss which can lie on a dusty shelf half a century and yet, if placed in water, grows green again. She wept so throughout the development and elaboration of the melody.

During the intermission before the second half, I questioned my aunt and found that the 'Prize Song' was not new to her. Some years before there had drifted to the farm in Red Willow County a young German, a tramp cow-puncher, who had sung in the chorus at Bayreuth when he was a boy, along with the other peasant boys and girls. Of a Sunday morning he used to sit on his gingham-sheeted bed in the hands' bedroom which opened off the kitchen, cleaning the leather of his boots and saddle, singing the 'Prize Song', while my aunt went about her work in the kitchen. She had hovered over him until she had prevailed upon him to join the country church, though his sole fitness for this step, in so far as I could gather, lay in his boyish face and his possession of this divine melody. Shortly afterward, he had gone to town on the Fourth of July, been drunk for several days, lost his money at a faro table, ridden a saddled Texas steer on a bet, and disappeared with a fractured collar-bone. All this my aunt told me huskily, wanderingly, as though she were talking in the weak lapses of illness.

'Well, we have come to better things than the old *Trovatore* at any rate, Aunt Georgie?' I queried, with a well meant effort at jocularity.

Her lips quivered and she hastily put her handkerchief up to her mouth. From behind it she murmured, 'And you have been hearing this ever since you left me, Clark?' Her question was the gentlest and saddest of reproaches.

The second half of the programme consisted of four numbers from the *Ring*, and closed with Siegfried's funeral march. My aunt wept quietly, but almost continuously, as a shallow vessel overflows in a rain-storm. From time to time her dim eyes looked up at the lights, burning softly under their dull glass globes.

The deluge of sound poured on and on; I never knew what she found in the shining current of it; I never knew how far it bore her, or past what happy islands. From the trembling of her face I could well believe that before the last number she had been carried out where the myriad graves are, into the grey, nameless burying grounds of the sea; or into some world of death vaster yet, where, from the beginning of the world, hope has lain down with hope and dream with dream and, renouncing, slept.

The concert was over; the people filed out of the hall chattering and laughing, glad to relax and find the living level again, but my kinswoman made no effort to rise. The harpist slipped the green felt cover over his instrument; the flute-players shook the water from their mouthpieces; the men of the orchestra went out one by one, leaving the stage to the chairs and music stands, empty as a winter cornfield.

I spoke to my aunt. She burst into tears and sobbed pleadingly. 'I don't want to go, Clark, I don't want to go!'

I understood. For her, just outside the concert hall, lay the black pond with the cattle-tracked bluffs; the tall, unpainted house, with weather-curled boards, naked as a tower; the crook-backed ash seedlings where the dishclothes hung to dry; the gaunt, moulting turkeys picking up refuse about the kitchen door.

SARAH ORNE JEWETT

The Flight of Betsey Lane

Sarah Orne Jewett (1849-1909) was born in South Berwick, Maine, the second of three daughters in a well-off family. She was a sickly rheumatic child and her father, a country doctor, took her on his rounds when she was away from school, bringing her into contact with a variety of people. She was educated at the village school and had four years' secondary education at a local academy. She decided early in life not to marry and her first story was published when she was eighteen. Her stories, both for children and adults, were published in periodicals, and her first collection Deerhaven, *using local New England subject matter, appeared in 1877. Her father, whom she was close to, died in 1878, and she never completely recovered from his death. A few years later she began a life-long friendship with Annie Fields, a woman fifteen years older than herself. She spent six months of each year with Mrs Fields after she was widowed, in Boston and on the coast, and they made four trips to Europe together. She had a life free of domestic responsibilities, both with Annie Fields and in her own home where one of her sisters did the housekeeping, and there were no children in either house. At the age of fifty-three, she was thrown from a carriage and injured, and the accident left her weakened and virtually unable to write. Her character was marked by a nostalgia for the past and a Peter Pan wish not to grow up ('she never put her doll away', Annie Fields wrote of her). She wrote short stories and, less successfully, novels, chiefly about New England, and is best known for* The Country of the Pointed Firs *(1896).*

One windy morning in May, three old women sat together near an open window in the shed chamber of Byfleet poorhouse. The wind was from the north-west, but their window faced the south-east, and they were only visited by an occasional pleasant waft of fresh air. They were close together, knee to knee, picking over a bushel of beans, and commanding a view of the dandelion-starred, green yard below, and of the winding, sandy road that led to the village, two miles away. Some captive bees were scolding among the cobwebs of the rafters overhead, or thumping against the upper panes of glass; two calves were bawling from the barnyard, where some of the men were at work loading a dump-cart and shouting as if everyone were deaf. There was a cheerful feeling of activity, and even an air of comfort, about the Byfleet poorhouse. Almost everyone was possessed of a most interesting past, though there was less to be said about the future. The inmates were by no means distressed or unhappy; many of them retired to this shelter only for the winter season, and would go out presently, some to begin such work as they could still do, others to live in their own small houses; old age had impoverished most of them by limiting their power of endurance; but far from lamenting the fact that they were town charges, they rather liked the change and excitement of a winter residence on the poorfarm. There was a sharp-faced, hard worked young widow with seven children, who was an exception to the general level of society, because she deplored the change in her fortunes. The older women regarded her with suspicion, and were apt to talk about her in moments like this, when they happened to sit together at their work.

The three bean pickers were dressed alike in stout brown ginghams, checked by a white line, and all wore great faded aprons of blue drilling, with sufficient pockets convenient to the right hand. Miss Peggy Bond was a very small, belligerent looking person, who wore a huge pair of steel-bowed spectacles, holding her sharp chin well up in air, as if to supplement an inadequate nose. She was more than half blind, but the spectacles seemed to face upward instead of square ahead, as if their wearer were always on the sharp lookout for birds. Miss Bond had suffered much personal damage from time to time, because she never took heed where she planted her feet, and so was always tripping and stubbing her bruised way through the world. She had fallen down hatchways and cellarways, and stepped composedly into deep ditches and pasture brooks; but she was proud of stating that she was upsighted, and so was her father before her. At the poorhouse, where an unusual malady was considered a distinction, upsightedness was looked upon as a most honourable infirmity. Plain rheumatism, such as afflicted Aunt Lavina Dow, whose twisted hands found even this light work difficult and tiresome – plain rheumatism was something of everyday occurrence, and nobody cared to hear about it. Poor Peggy was a meek and friendly soul, who never put herself forward;

she was just like other folks, as she always loved to say, but Mrs Lavina Dow was a different sort of person altogether, of great dignity and, occasionally, almost aggressive behaviour. The time had been when she could do a good day's work with anybody: but for many years now she had not left the town farm, being too badly crippled to work; she had no relations or friends to visit, but from an innate love of authority she could not submit to being one of those who are forgotten by the world. Mrs Dow was the hostess and social lawgiver here, where she remembered every inmate and every item of interest for nearly forty years, besides an immense amount of town history and biography for three or four generations back.

She was the dear friend of the third woman, Betsey Lane; together they led thought and opinion – chiefly opinion – and held sway, not only over Byfleet poorfarm, but also the selectmen and all others in authority. Betsey Lane had spent most of her life as aid-in-general to the respected household of old General Thornton. She had been much trusted and valued, and, at the breaking up of that once large and flourishing family, she had been left in good circumstances, what with legacies and her own comfortable savings; but by sad misfortune and lavish generosity everything had been scattered, and after much illness, which ended in a stiffened arm and more uncertainty, the good soul had sensibly decided that it was easier for the whole town to support her than for a part of it. She had always hoped to see something of the world before she died; she came of an adventurous, seafaring stock, but had never made a longer journey than to the towns of Danby and Northville, thirty miles away.

They were all old women; but Betsey Lane, who was sixty-nine, and looked much older, was the youngest. Peggy Bond was far on in the seventies, and Mrs Dow was at least ten years older. She made a great secret of her years; and as she sometimes spoke of events prior to the Revolution with the assertion of having been an eye-witness, she naturally wore an air of vast antiquity. Her tales were an inexpressible delight to Betsey Lane, who felt younger by twenty years because her friend and comrade was so unconscious of chronological limitations.

The bushel basket of cranberry beans was within easy reach, and each of the pickers had filled her lap from it again and again. The shed chamber was not an unpleasant place in which to sit at work, with its traces of seed corn hanging from the brown crossbeams, its spare churns, and dusty loom, and rickety wool-wheels, and a few bits of old furniture. In one far corner was a wide board of dismal use and suggestion, and close beside it an old cradle. There was a battered chest of drawers where the keeper of the poorhouse kept his garden-seeds, with the withered remains of three seed cucumbers ornamenting the top. Nothing beautiful could be discovered, nothing interesting, but there was something usable and homely about the place. It was the favourite and untroubled bower of the bean-pickers, to which they might retreat unmolested from the public apartments of this rustic institution.

Betsey Lane blew away the chaff from her handful of beans. The spring breeze blew the chaff back again, and sifted it over her face and shoulders. She rubbed it out of her eyes impatiently, and happened to notice old Peggy holding her own handful high, as if it were an oblation, and turning her queer, up-tilted head this way and that, to look at the beans sharply, as if she were first cousin to a hen.

'There, Miss Bond, 't is kind of botherin' work for you, ain't it?' Betsey inquired compassionately.

'I feel to enjoy it, anything I can do my own way so,' responded Peggy. 'I like to do my part. Ain't that old Mis' Fales comin' up the road? It sounds like her step.'

The others looked, but they were not far-sighted, and for a moment Peggy had the advantage. Mrs Fales was not a favourite.

'I hope she ain't comin' here to put up this spring. I guess she won't now, it's gettin' so late,' said Betsey Lane. 'She likes to go rovin' soon as the roads is settled.'

''T is Mis' Fales!' said Peggy Bond, listening with solemn anxiety. 'There, do let's pray her by!'

'I guess she's headin' for her cousin's folks up Beech Hill way,' said Betsey presently. 'If she'd left her daughter's this mornin', she'd have got just about as far as this. I kind o' wish she had stepped in just to pass the time o' day, long 's she wa'n't going to make no stop.'

There was a silence as to further speech in the shed chamber; and even the calves were quiet in the barnyard. The men had all gone away to the field where corn-planting was going on. The beans clicked steadily into the wooden measure at the pickers' feet. Betsey Lane began to sing a hymn, and the others joined in as best they might, like autumnal crickets; their voices were sharp and cracked, with now and then a few low notes of plaintive tone. Betsey herself could sing pretty well, but the others could only make a kind of accompaniment. Their voices ceased altogether at the higher notes.

'Oh my! I wish I had the means to go to the Centennial,' mourned Betsey Lane, stopping so suddenly that the others had to go on croaking and shrilling without her for a moment before they could stop. 'It seems to me as if I can't die happy 'less I do,' she added; 'I ain't never seen nothin' of the world, an' here I be.'

'What if you was as old as I be?' suggested Mrs Dow pompously. 'You've got time enough yet, Betsey; don't you go an' despair. I knowed of a woman that went clean round the world four times when she was past eighty, an' enjoyed herself real well. Her folks followed the sea; she had three sons an' a daughter married – all ship-masters, and she'd been with her own husband when they was young. She was left a widder early, and fetched up her family herself – a real stirrin', smart woman. After they'd got married off, an' settled, an' was doing well, she come to be lonesome; and first she tried to stick it out alone, but she wa'n't one that could; an' she got a notion she hadn't nothin' before her but her last sickness, and she wa'n't a person that enjoyed havin' other folks do for her. So one of her boys – I guess't was the oldest – said he was going to take her to sea; there was ample room, an' he was sailin' a good time o' year for the Cape o' Good Hope an' way up to some o' them tea-ports in the Chiny Seas. She was all high to go, but it made a sight o' talk at her age; an' the minister made it a subject o' prayer the last Sunday, and all the folks took a last leave; but she said to some she'd fetch 'em home something real pritty, and so did. An' then they come home t' other way, round the Horn, an' she done so well, an' was such a sight o' company, the other child'n was jealous, an' she promised she'd go a v'y'ge long o' each on 'em. She was as sprightly a person as ever I see; an' could speak well o' what she'd seen.'

'Did she die to sea?' asked Peggy, with interest.

'No, she died to home between v'y'ges, or she'd gone to sea again. I was to her funeral. She liked her son George's ship the best; 't was the one she was going on to Callao. They said the men aboard all called her "gran'ma'am," an' she kep' 'em mended up, an' would go below and tend to 'em if they was sick. She might 'a' been alive an' enjoyin' of herself a good many years but for the kick of a cow; 't was a new cow out of a drove, a dreadful unruly beast.'

Mrs Dow stopped for breath, and reached down for a new supply of beans; her empty apron was grey with soft chaff. Betsey Lane, still pondering on the Centennial, began to sing another verse of her hymn, and again the old women joined her. At this moment some strangers came driving round into the yard from the front of the house. The turf was soft, and our friends did not hear the horses' steps. Their voices cracked and quavered; it was a funny little concert, and a lady in an open carriage just below listened with sympathy and amusement.

'Betsey! Betsey! Miss Lane!' a voice called eagerly at the foot of the stairs that led up from the shed. 'Betsey! There's a lady here wants to see you right away.'

Betsey was dazed with excitement, like a country child who knows the rare pleasure of being called out of school. 'Lor', I ain't fit to go down, be I?' she faltered, looking anxiously at her friends; but Peggy was gazing even nearer to the zenith than usual, in her excited effort to see down into the yard, and Mrs Dow only nodded somewhat jealously, and said that she guessed 't was nobody would do her any harm. She rose ponderously, while Betsey hesitated, being, as they would have said, all of a twitter. 'It is a lady, certain,' Mrs Dow assured her; ''tain't often there's a lady comes here.'

'While there was any of Mis' Gen'ral Thornton's folks left, I wa'n't without visits from the gentry,' said Betsey Lane, turning back proudly at the head of the stairs, with a touch of old-world pride and sense of high station. Then she disappeared, and closed the door behind her at the stair foot with a decision quite unwelcome to the friends above.

'She needn't 'a' been so dreadful 'fraid anybody was goin' to listen. I guess we've got folks to ride an' see us, or had once, if we hain't now,' said Miss Peggy Bond, plaintively.

'I expect 't was only the wind shoved it to,' said Aunt Lavina. 'Betsey is one that gits flustered easier than some. I wish 't was somebody to take her off an' give her a kind of a good time; she's young to settle down 'long of old folks like us. Betsey's got a notion o' rovin' such as ain't my natur', but I should like to see her satisfied. She'd been a very understandin' person, if she had the advantages that some does.'

''T is so,' said Peggy Bond, tilting her chin high. 'I suppose you can't hear nothin' they're saying? I feel my hearin' ain't up to what it was. I can hear things close to me well as ever; but there, hearin' ain't everything; 't ain't as if we lived where there was more goin' on to hear. Seems to me them folks is stoppin' a good while.'

'They surely be,' agreed Lavina Dow.

'I expect it's somethin' particular. There ain't none of the Thornton folks left, except one o' the gran'darters, an' I've often heard Betsey remark that she should never see her more, for she lives to London. Strange how folks feels contented in them strayaway places off to the ends of the airth.'

The flies and bees were buzzing against the hot window panes; the handfuls of beans were clicking into the brown wooden measure. A bird came and perched on the window-sill, and then flitted away toward the blue sky. Below, in the yard, Betsey Lane stood talking with the lady. She had put her blue drilling apron over her head, and her face was shining with delight.

'Lor', dear,' she said, for at least the third time, 'I remember ye when I first see ye; an awful pritty baby you was, an' they all said you looked just like the old gen'ral. Be you goin' back to foreign parts right away?'

'Yes, I'm going back; you know that all my children are there. I wish I could take you with me for a visit,' said the charming young guest. 'I'm going to carry over some of the pictures and furniture from the old house; I didn't care half so much for them when I was younger as I do now. Perhaps next summer we shall all come over for a while. I should like to see my girls and boys playing under the pines.'

'I wish you re'lly was livin' to the old place,' said Betsey Lane. Her imagination was not swift; she needed time to think over all that was being told her, and she could not fancy the two strange houses across the sea. The old Thornton house was to her mind the most delightful and elegant in the world.

'Is there anything I can do for you?' asked Mrs Strafford kindly — 'anything that I can do for you myself, before I go away? I shall be writing to you, and sending some pictures of the children, and you must let me know how you are getting on.'

'Yes, there is one thing, darlin'. If you could stop in the village an' pick me out a pretty, little, small lookin' glass, that I can keep for my own an' have to remember you by. 'T ain't that I want to see me above the rest o' the folks, but I was always used to havin' my own when I was to your grandma's. There's very nice folks here, some on 'em, and I'm better off than if I was able to keep the house; but sence you ask me, that's the only thing I feel cropin' about. What be you goin' right back for? ain't you goin' to see the great fair to Pheladelphy, that everybody talks about?'

'No,' said Mrs Strafford, laughing at this eager and almost convicting question. 'No; I'm going back next week. If I were, I believe that I should take you with me. Goodbye, dear old Betsey; you make me feel as if I were a little girl again; you look just the same.'

For full five minutes the old woman stood out in the sunshine, dazed with delight, and majestic with a sense of her own consequence. She held something tight in her hand, without thinking what it might be; but just as the friendly mistress of the poorfarm came out to hear the news, she tucked the roll of money into the bosom of her brown gingham dress. "'T was my dear Mis' Katy Strafford,' she turned to say proudly. 'She come way over from London; she's been sick; they thought the voyage would do her good. She said most the first thing she had on her mind was to come an' find me, and see how I was, an' if I was comfortable; an' now she's goin' right back. She's got two splendid houses; an' said how she wished I was there to look after things – she remembered I was always her gran'ma's right hand. Oh, it does so carry me back, to see her! Seems if all the rest on 'em must be there together to the old house. There, I must go right up an' tell Mis' Dow an' Peggy.'

'Dinner's all ready; I was just goin' to blow the horn for the men-folks,' said the keeper's wife. 'They'll be right down. I expect you've got along smart with them beans – all three of you together'; but Betsey's mind roved so high and so far at that moment that no achievements of beanpicking could lure it back.

The long table in the great kitchen soon gathered its company of waifs and strays – creatures of improvidence and misfortune, and the irre-parable victims of old age. The dinner was satisfactory, and there was not much delay for conversation. Peggy Bond and Mrs Dow and Betsey Lane always sat together at one end, with an air of putting the rest of the company below the salt. Betsey was still flushed with excite-ment; in fact, she could not eat as much as usual, and she looked up from time to time expectantly, as if she were likely to be asked to speak to her guest; but everybody was hungry, and even Mrs Dow broke in upon some attempted confidences by asking inopportunely for a second potato. There were nearly twenty at the table, counting the keeper and his wife and two children, noisy little persons who had come from school with the small flock belonging to the poor widow, who sat just opposite our friends. She finished her dinner before any-one else, and pushed her chair back; she always helped with the house-work – a thin, sorry, bad-tempered-looking poor soul, whom grief had sharpened instead of softening. 'I expect you feel too fine to set with common folks,' she said enviously to Betsey.

'Here I be a-settin',' responded Betsey calmly. 'I don' know's I be-have more unbecomin' than usual.' Betsey prided herself upon her good and proper manners; but the rest of the company, who would have liked to hear the bit of morning news, were now defrauded of that pleasure. The wrong note had been struck; there was a silence after the clatter of knives and plates, and one by one the cheerful town charges disappeared. The beanpicking had been finished, and there was a call for any of the women who felt like planting corn; so Peggy Bond, who could follow the line of hills pretty fairly, and Betsey herself, who was still equal to anybody at that work, and Mrs Dow, all went out to the field together. Aunt Lavina laboured slowly up the yard, carrying a light splint-bottomed kitchen chair and her knitting-work, and sat near the stone wall on a gentle rise, where she could see the pond and the green country, and exchange a word with her friends as they came and went up and down the rows. Betsey vouchsafed a word now and then about Mrs Strafford, but you would have thought that she had been suddenly elevated to Mrs Strafford's own cares and the responsibilities attending them, and had little in common with her old associates. Mrs Dow and Peggy knew well that these high-feeling times never lasted long, and so they waited with as much patience as they could muster. They were by no means without that true tact which is only another word for unselfish sympathy.

The strip of corn land ran along the side of a great field; at the upper end of it was a field-corner thicket of young maples and walnut saplings, the children of a great nut-tree that marked the boundary. Once, when Betsey Lane found herself alone near this shelter at the end of her row, the other planters having lagged behind beyond the rising ground, she looked stealthily about, and then put her hand inside her gown, and for the first time took out the money that Mrs Strafford had given her. She turned it over and over with an astonished look: there were new bank bills for a hundred dollars. Betsey gave a funny little shrug of her shoulders, came out of the bushes, and took a step or two on the narrow edge of turf, as if she were going to dance; then she hastily tucked away her treasure, and stepped discreetly down into the soft harrowed and hoed land, and began to drop corn again, five kernels to a hill. She had seen the top of Peggy Bond's head over the knoll, and now Peggy herself came entirely into view, gazing upward to the skies, and stumbling more or less, but counting the corn by touch and twisting her head about anxiously to gain advantage over her uncertain vision. Betsey made a friendly, inarticulate little sound as they passed; she was thinking that somebody said once that Peggy's eyesight might be remedied if she could go to Boston to the hospital; but that was so remote and impossible an undertaking that no one had ever taken the first step. Betsey Lane's brown old face suddenly worked with excitement, but in a moment more she regained her usual firm expression, and spoke carelessly to Peggy as she turned and came alongside.

The high spring wind of the morning had quite fallen; it was a lovely May afternoon. The woods about the field to the northward were full of birds, and the young leaves scarcely hid the solemn shapes of a company of crows that patiently attended the corn-planting. Two of the men had finished their hoeing, and were busy with the construction of a scarecrow; they knelt in the furrows, chuckling, and looking over some forlorn, discarded garments. It was a time-honoured custom to make the scarecrow resemble one of the poorhouse family; and this year they intended to have Mrs Lavina Dow protect the field in effigy; last year it was the counterfeit of Betsey Lane who stood on guard, with an easily recognized quilted hood and the remains of a valued shawl that one of the calves had found airing on a fence and chewed to pieces. Behind the men was the foundation for this rustic attempt at statuary – an upright stake and bar in the form of a cross. This stood on the highest part of the field; and as the men knelt near it, and the quaint figures of the cornplanters went and came, the scene gave a curious suggestion of foreign life. It was not like New England; the presence of the rude cross appealed strangely to the imagination.

Life flowed so smoothly, for the most part, at the Byfleet poorfarm, that nobody knew what to make, later in the summer, of a strange disappearance. All the elder inmates were familiar with illness and death, and the poor pomp of a town pauper's funeral. The comings and goings and the various misfortunes of those who composed this strange family, related only through its disasters, hardly served for the excitement and talk of a single day. Now that the June days were at their longest, the old people were sure to wake earlier than ever; but one morning, to the astonishment of everyone, Betsey Lane's bed was empty; the sheets and blankets, which were her own, and guarded with jealous care, were carefully folded and placed on a chair not too near the window, and Betsey had flown. Nobody had heard her go down the creaking stairs. The kitchen door was unlocked, and the old watchdog lay on the step outside in the early sunshine, wagging his tail and looking wise, as if he were left on guard and meant to keep the fugitive's secret.

'Never knowed her to do nothin' afore 'thout talking it over a fortnight, and paradin' off when we could all see her,' ventured a spiteful voice. 'Guess we can wait till night to hear 'bout it.'

Mrs Dow looked sorrowful and shook her head. 'Betsey had an aunt on her mother's side that went and drownded of herself; she was as pritty-appearing woman as ever you see.'

'Perhaps she's gone to spend the day with Decker's folks,' suggested

Peggy Bond. 'She always takes an extra early start; she was speakin' lately o' going up their ways'; but Mrs Dow shook her head with a most melancholy look. 'I'm impressed that something's befell her,' she insisted. 'I heard her a-groanin' in her sleep. I was wakeful the forepart o' the night – 't is very unusual with me, too.'

''T wa'n't like Betsey not to leave us any word,' said the other old friend, with more resentment than melancholy. They sat together almost in silence that morning in the shed chamber. Mrs Dow was sorting and cutting rags, and Peggy braided them into long ropes, to be made into mats at a later date. If they had only known where Betsey Lane had gone, they might have talked about it until dinner-time at noon; but failing this new subject, they could take no interest in any of their old ones. Out in the field the corn was well up, and the men were hoeing. It was a hot morning in the shed chamber, and the woollen rags were dusty and hot to handle.

Byfleet people knew each other well, and when this mysteriously absent person did not return to the townfarm at the end of a week, public interest became much excited; and presently it was ascertained that Betsey Lane was neither making a visit to her friends the Deckers on Birch Hill, nor to any near acquaintances; in fact, she had disappeared altogether from her wonted haunts. Nobody remembered to have seen her pass, hers had been such an early flitting; and when somebody thought of her having gone away by train, he was laughed at for forgetting that the earliest morning train from South Byfleet, the nearest station, did not start until long after eight o'clock; and if Betsey had designed to be one of the passengers, she would have started along the road at seven, and been seen and known of all women. There was not a kitchen in that part of Byfleet that did not have windows toward the road. Conversation rarely left the level of the neighbourhood gossip: to see Betsey Lane, in her best clothes, at that hour in the morning, would have been the signal for much exercise of imagination; but as day after day went by without news, the curiosity of those who knew her best turned slowly into fear, and at last Peggy Bond again gave utterance to the belief that Betsey had either gone out in the early morning and put an end to her life, or that she had gone to the Centennial. Some of the people at table were moved to loud laughter – it was at supper-time on a Sunday night – but others listened with great interest.

'She never'd put on her good clothes to drownd herself,' said the widow. 'She might have thought 't was good as takin' 'em with her, though. Old folks has wandered off an' got lost in the woods afore now.'

Mrs Dow and Peggy resented this impertinent remark, but deigned to take no notice of the speaker. 'She wouldn't have wore her best clothes to the Centennial, would she?' mildly inquired Peggy, bobbing her head toward the ceiling. ''T would be a shame to spoil your best things in such a place. An' I don't know of her havin' any money; there's the end o' that.'

'You're bad as old Mis' Bland, that used to live neighbour to our folks,' said one of the old men. 'She was dreadful precise; an' she so begretched to wear a good alapaca dress that was left to her, that it hung in a press forty year, an' baited the moths at last.'

'I often seen Mis'Bland a-goin' in to meetin' when I was a young girl,' said Peggy Bond approvingly. 'She was a good-appearin' woman, an' she left property.'

'Wish she'd left it to me, then,' said the poor soul opposite, glancing at her pathetic row of children: but it was not good manners at the farm to deplore one's situation, and Mrs Dow and Peggy only frowned. 'Where do you suppose Betsey can be?' said Mrs Dow, for the twentieth time. 'She didn't have no money. I know she ain't gone far, if it's so that she's yet alive. She's be'n real pinched all the spring.'

'Perhaps that lady that come one day give her some,' the keeper's wife suggested mildly.

'Then Betsey would have told me,' said Mrs Dow with injured dignity.

On the morning of her disappearance, Betsey rose even before the pewee and the English sparrow, and dressed herself quietly, though with trembling hands, and stole out of the kitchen door like a plunderless thief. The old dog licked her hand and looked at her anxiously; the tortoise-shell cat rubbed against her best gown, and trotted away up the yard, then she turned anxiously and came after the old woman, following faithfully until she had to be driven back. Betsey was used to long country excursions afoot. She dearly loved the early morning; and finding that there was no dew to trouble her, she began to follow pasture paths and short cuts across the fields, surprising here and there a flock of sleepy sheep, or a startled calf that rustled out from the bushes. The birds were pecking their breakfast from bush and turf; and hardly any of the wild inhabitants of that rural world were enough alarmed by her presence to do more than flutter away if they chanced to be in her path. She stepped along, lightfooted and eager as

a girl, dressed in her neat old straw bonnet and black gown, and carrying a few belongings in her best bundle-handkerchief, one that her
only brother had brought home from the East Indies fifty years
before. There was an old crow perched as sentinel on a small, dead
pine tree, where he could warn friends who were pulling up the
sprouted corn in a field close by; but he only gave a contemptuous caw
as the adventurer appeared, and she shook her bundle at him in
revenge, and laughed to see him so clumsy as he tried to keep his footing on the twigs.

'Yes, I be,' she assured him. 'I'm a-goin' to Pheladelphy, to the
Centennial, same 's other folks. I'd jest as soon tell ye's not, old
crow'; and Betsey laughed aloud in pleased content with herself and
her daring, as she walked along. She had only two miles to go to the
station at South Byfleet, and she felt for the money now and then, and
found it safe enough. She took great pride in the success of her
escape, and especially in the long concealment of her wealth. Not a
night had passed since Mrs Strafford's visit that she had not slept with
the roll of money under her pillow by night, and buttoned safe inside
her dress by day. She knew that everybody would offer advice and
even commands about the spending or saving of it; and she brooked
no interference.

The last mile of the footpath to South Byfleet was along the railway
track; and Betsey began to feel in haste, though it was still nearly two
hours to train time. She looked anxiously forward and back along the
rails every few minutes, for fear of being run over; and at last she
caught sight of an engine that was apparently coming toward her, and
took flight into the woods before she could gather courage to follow
the path again. The freight train proved to be at a standstill, waiting at
a turnout; and some of the men were straying about, eating their early
breakfast comfortably in this time of leisure. As the old woman came
up to them, she stopped too, for a moment of rest and conversation.

'Where be ye goin'?' she asked pleasantly; and they told her. It was
to the town where she had to change cars and take the great through
train; a point of geography which she had learned from evening talks
between the men at the farm.

'What'll ye carry me there for?'

'We don't run no passenger cars,' said one of the young fellows,
laughing. 'What makes you in such a hurry?'

'I'm startin' for Pheladelphy, an' it's a gre't ways to go.'

'So 't is; but you're consid'ably early, if you're makin' for the eight
-forty train. See here! you haven't got a neddle an' thread 'long of you

in that bundle, have you? If you'll sew me on a couple o' buttons, I'll give ye a free ride. I'm in a sight o' distress, an' none o' the fellows is provided with as much as a bent pin.'

'You poor boy! I'll have you seen to, in half a minute. I'm troubled with a stiff arm, but I'll do the best I can.'

The obliging Betsey seated herself stiffly on the slope of the embankment, and found her thread and needle with utmost haste. Two of the train men stood by and watched the careful stitches, and even offered her a place as spare brakeman, so that they might keep her near; and Betsey took the offer with considerable seriousness, only thinking it necessary to assure them that she was getting most too old to be out in all weathers. An express went by like an earthquake, and she was presently hoisted on board an empty box-car by two of her new and flattering acquaintances, and found herself before noon at the end of the first stage of her journey, without having spent a cent, and furnished with any amount of thrifty advice. One of the young men, being compassionate of her unprotected state as a traveller, advised her to find out the widow of an uncle of his in Philadelphia, saying despairingly that he couldn't tell her just how to find the house; but Miss Betsey Lane said that she had an English tongue in her head, and should be sure to find whatever she was looking for. This unexpected incident of the freight train was the reason why everybody about the South Byfleet station insisted that no such person had taken passage by the regular train that same morning, and why there were those who persuaded themselves that Miss Betsey Lane was probably lying at the bottom of the poorfarm pond.

'Land sakes!' said Miss Betsey Lane, as she watched a Turkish person parading by in his red fez, 'I call the Centennial somethin' like the day o' judgement! I wish I was goin' to stop a month, but I dare say 't would be the death o' my poor old bones.'

She was leaning against the barrier of a patent popcorn establishment, which had given her a sudden reminder of home, and of the winter nights when the sharp-kernelled little red and yellow ears were brought out, and Old Uncle Eph Flanders sat by the kitchen stove, and solemnly filled a great wooden chopping-tray for the refreshment of the company. She had wandered and loitered and looked until her eyes and head had grown numb and unreceptive; but it is only unimaginative persons who can be really astonished. The imagination can always outrun the possible and actual sights and sounds of the world; and this plain old body from Byfleet rarely found anything rich and splendid enough to surprise her. She saw the wonders of the West and the splendours of the East with equal calmness and satisfaction; she had always known that there was an amazing world outside the boundaries of Byfleet. There was a piece of paper in her pocket on which was marked, in her clumsy handwriting, 'If Betsey Lane should meet with accident, notify the selectmen of Byfleet'; but having made this slight provision for the future, she had thrown herself boldly into the sea of strangers, and then had made the joyful discovery that friends were to be found at every turn.

There was something delightfully companionable about Betsey; she had a way of suddenly looking up over her big spectacles with a reassuring and expectant smile, as if you were going to speak to her, and you generally did. She must have found out where hundreds of people came from, and whom they had left at home, and what they thought of the great show, as she sat on a bench to rest, or leaned over the railings where free luncheons were afforded by the makers of hot waffles and molasses candy and fried potatoes; and there was not a night when she did not return to her lodgings with a pocket crammed with samples of spool cotton and nobody knows what. She had already collected small presents for almost everybody she knew at home, and she was such a pleasant, beaming old country body, so unmistakably appreciative and interested, that nobody ever thought of wishing that she would move on. Nearly all the busy people of the Exhibition called her either Aunty or Grandma at once, and made little pleasures for her as best they could. She was a delightful contrast to the indifferent, stupid crowd that drifted along, with eyes fixed at the same level, and seeing, even on that level, nothing for fifty feet at a time. 'What be you making here, dear?' Betsey Lane would ask joyfully, and the most perfunctory guardian hastened to explain. She squandered money as she had never had the pleasure of doing before, and this hastened the day when she must return to Byfleet. She was always inquiring if there were any spectacle sellers at hand, and received occasional directions; but it was a difficult place for her to find her way about in, and the very last day of her stay arrived before she found an exhibitor of the desired sort, an oculist and instrument-maker.

'I called to get some specs for a friend that's upsighted,' she gravely informed the salesman, to his extreme amusement. 'She's dreadful troubled, and jerks her head up like a hen a-drinkin'. She's got a blur a-growin' an' spreadin', an' sometimes she can see out to one side on 't, and more times she can't.'

'Cataracts,' said a middle-aged gentleman at her side; and Betsey Lane turned to regard him with approval and curiosity.

''T is Miss Peggy Bond I was mentioning, of Byfleet poorfarm,' she explained. 'I count on gettin' some glasses to relieve her trouble, if there's any to be found.'

'Glasses won't do her any good,' said the stranger. 'Suppose you come and sit down on this bench, and tell me all about it. First, where is Byfleet?' and Betsey gave the directions at length.

'I thought so,' said the surgeon. 'How old is this friend of yours?'

Betsey cleared her throat decisively, and smoothed her gown over her knees as if it were an apron; then she turned to take a good look at her new acquaintance as they sat on the rustic bench together. 'Who be you, sir, I would like to know?' she asked, in a friendly tone.

'My name's Dunster.'

'I take it you're a doctor,' continued Betsey, as if they had overtaken each other walking from Byfleet to South Byfleet on a summer morning.

'I'm a doctor; part of one at least,' said he. 'I know more or less about eyes; and I spend my summers down on the shore at the mouth of your river; some day I'll come up and look at this person. How old is she?'

'Peggy Bond is one that never tells her age; 't ain't come quite up to where she'll begin to brag of it, you see,' explained Betsey reluctantly; 'but I know her to be nigh to seventy-six, one way or t'other. Her an' Mrs Mary Ann Chick was same year's child'n, and Peggy knows I know it, an' two or three times when we've be'n in the buryin'-ground where Mary Ann lays an' has her dates right on her headstone, I couldn't bring Peggy to take no sort o' notice. I will say she makes, at times, a convenience of being upsighted. But there, I feel for her – everybody does; it keeps her stubbin' an' trippin' against everything, beakin' and gazin' up the way she has to.'

'Yes, yes,' said the doctor, whose eyes were twinkling. 'I'll come and look after her, with your town doctor, this summer – some time in the last of July or first of August.'

'You'll find occupation,' said Betsey, not without an air of patronage. 'Most of us to the Byfleet Farm, has got our ails, now I tell ye. You ain't got no bitters that'll take a dozen years right off an ol' lady's shoulders?'

The busy man smiled pleasantly, and shook his head as he went away. 'Dunster,' said Betsey to herself, soberly committing the new name to her sound memory. 'Yes, I mustn't forget to speak of him to the doctor, as he directed. I do' know now as Peggy would vally her-self quite so much accordin' to, if she had her eyes fixed same as other folks. I expect there wouldn't been a smarter woman in town, though, if she'd had a proper chance. Now I've done what I set to do for her, I do believe, an' 't wa'n't glasses neither. I'll git her a pritty little shawl with that money I laid aside. Peggy Bond ain't got a pritty shawl. I always wanted to have a real good time, an' now I'm havin' it.'

Two or three days later, two pathetic figures might have been seen crossing the slopes of the poorfarm field, toward the low shores of Byfield pond. It was early in the morning, and the stubble of the lately mown grass was wet with rain and hindering to old feet. Peggy Bond was more blundering and liable to stray in the wrong direction than usual; it was one of the days when she could hardly see at all. Aunt Lavina Dow was unusually clumsy of movement, and stiff in the joints; she had not been so far from the house for three years. The morning breeze filled the gathers of her wide gingham skirt, and ag-gravated the size of her unwieldy figure. She supported herself with a stick, and trusted beside to the fragile support of Peggy's arm. They were talking together in whispers.

'Oh, my sakes!' exclaimed Peggy, moving her small head from side to side. 'Hear you wheeze, Mis' Dow! This may be the death o' you; there, do go slow! You set here on the side-hill, an' le' me go try if I can see.'

'It needs more eyesight than you've got,' said Mrs Dow, panting between the words. 'Oh! to think how spry I was in my young days, an' here I be now, the full of a door, an' all my complaints so aggra-vated by my size. 'T is hard! 't is hard! but I'm a-doin' of all this for pore Betsey's sake. I know they've all laughed, but I look to see her ris' to the top o' the pond this day – 't is just nine days since she de-parted; an' say what they may, I know she hove herself in. It run in her family; Betsey had an aunt that done just so, an' she ain't be'n like herself, a-broodin' an' hivin' away alone, an' nothin' to say to you an' me that was always such good company all together. Somethin' sprung her mind, now I tell ye, Mis' Bond.'

'I feel to hope we sha'n't find her, I must say,' faltered Peggy. It was plain that Mrs Dow was the captain of this doleful expedition. 'I guess she ain't never thought o' drowndin' of herself, Mis' Dow; she's gone off a-visitin' way over to the other side o' South Byfleet; some thinks she's gone to the Centennial even now!'

'She hadn't no proper means, I tell ye,' wheezed Mrs Dow

indignantly; 'an' if you prefer that others should find her floatin' to the top this day, instid of us that's her best friend', you can step back to the house.'

They walked on in aggrieved silence. Peggy Bond trembled with excitement, but her companion's firm grasp never wavered, and so they came to the narrow, gravelly margin and stood still. Peggy tried in vain to see the glittering water and the pond lilies that starred it; she knew that they must be there; once, years ago, she had caught fleeting glimpses of them, and she never forgot what she had once seen. The clear blue overhead, the dark pine woods beyond the pond, were all clearly pictured in her mind. 'Can't you see nothin'?' she faltered; 'I believe I'm wuss'n upsighted this day. I'm going to be blind.'

'No,' said Lavina Dow solemnly; 'no, there ain't nothin' whatever, Peggy. I hope to mercy she ain't' –

'Why, whoever'd expected to find you 'way out here!' exclaimed a brisk and cheerful voice. There stood Betsey Lane herself, close behind them, having just emerged from a thicket of alders that grew close by. She was following the short way homeward from the railroad.

'Why, what's the matter, Mis' Dow? You ain't overdoin', be ye? an' Peggy's all of a flutter. What in the name o' natur' ails ye?'

'There ain't nothin' the matter, as J knows of,' responded the leader of this fruitless expedition. 'We only thought we'd take a stroll this pleasant mornin',' she added, with sublime self-possession. 'Where've you be'n, Betsey Lane?'

'To Pheladelphy, ma'am,' said Betsey, looking quite young and gay, and wearing a townish and unfamiliar air that upheld her words. 'All ought to go that can; why, you feel's if you'd be'n all round the world. I guess I've got enough to think of and tell ye for the rest o' my days. I've always wanted to go somewheres. I wish you'd be'n there, I do so. I've talked with folks from Chiny an' the back o' Pennsylvany; and I see folks way from Australy that 'peared, as well as anybody; an' I see how they make spool cotton, an' sights o' other things; an' I spoke with a doctor that lives down to the beach in the summer, an' he offered to come up 'long in the first of August, an' see what he can do for Peggy's eyesight. There was di'monds there as big as pigeon's eggs; an' I met with Mis' Abby Fletcher from South Byfleet depot; an' there was hogs there that weighed risin' thirteen hundred –'

'I want to know,' said Mrs Lavina Dow and Peggy Bond, together.

'Well, 't was a great exper'ence for a person,' added Lavina, turning ponderously, in spite of herself, to give a last wistful look at the smiling waters of the pond.

'I don't know how soon I be goin' to settle down,' proclaimed the rustic sister of Sindbad. 'What's for the good o' one's for the good of all. You just wait till we're setting together up in the old shed chamber! You know, my dear Mis' Katy Strafford give me a han'some present o' money that day she come to see me; and I'd be'n a-dreamin' by night an' day o' seein' that Centennial; and when I come to think on 't I felt sure somebody ought to go from this neighbourhood, if 't was only for the good o' the rest; and I thought I'd better be the one. I wa'n't goin' to ask the selec'men neither. I've come back with one-thirty-five in money, and I see everything there, an' I fetched ye all a little somethin'; but I'm full o' dust now, an' pretty nigh beat out. I never see a place more friendly then Pheladelphy; but 't ain't natural to a Byfleet person to be always walkin' on a level. There, now, Peggy, you take my bundle-handkercher and the basket, and let Mis' Dow sag on to me. I'll git her along twice as easy.'

With this the small elderly company set forth triumphant toward the poorhouse, across the wide green field.

Acknowledgements and bibliographical notes on first publication

The short stories in this collection first appeared as follows:

Clara Schiavolena, 'Clementina' (translated by Miranda Miller) is published for the first time here. Published by permission of the author.

Henry Handel Richardson, 'The Bathe', in *The End of a Childhood and Other Stories*, London, Heinemann, 1934 (re-issued as *The Adventures of Cuffy Mahony and Other Stories*) and used by permission of Angus and Robertson Publishers, Australia.

Alix Kates Shulman, 'A Story of a Girl and her Dog', in *13th Moon*, Vol III, 1, Winter 1975. Published by permission of the author.

Evelyn Sharp, 'The Game that Wasn't Cricket', in *Rebel Women*, London, A.C. Fifield, 1910.

The extract from *A Young Girl's Diary*, by Greta Lainer, was first published by Internationaler Psychoanalytischer Verlag, Leipzig, Vienna, Zurich, 1919; English translation by Eden and Cedar Paul, London, Allen and Unwin, 1921.

Eliza Haywood, 'Aliena's Story', in *The Female Spectator*, originally published between 1744-6 and re-issued in 1748 and 1771.

Caroline Norton, 'Kate Bouverie', in *Tales and Sketches in Prose and Verse*, London, E. Churton, 1850.

Aphra Behn, 'The Adventure of the Black Lady', published 1696.

Mary Webb, 'In Affection and Esteem', in *Armour Wherein he Trusted*, London, Jonathan Cape, 1929.

Mary Delarivière Manley, 'The Physician's Stratagem', in *The Power of Love: in seven novels*, London, 1720.

Dorothy Richardson, 'Christmas Eve', in *Art and Letters*, 3, Winter 1920. Reprinted by permission of Mark Paterson & Associates.

Eliza Linton, 'Two Cousins', in *With a Silken Thread and Other Stories*, London, Chatto and Windus, 1880.

Françoise Mallet-Joris, 'Marie', in *Cordelia*, Paris, René Julliard, 1956; English translation by Peter Green, London, W.H. Allen, 1965. Reprinted by permission of W.H. Allen.

Margaret Cavendish, 'The Matrimonial Agreement', in *Natures Pictures Drawn by Francies Pencil to the Life*, for J. Martin and J. Allestryie, London, 1656.

Janet Frame, 'The Bedjacket', in *The Lagoon*, Christchurch, New Zealand, The Caxton Press, 1951. Reprinted by permission of the author.

Elizabeth Robins, ''Gustus Frederick', in *Below the Salt*, London, William Heinemann, 1896. (Published under the pseudonym C.E. Raimond.) Reprinted by permission of William Heinemann.

Margaret Oliphant, 'A Story of a Wedding Tour', in *A Widow's Tale and Other Stories*, Edinburgh, Blackwood, 1898.

Kate Chopin, 'A Pair of Silk Stockings', in *Vogue*, 16 September 1897; reprinted in *Portraits*, Helen Taylor (ed), London, The Women's Press, 1979.

Mary Wilkins, 'A New England Nun', in *A New England Nun and Other Stories*, New York, Harper, 1891; London, Osgood, 1891.

June Arnold, *Sister Gin*, Plainfield, Vermont, Daughters Publishing Co Inc, 1975; London, The Women's Press, 1979. Reprinted by permission of the author.

Willa Cather, 'A Wagner Matinée', in *The Troll Garden*, New York, McClure Phillips, 1905.

Sarah Orne Jewett, 'The Flight of Betsey Lane', in *A Native of Winby and Other Tales*, Boston, Houghton Mifflin, 1893.

Acknowledgements and bibliographical notes on first publication

The short stories in this collection first appeared as follows:

Clara Schiavolena, 'Clementina' (translated by Miranda Miller) is published for the first time here. Published by permission of the author.

Henry Handel Richardson, 'The Bathe', in *The End of a Childhood and Other Stories*, London, Heinemann, 1934 (re-issued as *The Adventures of Cuffy Mahony and Other Stories*) and used by permission of Angus and Robertson Publishers, Australia.

Alix Kates Shulman, 'A Story of a Girl and her Dog', in *13th Moon*, Vol III, 1, Winter 1975. Published by permission of the author.

Evelyn Sharp, 'The Game that Wasn't Cricket', in *Rebel Women*, London, A.C. Fifield, 1910.

The extract from *A Young Girl's Diary*, by Greta Lainer, was first published by Internationaler Psychoanalytischer Verlag, Leipzig, Vienna, Zurich, 1919; English translation by Eden and Cedar Paul, London, Allen and Unwin, 1921.

Eliza Haywood, 'Aliena's Story', in *The Female Spectator*, originally published between 1744-6 and re-issued in 1748 and 1771.

Caroline Norton, 'Kate Bouverie', in *Tales and Sketches in Prose and Verse*, London, E. Churton, 1850.

Aphra Behn, 'The Adventure of the Black Lady', published 1696.

Mary Webb, 'In Affection and Esteem', in *Armour Wherein he Trusted*, London, Jonathan Cape, 1929.

Mary Delarivière Manley, 'The Physician's Stratagem', in *The Power of Love: in seven novels*, London, 1720.

Dorothy Richardson, 'Christmas Eve', in *Art and Letters*, 3, Winter 1920. Reprinted by permission of Mark Paterson & Associates.

Eliza Linton, 'Two Cousins', in *With a Silken Thread and Other Stories*, London, Chatto and Windus, 1880.

Françoise Mallet-Joris, 'Marie', in *Cordelia*, Paris, René Julliard, 1956; English translation by Peter Green, London, W.H. Allen, 1965. Reprinted by permission of W.H. Allen.

Margaret Cavendish, 'The Matrimonial Agreement', in *Natures Pictures Drawn by Francies Pencil to the Life*, for J. Martin and J. Allestryie, London, 1656.

Janet Frame, 'The Bedjacket', in *The Lagoon*, Christchurch, New Zealand, The Caxton Press, 1951. Reprinted by permission of the author.

Elizabeth Robins, ''Gustus Frederick', in *Below the Salt*, London, William Heinemann, 1896. (Published under the pseudonym C.E. Raimond.) Reprinted by permission of William Heinemann.

Margaret Oliphant, 'A Story of a Wedding Tour', in *A Widow's Tale and Other Stories*, Edinburgh, Blackwood, 1898.

Kate Chopin, 'A Pair of Silk Stockings', in *Vogue*, 16 September 1897; reprinted in *Portraits*, Helen Taylor (ed), London, The Women's Press, 1979.

Mary Wilkins, 'A New England Nun', in *A New England Nun and Other Stories*, New York, Harper, 1891; London, Osgood, 1891.

June Arnold, *Sister Gin*, Plainfield, Vermont, Daughters Publishing Co Inc, 1975; London, The Women's Press, 1979. Reprinted by permission of the author.

Willa Cather, 'A Wagner Matinée', in *The Troll Garden*, New York, McClure Phillips, 1905.

Sarah Orne Jewett, 'The Flight of Betsey Lane', in *A Native of Winby and Other Tales*, Boston, Houghton Mifflin, 1893.